Beyond ISO 9000

Beyond ISO 9000

How to Sustain Quality in a Dynamic World

William A. Stimson

AMACOM
American Management Association
New York • Atlanta • Boston • Chicago • Kansas City • San Fransisco • Washington, D.C.
Brussels • Mexico City • Tokyo • Toronto

This book is available at a special discount when ordered in bulk quantities. For information, contact Special Sales Department, AMACOM, a division of American Management Association, 1601 Broadway, New York, NY 10019.

Library of Congress Cataloging-in-Publication Data

Stimson, William A.

Beyond ISO 9000 : how to sustain quality in a dynamic world / William A. Stimson.

p. cm.

Includes index.

ISBN 0-8144-0392-1

1. ISO 9000 Series Standards. I. Title.

TS 156.6.S79 1998

658.5′62—dc21 97-38495

CIP

Printing number

10 9 8 7 6 5 4 3 2 1

To **Patrick, Christine, Jennifer, Stephanie,** and **Aaron**
My son and his family—a source of joy and pride

Table of Contents

Preface

The United States was born in innovation. Having arrived here, no one knew what to do next; it is highly probable that brainstorming became the primary means of finding direction. Novelty and pioneering were the rule for 200 years. As a result, flexibility of notion is ingrained in the American spirit. Yes, we have our mind-sets, our biases, and our chauvinism, just as everyone does. But it is arguably easier to introduce a new idea in the United States than anywhere else. This doesn't mean that we have a corner on novelty, but it does mean that we are susceptible to it and consider innovation a virtue.

The world of business is no exception. We will try anything, anytime. Consultants, gurus, and psychologists of every shape and persuasion find access to our boardrooms to advance their ideas. Consider how readily business management got aboard strategic planning, then reengineering, then transformation, and now back to strategic planning again.

New ideas carry a risk, of course. They often require an investment up front, before their advantages and disadvantages are clear. Some of the ideas fail quickly, perhaps not quickly enough to prevent significant loss. Ford's introduction of the Edsel comes to mind. Others, like just-in-time, seem to work in some places but not others. Debate goes on about them, with partisans pro and con choosing up sides.

ISO 9000 is one of these ideas. It is a set of quality management standards conceived and developed in Europe. Many of its opponents are against any standard at all, which by definition is a constraint. Others object to any idea that is not native. Still others complain that for all their structure—and installation and maintenance costs—ISO standards do not ensure quality of product.

Despite these objections, ISO 9000 is winning out. As of this writing, about 15,000 American companies have acquired this certification. Resistance is still strong, but a good idea inevitably triumphs, and this book will show that ISO 9000 is a good idea. Modern business organizations are too complex to rely completely on quality control procedures, even those using the latest statistical techniques. The integration of marketing, design, manufacturing, service, and transfer functions, all subject to external forces, is absolutely necessary in order to maintain competitiveness. The nation's business leaders and literature agree on this issue, but the idea that *quality* might be the unifying law of business processes is a growing notion and the basis of this book.

What about the argument that ISO 9000 standards do not ensure product quality? This argument is incorrect. It assumes that there is no correlation between management and objectives. But the provision of direction to objectives is the sole purpose of management. There is logically a positive correlation between the management of quality and the quality of product. This correlation will vary from company to company; the purpose of this book is to show how to improve that correlation.

What does an ISO 9000 process standard do for you? Its major benefit is that it enables stability of form. This notion is underappreciated in an innovative society, and so is examined in considerable detail in Chapters 12 and 27. It is sufficient here to recognize that stability is an extremely important property of dynamic systems, so that its achievement is absolutely necessary. An ISO 9000 management standard enables stability by the enforcement of systematic conduct of business through documented activity. This stability is beneficial to both the manufacturer or provider of service and the customer, who can rely on a consistent level of quality at a given price. The producer can project costs and profits into any arbitrary environment, provided that an effective ISO operation can be sustained.

Oops! I said it—"sustain." I may have stumbled on an uneasy notion in the back of your mind. Whether you are now certified or are just pondering going for it, you may wonder whether ISO 9000 is a bottomless pit. Is sustainability feasible? Is the game worth the price of admission?

Sustainability has two components. The first is organizational and pertains to leadership and marketability. *Leadership* refers to management's ability to adapt and integrate company resources in a dynamic environment. ISO 9000 does not replace management. It does enforce processes that are sufficiently systematic so that management can spend less time on fire drills and more time on leadership. *Marketability* addresses the reality of the producer-customer relation: It does no good to be the best if no one is aware of it. ISO 9000 is not meant to be a marketing advantage, but it is indeed.

The second component is technical and has to do with the dynamics of operations, whether they are production, service, or support. Dynamic operations are characterized by three properties: stability, capability, and improvability. ISO 9000 does not do any of this for you, but it makes these properties controllable.

The facts are these: ISO 9000 certification is necessary in our global business environment. Your customers are going to require it of you sooner than you think. Properly implemented, the standard establishes stability in all your operations. Although stability is an essential property of an industrial process, it is not sufficient. It is only the first dynamic needed for successful performance of manufacturing or service. We need capability and improvability also. We can define these properties loosely in this way: A stable process provides a constant level of quality; a capable process provides quality that is acceptably close to a target value; an improvable process provides the ability to track an increasingly improved target value.

ISO requirements do not ensure sustainability, but they put you in command of a system that can get you there. A company that is organized to ISO conformance is in a position to go the extra step and incorporate sustainable operations. It costs no more. This book shows how to achieve sustainability within the context of an ISO 9000 program. Every requirement of the international standard is maintained, but we go beyond the minimum to strategic management and to capable and improvable structures. The objective, after all, is an effective, sustainable quality system, ISO 9000 or not. We will achieve this quality system by using an ISO 9001 nucleus and then going beyond it.

Therefore, this book is not a cookbook that takes you one step at a time to achieve certification. It does show how to organize sustainable and capable processes, but its main purpose is to generate thought about better ways to do things. No matter the company or nature of business, thinking about "why" as well as "how" leads to both form and substance. We are encouraged to build processes that are stable, capable, and improvable. They adapt to changes in the environment and are immune to political winds. They are sustainable.

Notes on Style

ISO 9000 is itself not a standard but is the name of a series of standards: ISO 9001, ISO 9002, and ISO 9003. ISO 9001 is the most comprehensive of the set, but each has its own purpose. In order to accommodate reference to one or the other, I use the following convention. The term *ISO 9000*, or the term *Standard*, refers to any one or all three standards. This convention is used because a single term is easier to read and to write than is the triad *ISO 9001, ISO 9002, and ISO 9003*. On occasion it is necessary to refer explicitly to the comprehensive standard ISO 9001, the only standard with a full set of twenty requirements. The context makes the reference clear. *ISO 9001* refers specifically to ISO 9001 only.

The use of English is adapting to reflect that women are assuming their rightful place in the industrial and business world. In accordance with this reality, I use the following convention in this book: about one third of pronouns are *him*, about one third *her*, and about one third *them*. There is no use of the convention *him/her*, which I believe makes reading difficult.

This book encourages the reader to undertake a dynamic enterprise, to go "beyond ISO 9000." Understanding how to do this is a major challenge. I want to work together with the reader on this task. Accordingly, throughout this book I often use the pronoun *we*. This is not meant to be pedantic or to take an editorial posture but to show you, the readers, that we are working together to arrive at this goal.

Acknowledgments

Books are generally a product of the author's learning and experience. This book is no exception. However, both learning and experience are two-way streets. They are subject to a kind of Newton's third law: For every action there is a reaction. If I have learned anything from an experience, then there is logically a contributor to that knowledge.

All this is by way of recognizing that there are many contributors to this book. The first is Larry Tate, vice president for quality, Comdial Corporation, Charlottesville, Virginia. Larry has been a mentor, an adviser, and a friend. An experienced and successful implementor of an ISO 9001 quality system himself, Larry represents the modern view of the notion of quality as it is applied in the real world. Many of my ideas go to Larry Tate for a reality check.

A good quality system is responsive to a wide variety of productive processes. Nevertheless, every process is unique in some sense, and it takes great skill to adapt system to process, and conversely. Ian Mills, quality assurance manager for Liberty Fabrics, and Carmine Covais, quality assurance manager for Klöckner Pentaplast of America (both companies of Gordonsville, Virginia), have contributed to this book by providing rubber-meets-the-road insight into quality systems applications.

One of the benefits of my job is the opportunity to meet entrepreneurs. For every two things that they might learn from me, I learn twenty from them. Entrepreneurs hold my admiration because they are the men and women who make our economy work, who risk all to achieve their dream, and in so doing, sustain the rest of us. Two such entrepreneurs are Tom and Deanna Hall, of Acme Design Technology, Crozet, Virginia. Their wisdom and effort have contributed importantly to this book.

Another entrepreneur is Tom Hubbard, of INOVA Corporation, Charlottesville, Virginia. INOVA competes in the world of high technology, and the ability of Tom and his team to integrate their business and diverse engineering activities provides a clarifying view on how horizontal integration can be done. One of the propositions of this book is that good business practices and quality practices are the same thing. INOVA's operations support this hypothesis.

Richard Goldbach, president and CEO of Metro Machine Corporation, Norfolk, Virginia, and Senior V.P. Ken Newman gave me a second demonstration of this proposition. No one talks about quality per se at Metro. Quality, production, and business procedures are not distinguished. Yet detailed analysis of Metro's operations reveals that company processes meet or exceed any of the popular quality standards.

There is a final acknowledgment that must be made. It has nothing to do with quality theory, standards, or processes. It has to do with integrity, a fundamental virtue without which there can be no quality. The person remains unknown to me. He was a welder, an employee of Metro Machine. He was welding a pipe down in the depths of a ship, five decks below the main deck, in a dark, dank space. The pipe was mounted against the bulkhead, near the deck, so that the welder had only a few inches of clearance in which to weld, and had to double over to do it. No one was watching him. If he fudged, if he took the easy way, no one would know for a long time, and he would never be blamed. But he did not fudge. He did his best. Unannounced, a quality inspector showed up, and with a mirror, examined the bulkhead side of the weld. It was beautiful. I was proud to be a human being that morning and so full of emotion that I dared not speak, afraid to embarrass those there. Even today, it is hard to put in words what I felt; we do not talk about these things. I had witnessed quality.

Part One
Sustainability

Chapter 1

The ISO and Quality: An Overview

Formal work standards have been with us for centuries—since the Middle Ages at least. The famous European craft guilds of the eleventh to fifteenth centuries had as an important objective the development and maintenance of high standards of finished work. This quality prevailed in furniture, cathedrals, and châteaus, and we still marvel at the results. Craftsmen were divided into three categories: master, journeyman, and apprentice, and the quality of one's work had to be demonstrated in order to gain admission to the guild. Within a shop, the quality of the product was ensured by its inspection by the master. These ideas are indicated by the Guild Act of eleventh-century England, whereby representatives of the king were invested with the power to enforce uniformity in "places of manufacture where the wardens of the crafts were appointed to see the work to be good and right and to reform what defects they should find therein, and thereupon inflict due punishment upon offenders and to stamp only good work with the seal of approval" (Hashim and Khan, 1990).

The idea of ensuring product quality by use of inspection to a product standard has remained with us through the centuries and is still used today, but with decreasing frequency. Even the development of mass production did not eliminate this practice; industry simply adopted statistical methods to deal with the larger number of products. In other words, through most of history, the basis of quality has been the product standard.

World War II forced a different idea. Production levels increased to unimaginable heights. In addition, the result of poor product quality could be awful, even catastrophic. Mass production of bullets with too little powder, of shells with too much, or of cannon barrels with fault fracture could lead to unrecoverable losses in the age of blitzkrieg. At the same time, the techniques of systems analysis were developing so that it became possible to determine methods of ensuring *process quality* as opposed to *product quality*. The basis of process quality is the notion that if the process is good, the product will be good too, even in mass production.

Quality, of course, is not the only reason for using standards. Another is uniformity. The coalitions of World War II required some means of uniformity of product. The industrial practices of the Axis forces are not readily available, but we know that the Allies did develop standards, including process standards. Unfortunately, uniformity from ally to ally was not realized because each nation developed its own standards, so the opportunity was missed. Both England and the United States developed process standards during the war, which eventually led to today's British Standard (BS) 5750 and the Mil-Q-9858 quality system standards, respectively.

These standards were used differently in the postwar era, however. England encouraged the use of BS 5750 in the private sector as well as in defense. The United States, holding to its traditional belief that government has little business in the marketplace, maintained a policy of laissez-faire, so the Mil-Q-9858 process standard has been limited to the defense industry and caveat emptor remains the fundamental principle of the market.

In fact, quality took a turn for the worse. Unchallenged during nearly two generations, American manufacturers let quality slide. The abandonment of product quality in American industry following World War II has been so well documented that I will not expand on it here, only mentioning in passing the term *planned obsolescence* of American products during the 1950s through the 1970s.

Meanwhile, in the postwar rebuilding period, everyone else took the opportunity to do it right the second time around. Both Japan and Europe began to focus on process quality. Japan's achievements in the quality of its mass production are well identified. In Europe, in addition to England's broad use of BS 5750, the continental nations initiated process standards, such as France's NFX 50. In particular, the challenge of postwar Japan brought us to our senses. We Americans began to realize that our economy was global. We would and did purchase foreign products if we believed that those products had superior quality. Strategies such as import quotas and appeals to patriotism didn't seem to work. When all else failed, American industry understood the message and began a return to manufacturing quality product. An increasing number of companies are now getting on board. The overpowering reality is that the global market encourages treaties such as the North American Free Trade Agreement (NAFTA) and the General Agreement on Tariffs and Trade (GATT), which define standards of trade, production, and service.

The International Organization for Standardization

Following World War II, continual efforts were made by European nations to form a single economic force. The GATT was an important early milestone, achieved in 1947. By 1979, European nations succeeded in overcoming nationalistic barriers sufficiently to form a sizable free trade group, the European Economic Community, of sixteen nations and growing. One of the many factors in this community was a rebirth of the idea that uniformity could be achieved through common standards and that this uniformity was necessary. Another factor was recognition of quality standards as a mechanism for leveling the competitive field. The International Organization for Standardization (ISO), established in Switzerland in 1946, assumed responsibility for overseeing the standards agreements of various member nations.

The basis of a universal quality standard lies in government overview of the registrars, all of them private. Whether in Canada or Denmark, when you seek ISO certification, the certifying party is a private company. In the free-market world, no government controls quality or production; the marketplace controls these things. However, to ensure that standards are uniform and inviolate, governments oversee the overseers—except in the United States.

The distinction between the American and European approaches to quality system standards is made clear by a comparison of the quality structures used in the United Kingdom and in the United States. The British government has encouraged all companies to register, creating agencies to accredit registration bodies and to authorize training. BS 5750 is publicized throughout the United Kingdom to increase awareness and gain acceptance among the population. Exhibit 1-1, from Johnson (1993), depicts the British organization on the right. Accreditation is conferred by the United Kingdom Assessment Service (UKAS), under the auspices of the Department of Trade and Industry. In contrast, in the U.S. structure (shown on the left), the government remains apart. Overview of the U.S. quality system has been assumed by the American Society for Quality (ASQ) and by the American National Standards Institute (ANSI), jointly accredit-

Exhibit 1-1. The U.K. and U.S. quality system structures.

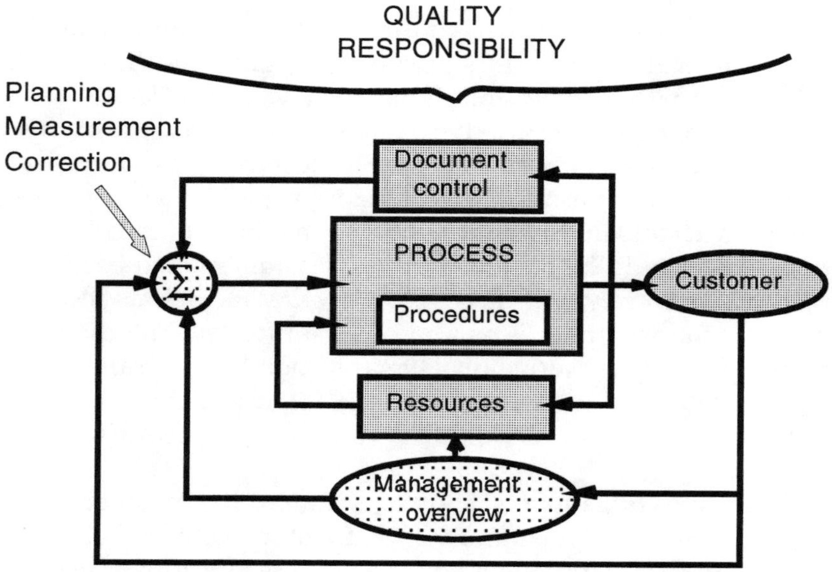

Adapted and reprinted by permission of Perry Johnson, Inc.

ing through the Registrar Accreditation Board (RAB). The ANSI-ASQC have also jointly issued a series of standards known as Q9000, which are identical to the ISO 9000 series.

Whether in the British or American system, the accredited registrars are private companies. They are authorized to certify manufacturers and providers of service to one of the ISO 9000 standards. The certified companies are called suppliers in the ISO vernacular. In the United States, some of these certified companies are government agencies—for example, the Naval Surface Warfare Center, Cardrock, Maryland. Nevertheless, the ISO certifier of a government agency is a private company.

ISO 9000 (1994) Quality System Standards

ISO 9000 is a series of quality system standards comprising three quality system models:

1. *ISO 9001* Quality Systems: Model for Design, Development, Production, Installation, and Servicing
2. *ISO 9002* Quality Systems: Model for Production and Installation
3. *ISO 9003* Quality Systems: Model for Final Inspection and Test

ISO 9001 applies to companies that design and produce products. ISO 9002 is a subset of ISO 9001 and applies to companies that produce and install products or services, but that have no design function. ISO 9003 is a subset of ISO 9002 and applies to those companies that neither design nor produce, but which only inspect or test products. Paragraph 4.0 is the quality requirements paragraph for all the ISO standards and contains the identical set of clauses in each model, except that in the 1994 revision of the set inappropriate clauses were declared inapplicable for that model. Thus, ISO 9002 is exactly ISO 9001, but with several quality requirements declared inapplicable in paragraph 4; ISO 9003 is exactly ISO 9002, but with several more quality requirements declared inapplicable in paragraph 4.

ISO 9000 is a set of very general quality system standards, applicable to every business engaged in production or service.

However, it is comprehensive in scope and specific about rules of evidence. A company that hopes to meet these strict criteria must develop a quality system that is equally specific and systematic. Before going into the implementation and maintenance of an ISO 9000 quality system, we need a few definitions to establish important references and provide a common understanding of objectives.

A Working Definition of Quality

Quality, like beauty, is in the eye of the beholder. We do not need to define quality in order to recognize it because our sense of it derives from the heart and our intuition. We know it when we see it. Still, quality is not quite beauty, although it can be beautiful. A sunset is beautiful. A horse at the run is beautiful. We associate quality with beauty when we speak about some characteristic of a creation; thus a painting might be beautiful. We study about art in order to better appreciate it and to express our appreciation to others. We study such characteristics as color and texture, form and position, light and shade, and finally, without meaning to, we arrive at a definition of its quality. It is only by defining quality that we are able to express to a manufacturer what it is that we want.

The manufacturer, too, needs a definition of quality that can be understood and implemented on the factory floor. It is on the production line that quality is physically put into a product or not. So to begin, we need a workable definition of quality. It is not as easy as you might think; consider the candidates in Exhibit 1-2.

The first is a shortened version from ISO 8402. The remainder are from Deming (1986), Juran (1992), and Crosby (1979),

Exhibit 1-2. Definitions of quality.

Author	*Definition of Quality*
International Organization for Standardization	Sum of properties of a product that satisfies customer needs
W. Edwards Deming	Continuous improvement
Joseph Juran	Fitness for use
Phillip Crosby	Conformance to requirements

respectively. All of these definitions are intuitively satisfying and are widely accepted. The last three are at least concise. Thinking about them, though, we note important nuances of difference among them. The definition used by the ISO is too abstract to be understood on the factory floor. Factory workers rarely ever talk to an outside customer. Moreover, the ISO definition is quite lengthy in its full form. Deming's definition is short and sounds good, two reasons why we see it so often in corporate mission statements. However, improvability must be rigorously defined and implemented or it quickly diminishes to a motherhood statement. Improvability is not easy to implement. A considerable time is spent in this book discussing it and the discipline needed to achieve it.

Juran's definition is open to loose interpretation: If it's good enough, then it's OK. For example, a product that is unfit for its primary market but that can be used in a secondary market satisfies this definition of quality. This is called product regrade and cannot be said to be a quality activity, as we shall see in Chapter 23.

The most utilitarian definition is Crosby's. It can be brought to bear directly on service industries, whose workers usually deal directly with customers. However, it is less useful in manufacturing because workers on the factory floor—who, in the end, are responsible for a quality product—never get to see the customer requirements. All they see are the specifications of the job order. Having interviewed hundreds of factory workers on the definition of quality, the best answer I ever received was, "I don't know. I just do what's on the job order." We shall start from there and define quality to suit what the worker sees, paraphrasing Crosby somewhat:

Quality is conformance to specifications.

Of course, this definition carries with it the burden of ensuring that the specifications are a correct representation of the requirements. How this is done is discussed in the design control and contract review clauses in Chapters 15 and 25. Once we have agreed on a common definition of quality, other important definitions follow, as shown in Exhibit 1-3.

The philosophical structure of the ISO program is apparent from this list of definitions. We begin by defining quality in a way

Exhibit 1-3. Key definitions regarding quality.

Quality	Conformance to specifications
Quality policy	The will and direction of a company with regard to quality, as established by top management
Quality management	The management function that determines and implements the quality policy
Quality system	The organizational structure, responsibilities, procedures, processes, and resources for implementing quality management

that best suits our particular business. It is not necessary to adopt the ISO definition; any one of the well-established definitions is acceptable. We have adapted Crosby's because specifications can be related directly to structures of capability and improvability, whose attainment is the objective of this book. Then given an understanding of what quality means, other definitions follow logically from it. A quality policy is required as a fundamental expression of the will and direction of the company. Management responsibilities are defined and assigned in order to carry out the policy, and a quality system is developed as a structure to achieve quality throughout the organization. The breadth of the quality system is substantial, encompassing company functions, activities, documentation, and resources. There are, of course, some functions that do not bear directly on the quality of product or service, but they are few in an efficient organization. The quality system is therefore a major responsibility of management and the demonstration of its will and belief in quality.

Why Get ISO Certification?

In my middle age I used to ride ships, and in the isolation of life at sea, during quiet moments, young officers who found themselves in career crisis would sometimes come to me to discuss civilian life. Most of them had no idea about it, but were torn between the conflicting demands of Navy and family. I would tell them that before they abandoned a naval career they should reflect on why they chose it to begin with. Many of the reasons were still there, and they would be unhappy if they changed.

And so it is with ISO. Obtaining an ISO 9000 quality standard certification requires a major investment of time, effort, and money. If you are not yet certified, why bother? If you are, is it worth it? Exhibit 1-4 shows why certification is a good idea. And the first reason given is the very best: We need a first-class quality system if we want to make first-class products.

Some companies put most of their quality budget into advertising, but they are kidding themselves. At best they are dealing in folklore; at worst they are relying on the maxim attributed to P. T. Barnum, "There's a sucker born every minute." But customers are becoming more sophisticated and you need quality to get them and keep them. The only way to maintain quality is with a systematic process. Advertising announces quality, but it doesn't create it. Nor do the exhortations of higher management. A quality system is the only way to get there.

So the main reason for certification is straightforward: To have a quality system that is stable, comprehensive, and consistent. ISO 9000 will give you that. The second reason is even more

Exhibit 1-4. Reasons for ISO certification.

important, survival. ISO 9000 is taking on the dimensions of a *seal of approval*. More and more companies are going for it, including your competition. Each competitor that achieves ISO certification while you stand around thinking about it gains at least one year's head start in pursuing market share.

Increasingly, companies are requiring their suppliers to become ISO-certified. Even companies that are now your clients may adopt an ISO-only supplier policy, leaving you out in the cold. This decision is usually made at the highest corporate level, often in a city distant from your local customer contacts. Thus, even if your local reputation is solid, you may find yourself losing customers whose supplier choices have been overruled by their home office.

Global competition is another ISO motivation. It is both a threat and an opportunity. The overseas producers are going to market in your backyard. Conversely, the expansion of trade agreements will allow you to compete in theirs. Even if your present five-year strategic plan does not call for foreign sales, the next five-year plan very well may include it. The time for basic preparation is now, and ISO certification is a fundamental advantage.

Finally, there are major clients and government agencies that have already adopted a policy of ISO-only suppliers. This market, now closed to you, opens up when you obtain this basic qualification.

Getting There and Staying There

It takes significant time and effort to obtain ISO certification, usually a year or more. The structure required to achieve this goal is shown in Exhibit 1-5, the certification phase. The supplier is you. You need to develop a quality system that is in conformance with one of the standards of ISO 9000 and to implement the program with an organizational structure as shown, supported with documentation. You lay out policies, the scope of the quality system, and objectives. It's here that you decide whether to patch your old system or start anew, and whether to meet the minimum requirements or go for a stable and capable quality system. It's here that you define the quality

Exhibit 1-5. Certifying and sustaining an ISO quality system.

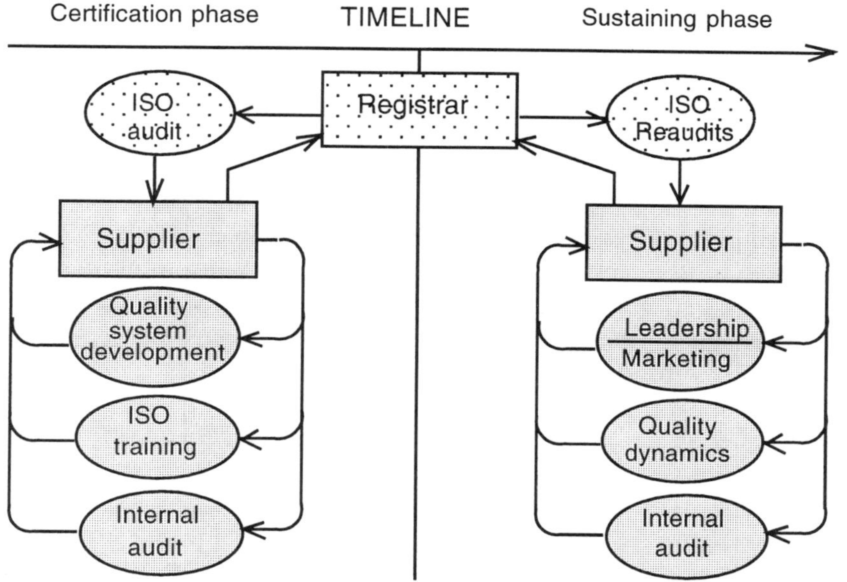

manual and choose a management representative (MR) who will bird-dog the ISO program through to certification.

You will need ISO training for your key personnel and will need to create and maintain a permanent internal quality audit (IQA) team. The importance of this team to certification cannot be overemphasized. There is a slogan: Quality is everyone's business. This is a motherhood statement in some companies, but let's assume that in your company it is true. Nevertheless, there is a difference between responsibility and accountability, which will be expanded upon later in this book. The management representative is accountable for the quality system and the IQA team is the MR's agent. As I mentioned, the certifying phase is itself a prolonged effort and the IQA team is a vital force in sustaining it until the goal is reached.

Although the certifying phase usually lasts from twelve to eighteen months, the sustaining phase has an infinite operational horizon. The two structures look similar—in fact, both phases use a feedback loop. The basic feedback structure is extremely important, and we shall see it over and over again throughout the book. One element of the structure remains the same in both phases—internal audit. The IQA team plays a permanent major role in a sustainable ISO 9000 quality system.

As for the rest, the difference in the phases is one of focus. Given that the quality system conforms to the requirements, you sustain it over the long term by concentrating on quality dynamics. A quality system is like any other kind of system; it is, in the words of R. E. Kalman (1969), a "dynamical process." The dynamic properties that you must be concerned with are stability, capability, and improvability. You must implement these properties in each of the twenty requirements of the ISO 9001 quality standard.

ISO training does not appear in the structure of the sustaining phase. Training does not stop; indeed, training of all kinds is one of the basic ISO requirements. But it is a question of focus in the postcertification period. We assume that the operational quality system is working with all of the requirements ongoing and conforming, including training.

Management, too, has its ISO responsibilities defined in the certification phase and continuing in the sustaining phase. But now you need a refocus, a concentration on leadership. Prior to certification you had the ISO challenge as a rallying point for corporate momentum. After certification, you enter a quiescent period when the ISO program loses its center-stage visibility and is not likely to get better, the cost of business goes on, production schedules must be met, competition continues to hound you, and so on. In simple terms, the flush of victory fades in the onslaught of daily business. Leadership can ensure that the opportunity is pursued to build on the purpose and the power of the ISO 9000 program. Leadership is a form of management that is discussed in Chapter 2.

Marketing is an additional key to sustaining ISO certification. Again, you must go beyond the ISO 9000 requirements of marketing, which focus on customer satisfaction. In the sustaining phase, you continue with customer satisfaction in order to maintain conformance, but you want to ensure customer *awareness* of your new capability and its advantages. Moreover, awareness is a two-way street. You will sustain a quality position by tracking changes and trends in customer requirements—this, too, is primarily a marketing activity.

The Charlottesville, Virginia, newspaper *Daily Progress,* in a September 8, 1996, editorial, said that sustainability is an old-fashioned idea whose time has come and gone and come back again. You will shall see in Chapter 2 the rebirth of still another old-fashioned idea, strategic planning. Indeed, the two notions are related in that they are concerned with the future. If these are old-fashioned ideas, then let's have more of them.

Summary

Quality has been defined as conformance to specifications, and standards are needed to achieve it. Modern commerce and industry require both product and process standards, the latter being a relatively new idea. The most universal process standards are those within the ISO 9000 framework. Obtaining ISO certification to a quality system standard requires a short-term certification effort and a long-term sustaining effort. A sustaining quality system must go beyond the ISO framework itself and incorporate the notions of leadership and marketing, and the dynamic properties of stability, capability, and improvability.

References

ANSI/ISO/ASQC. *A8402-1994. American National Standard: Quality Management and Quality Assurance—Vocabulary.* American Society for Quality Control, 1994.

ANSI/ISO/ASQC. *Q9004-1-1994. American National Standard: Quality Management and Quality System Elements and Guidelines.* American Society for Quality Control, 1994.

"Common sense gets new name." *Charlottesville Daily Progress,* September 8, 1996, page D2.

Crosby, P. B. *Quality is Free.* New York: McGraw-Hill, 1979.

Deming, W. E. *Out of the Crisis.* Cambridge: Massachusetts Institute of Technology, Center for Advanced Engineering Study, 1986.

Hashim, Mohammad, and Mujeeb Khan. "Quality Standards—Past, Present, and Future." *Quality Progress,* June 1990, pp. 56–59.

Juran, J. M. *Juran on Quality by Design.* New York: Free Press, 1992.

Johnson, Perry. *ISO 9000: Meeting the New International Standards.* New York: McGraw-Hill, 1993.
Kalman, R. E., R. L. Falb, and M. A. Arbib. *Topics in Mathematical System Theory.* New York: McGraw-Hill, 1969.

Chapter 2
Leadership

Leadership is a highly prized quality in the military profession, defined, understood, and explicitly cultivated. In the business community, the term is used infrequently, indirectly, reservedly, and sometimes uneasily. It seems that leadership suggests something autocratic to many people, so the preferred term is management. When leadership is discussed, the usual approach is to talk about certain positive aspects perceived to be associated with it rather than to discuss the notion itself. For example, Blanding (1991) writes that employee stress increases when management displays wishy-washy behavior. Presumably then, leadership invokes assertive behavior. Laudon and Laudon (1991) write that leadership has various styles, e.g., democratic, authoritarian, bureaucratic. This concept allows a classification of leadership without yet telling us what it is.

Deming (1986) identified leadership as a quality characteristic in one of his fourteen points, but chose not to define it explicitly. Rather, he said that the job of management is not supervision but leadership, which is best manifested by helping workers to do their job. Of course, this implies that managers have experience in the job also. Champy (1995) reinforces this idea, pointing out that at Intel, management was encouraged to get hands-on experience. In this way they could help subordinates, thus gaining a "perspective of leadership rather than management."

Tomasko (1987) also distinguishes leadership and management, but in a different way, saying that the latter role is perceived as a concern with day-to-day operations while the former is a visionary role, looking to the future. There is a great deal of truth to this idea because leaders are pathfinders; however, not all pathfinders are leaders.

Sometimes we find the term used inappropriately. For example, we might hear of IBM's loss of leadership in the personal computer market. If the speaker is referring to market share, then the use is wrong. Market share is not leadership, although it can be the result of leadership.

ISO 9000 does not mention the word. If leadership is not a requirement in the certifying phase, then why is it necessary in the sustaining phase? The answer is that when going for ISO 9000 certification, the goal is well defined and the path is well known. However, this is not the case with sustaining it, when the path is unknown or unclear. Leadership can define and achieve the goal of sustainability, but we must be explicit about it. If you have never seen an elephant, you can understand quite a bit about it just by following its trail; it is best, however, to see one. So also the notion of leadership. It is best to define it, then show how it can help to achieve sustainability.

Although a discussion of leadership on its own merits is rare in the business community, there is always an exception that proves the rule. One of the best is by Thomas R. Horton (1992), a former CEO of the American Management Association. His exposition on leadership is descriptive, inclusive, and well written, albeit focusing on CEOs. Leadership may start at the top, but it must be found at all levels of the command structure if decisions are to be delegated to the necessary level. If we want a very brief statement of the meaning of leadership we can turn to the U.S. Army (1994), where the matter is crucial. Interestingly, the Army's definition is not in military terms and can be applied directly to the business world:

> *Leadership is the process of influencing others to accomplish the mission by providing purpose, direction, and motivation.*

We shall use this definition as our guide to sustainability, expanding in this chapter on its key ideas: mission, purpose, direction, and motivation. These components of leadership can be implemented very simply through the process of dynamic quality planning.

Leadership Through Dynamic Planning

STRATEGIC PLANNING—IT'S BACK! So proclaimed *Business Week* on the cover of its August 26, 1996, issue. The story described a cycle of executive management objectives from strategic planning to reengineering to downsizing to transformation and back to strategic planning—this time, of course, with a difference. We cannot go back, perish the thought, except that it was never necessary to go through the cycle in the first place. If we are planning correctly and leading our companies dynamically, we don't need these cycles. What has been left unsaid is that major efforts such as reengineering, downsizing, and transformation are compensations for having been wrong.

We downsized because we guessed wrong about the future market. We reorganized because our existing structures could not adjust or respond to a changing environment. And of course, since Americans like novelty, the notion of making drastic changes for the sake of change became the thing to do even if the company was not in trouble. The CEO or general manager, having paid dearly to attend a lecture by one of the evangelists of change, would rush back to the plant saying, "We gotta reengineer! Everyone's doing it. We'll be left behind."

A leader keeps an eye on the horizon, then plans accordingly, for vision is necessary but not sufficient. But what do we look for on the horizon and how do we plan in order to avoid going through cycles of wrong judgments? It seems to me that there is only one icon—quality—and there is only one way to plan—dynamically.

There is too much worrying about what the competition is doing, what the gurus are saying, whether the economy is growing. All of these things constitute our environment and are factors in planning, but they are not goals on the horizon. On the other hand, quality is so broad and pervasive, so oriented to the customer, that when fully pursued it can serve as the only goal needed. When a small business begins, what is its sole focus? Satisfying the customer with a product that exceeds expectations. And how does this goal get lost as a company grows? My father used to say that the most efficient business is a one-man popcorn-vendor operation. The producer-customer relationship is direct, and affordable quality is the sole criterion. The vendor works to that single goal and everything else is addressed in doing so: competition, organization, economics. These factors are not goals but become issues to be resolved in getting to the goal. The goal is quality.

Dynamic quality planning is the way to the goal. *Dynamic* refers to the recognition that both the company (the system) and the world we operate in (the environment) change. The change can be met through adaptive design in both the organization and in the planning that will make the company capable and improvable. As you will see in Chapter 4, a strict by-the-book implementation of ISO 9000 may get you certified, but it won't make you capable. ISO 9000 enhances stability, but it does not ensure capability. And yet it costs no more to do the thing right, to build an organizational structure that is robust and that will endure. *Planning* capable processes requires a focus on dynamic response and on quality. In this kind of planning, *quality* is an adjective. You don't just plan quality; you plan *with* quality. Here and throughout this book, quality is both a goal and a mode, a way of doing something. When you plan with quality to build proactive structures, you use a methodology discussed in great detail later in this chapter.

The idea is to build processes that adapt automatically to both internal and external disturbances. The term *disturbance* has no negative connotation here; it is simply a force acting upon the system. Internal disturbances originate within the company and can be benign, such as ideas on improvement, or they can be adverse—say, machine failure or labor strife. External disturbances originate outside the company, are called *driving forces,* and include such things as parts deliveries or market demand. The processes that you design and build will operate in accordance with how they are built, no better and no worse. Thus, we shall begin our description of dynamic quality planning with a top-down approach—what you want to do and why.

Corporate Philosophy

The term *bottom line* is in such widespread use today that it has taken on a certain prestige, as though it had the status of a philosophy. What precisely does it mean? As a fad term, *bottom line* refers to the crux of a problem, but when it is used in a business sense it refers to profit. Profit is seen, at least superficially, as the endgame of business. Consider Eli Goldratt's viewpoint in his book *The Goal* (1986). The title describes the central idea: The sole objective of a manufacturing organization is to make money.

Several years ago I attended a meeting presided over by the president of a small service company. He managed to say "bottom line" half a dozen times within the first fifteen minutes, presumably because that was his orientation. Moreover, he was surrounded by the accoutrements of success: his own corporate headquarters, fashionable office furnishings, and a Mercedes in his parking slot. The conclusion seems to be that if you focus on the bottom line, if you keep the making of money as your primary goal, then your company will be successful.

But there is another point of view. Jim Collins and Jerry Porras (1994) have identified what they call "visionary companies," describing them this way: "They have a basic set of core values and a sense of enduring purpose—a reason for existence—that changes seldom, if ever. These values and sense of purpose go far beyond just making money."

Although they conflict, both notions are correct. You cannot ignore the bottom line, which must be a tactical objective if you are to stay in business. The idea that there is something negative or immoral about profit is a vigorous holdover from the Middle Ages with champions in the United States even today. A society maintains its civilization through a cooperative stewardship of its resources, and no economic system has been more efficient at this than free enterprise. Using this profit-oriented system, we have been able to feed our citizens continually for over 300 years, and few nations can make that claim. On the other hand, altruistic economic systems have failed on large scale, at least under the banner of communism. So we can accept the idea of profit as a necessary motivation, well suited to the human psyche, and this can lead to efficient tactical decisions.

Strategic decisions, though, require a broad perspective, a consideration of things that may come to be or of an environment as yet undefined. Collins and Porras were speaking of visionary companies that are preparing for the future. A cursory review of some dynamic forces in our economy shows why. For example, environmental protections are an increasingly dominant force in the world's decision making, as manifested by the impending adoption of the ISO 14000 standard by many industrial nations. Social forces influence what companies make, how they make it, and where they sell those products. International forces invade our markets with their goods, and consumers buy those goods unless we can produce them better or cheaper. On the other hand, if we want to sell our goods in foreign markets, we must learn something of those cultures. We are no longer the only producer in town.

These considerations indicate that to be successful in the long term, companies need to produce quality and managers need a broad view of the world and of their place in it. In other words, companies are subject to the same forces as are individuals. So if you want to make a quality product and do it forever, then you need a core philosophy that will get you where you want to go. Hayes and Wheelwright (1984) provide an appropriate definition of company philosophy, which is paraphrased by inserting the word *quality*:

> *A set of guiding principles, driving forces, and ingrained attitudes that help communicate quality goals, plans, and policies to all employees and that are reinforced through conscious and subconscious behavior at all levels of the organization.*

This definition is a good one for our purposes because it integrates the notions of quality policy, goals, and systems with commitment. The commitment is pervasive, including that of both top management and employees. The commitment of executive management is absolutely required in order to initiate tactical and strategic change. The commitment of employees is necessary because you simply do not have a company (unity) without it. The trend today is to recognize the importance of a unified force by referring to employees as associates and to reduce hierarchy by renaming supervisors as coordinators. I am not sure how effective this is over the short term; critics protest that it is just social engineering. I believe that it will be effective over the long term, however. The whole idea of equality in

America is social engineering, but it seems to work. Americans are descended from one side of aristocracy or the other and we reject the notion. A class system exists in other democracies, such as France and England, but it does not work here. The way to get Americans to work together is to show them that it is in their self-interest to do so.

A company's philosophy is sometimes articulated in a mission statement, which is always put in the perspective of the customer. Some critics claim that this is merely blowing smoke, but I don't think so. It is true that words allow nonbelievers to pass as believers, but this has been true throughout history. A mission statement serves two purposes. First, it summarizes a corporate philosophy in a few words; second, it gives authority to the words. If you say them often enough you will eventually accept them as your reason for being. Yes, we all work for a living but we work *well* if we believe in what we do.

Mission statements tend to be "blue sky" goals in the following vein: "to build a profitable, continuously improvable company, using advanced technology gained through continuing product development, in order to meet or exceed customer expectations."

A company has only one mission statement and it applies throughout the company. It is everyone's mission. It is called "blue sky" because it represents goals that are never attained; they are always just over the horizon. You continue to pursue them forever, and this pursuit provides direction for the company. It offers focus and influences decisions. The mission statement helps keep the company within its areas of competence without impeding choices. You can go after a new market niche and have a reasonable chance for success, other conditions being favorable, but if the niche is outside the company mission, then there is less chance for success. An efficient company amasses expertise, resources, and wisdom in accordance with its mission; outside its mission, these factors diminish and the risks increase.

Strategic and Tactical Planning

Collins and Porras found that visionary companies invested for the future more than did other companies. This implies that visionary companies are masters of strategic planning. A review of the current business literature shows how important this kind of planning has become for today's international markets. Byrne (1996) reports a general consensus among executive management that long-term planning is the single most important issue, albeit changed somewhat in character. Today's planning is a mix of strategic and tactical planning along the lines presented in Stimson's *The Robust Organization* (1996). Let's examine that mix and why it is important.

Most people agree that strategic planning refers to the long term—say, greater than five years—and tactical planning for the near term—say, less than five years. Each has its proponents, who endorse the one and belittle the other. Strategic planning is, of course, top down, or done by those trained to plan for the future and to provide direction. They first set up a proper organization, then the business takes care of itself, leaving them free to consider strategy. However, if the structure is fixed, then it cannot respond to change; if the structure is adaptive, then it will require timely management decisions at all levels. On the other hand, tactical proponents such as Abell (1993) point out that near-term planning uses the systems in place and so needs the bottom-up expertise of employees and supervisors. Steven Hewitt (1994) agrees, believing that high-level planning without bottom-up input is blue-sky thinking and cannot be effective.

Dynamic quality planning includes both strategic and tactical planning in balance, and Gibson (1990) explains why. Strategic planning establishes goals and objectives and considers the planning environment. Because this view is general, it does not provide the detail needed to resolve daily issues. Tactical planning addresses the here and now. It provides immediate and effective solutions for near-term problems because it is done by system experts. But as Gibson points out, the shortcomings of bottom-up thinking are that it tends to focus on short-term problems, producing ever decreasing incremental improvements. Most adversely, it locks in current technology and structure. Your competition will kill you if you rely heavily on just one or the other of these approaches to planning.

Top-down planning is characterized by a general approach to issues, focusing on direction. Generalizing allows us to look at the big picture, taking into account the system, its driving forces, and its environment. This long-term view is absolutely necessary in order to anticipate the potential changes that may occur. No one can predict the future, but we increase our foresight if we imagine at least what is possible within a given time horizon.

Bottom-up planning considers the day-to-day picture as viewed by experts who must deal with it. The technical expertise is here. For example, the workers on the line and their supervisors are best qualified to resolve problems, including long-term problems, that derive from day-to-day details.

Characteristics of Planning Dynamically

Top-down and bottom-up planning, although distinct, are not mutually exclusive. They can be used effectively and simultaneously to achieve different objectives. For example, top-down planning tells you where to go and maybe how to make some broad strokes of the brush while bottom-up planning provides the detail to make things work. Top-down planning envisions improvements of a completely different kind while bottom-up planning provides the incremental improvements necessary for a dynamic system. This integration of planning styles is characterized by five elements: a time horizon, a hierarchy of goals, a system infrastructure, a formal methodology, and controls.

The time horizon refers to the period of the plan, which should extend beyond the performance to include both the activity and time needed to observe results. No one has the wisdom to see forever. There is a time constraint to all plans.

We reach distant goals by meeting a series of intermediate goals whose attainment provides a measurement of progress. The major goals are supported by a hierarchy of lower-level goals whose attainment leads to the next higher level of goals. This supporting structure serves two purposes: It orders the achievement of objectives, and it engages the company. Every goal is attained by some order of activity, usually the attainment of lesser goals. The tragic inability of the Irish over the centuries to throw off English occupation of their land has been recounted many times, by Thomas Flanagan (1988), for example, in his book *The Tenants of Time*. The tale is a long sequence of plans with a single goal and no supporting objectives preceding it. A typical example is a battalion of French soldiers landing in support of an Irish rebellion and no Irish battalions put together to join them. Another is a ship lying offshore, loaded with arms, with no one assigned to off-load the cargo. In each case, the main goal was well conceived by strategic planners: Irish leaders in Paris in 1790 convinced the French to commit forces in Ireland to tie up the English; Irish leaders in Berlin in 1915 convinced the Germans to arm Irish freedom fighters. But in both cases the superstructure of subordinate goals was not there.

I use these examples because of their dramatic impact—in both cases a great loss of life ensued. Inadequate business planning may not cause loss of life, but nonsupport of goals still leads to defeat. A commitment to go after a particular market must be coordinated with a productive capacity that can meet that market. And sometimes subordinate goals exist, but they serve at cross-purposes. For example, in 1982 the U.S. Navy decided to place modern surface combatants in private shipyards. This goal had to be supported by a lesser objective, the certification of these shipyards to work on modern ship systems. Certification was costly because of the increased training required; presumably this cost could be offset by a well-established system of negotiated procurement. Unfortunately, in the same year the Navy initiated a counterobjective of lowest-bid awards. The more likely that a shipyard had the expertise to repair modern surface combatants, the less likely it could win a contract. As of this writing these conflicting objectives have not been resolved.

An effective plan requires an organizational hierarchy integrated horizontally as well as vertically. In this way, quality processes can be deployed across functions with no loss in ownership. The integrated organizational structure is supported by a parallel integration of functions and resources, which are formalized and systematic in order to achieve stability. In fact, ISO 9000 looks closely at the formality of processes, requiring a duality of organization and documentation. The ISO standards recognize that group achievement is possible only through cooperation of skills and expertise realized through organizational and functional structures. The organizational structure provides form and the functional structure provides substance.

Both can be designed for stability and capability, whose properties are the whole justification for structure. Business and industrial organizations are human-in-the-loop, which means that a decision system is required to respond to multiple input environments.

Finally, dynamic quality planning calls for a control process for data collection and analysis, metrics for measuring of progress, and feedback for tracking and improvement. Measurement is required for control; control is required in order to reach the targets. I have long been fascinated with the resistance to measurement that occurs in both government and industry. Admittedly, measurement is not free, so an industry might be reluctant to do it. And results can be embarrassing, so government agencies might be reluctant, too. There are companies that do not know how much of their overall production is regrade, nor how much is scrap. There are government agencies that cannot describe their effectiveness in numbers. In short, you can't know where you are relative to a goal unless you make measurements.

Elements of a Dynamic Quality Plan

Some things must be put into a planning process in order to have dynamic quality planning, and there is strong consensus on what these things ought to be. For example, Abell, Cuppello (1994), Juran (1992), and Stahl and Grigsby (1992) all present similar elements for this kind of planning. There will be committees, policies, goals, deployment, and evaluation. These elements satisfy the character of dynamic planning that has been described.

Committees

An executive quality council consisting of senior-level management provides policy and goals for the corporate quality program. The council may be supported by lower-level quality committees representing all levels of the company. Goals suggest an ordering process, and this is achieved through some logical structure of forums. Forums can enhance dynamic planning because of the opportunity for free-ranging ideas, oriented to some specific goal. For example, Juran states that an executive-level quality council is fundamental to the success of quality planning. Strategy is the purview of executive management, and without participation at this level quality will not happen. On the other hand, quality by mandate is not usually successful either, so lower-level quality committees can be useful also. All employees participate in these committees and communication is open. A unifying thread is established by using members of higher-level committees as chairpersons of lower-level committees. The appropriate number of such committees depends on the size of the company, the range of its functions, and its geographical deployment.

A quality forum is not a meeting to discuss quality. These meetings do take place, but in general they are a bad idea. Treating quality as a noun often results in gestures of form over substance. Again, quality is a mode, a way of doing business. Thus, the substance of a quality meeting should be the normal subjects of business, viewed in regard to the principles of quality. Consider, for example, a production meeting. The topic might concern the schedule of a given project. The meeting should be attended by persons with the authority to resolve the issues, and all players concerned with that schedule should be present, their input solicited irrespective of rank but according to their expertise. Existing problems are identified, analyzed, and assigned for action, with an appropriate target date for solution. Circumstances that can contribute to potential problems are discussed with the view toward anticipating and avoiding an impact on the critical path. In other words, both corrective and preventive actions are assigned for execution. A production meeting conducted in this manner is a quality meeting even though the word *quality* may never be used. Quality is a way of life, not a slogan.

Policies

Policies are action statements derived from the corporate mission. In terms of quality, executive management is responsible for developing and implementing such policy. The literal interpretation of this statement is that a company needs a policy regarding quality, but the policy as such is too narrow to lead to capable systems. In an important sense, *policy* and *quality policy* are redundant terms. Every policy should reflect the principles of quality. But a policy that is delineated as a quality policy is probably not worth much, as it tends to be isolated from the general activity of the organization. So for the remainder of this discussion, *policy* is used in a holistic sense. With this holistic view, there is a logical thought process involved in the leadership to meet any objective, a notion that will be explored in the next several paragraphs.

Policies reflect thought, and thought is based on a philosophy. Thus we see why companies in business require a philosophy. Studies show that companies with a driving philosophy last longer and tend to make better decisions in a changing environment than do companies whose sole purpose is to make money. As mentioned earlier, Collins and Porras call such companies visionary and claim that, having identified a fixed core ideology, they are free to change everything else. For this reason, visionary companies are highly adaptable to changing external forces without losing their way. Adaptability is a necessary property for building capable and sustainable systems.

A company's philosophy must be articulated in a form that can be implemented. One way is to express corporate policies as guidelines for action, to which goals can be assigned. This translation from ideas to results is shown in Exhibit 2-1, with the philosophy, mission, policies, and goals tied together. This closed-loop control configuration is fundamental to capability, and it will be used throughout the analysis of the twenty requirements of the Standard.

The nuances of Exhibit 2-1 bear some explanation. There is always feedback from goals to the policies from which those goals are derived, both to verify that the policies are followed and to validate the policies themselves. Monk (1995) provides an interesting example of policy validation. The Alaskan salmon industry decided on a policy of opposition to salmon farming in order to maintain its traditional commercial fleet. One goal was to obtain a federal ban on the import of Norwegian farmed salmon. This was achieved but proved worthless owing to replacement imports from Chile. At this writing, the Alaskan

Exhibit 2-1. Closed-loop transition of ideas to action.

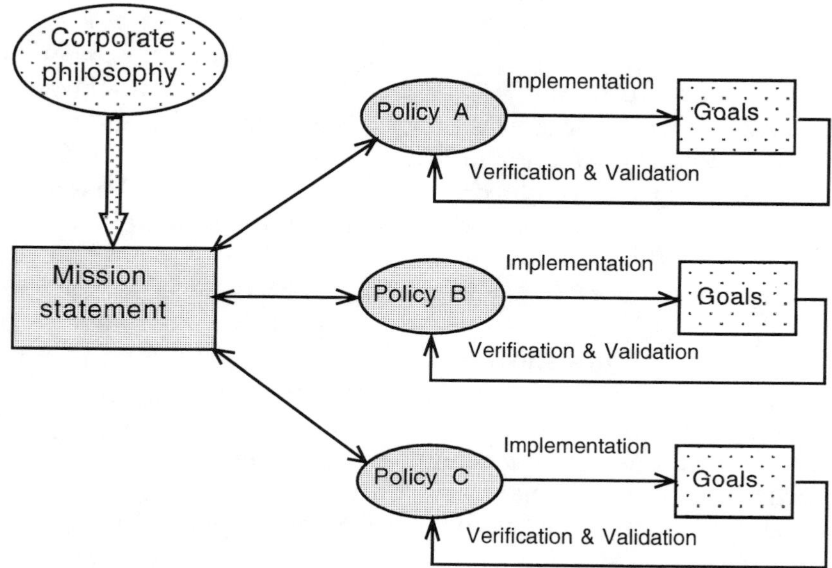

industry appears to have two alternatives: Try for a ban against Chilean imports as well, or change its policy. If the industry succeeds in banning Chilean imports, will it face yet a third competitor? And a fourth and a fifth? This example makes clear the need to validate policies.

As another example, consider a manufacturer of industrial air conditioners that decides to branch out into the residential market and determines some goals in line with this policy. The company may find, however, that having a substantial reputation in the industrial market means little in the residential area and, in fact, its products have a capability that overprices the competition. The company's new policy clearly needs to be reviewed. The new policy could well have been—indeed, should have been—in line with the company mission, but the company mission was not reviewed. There was no feedback from mission to philosophy, or the fixed-core ideology that Collins and Porras say characterizes the visionary company.

Policies, then, are action statements that implement the corporate philosophy expressed in the mission statement. Policies must lead to goals that are recognizable and achievable. They may vary from company to company, but Juran lists common characteristics of policies. They should:

1. Meet the needs of customers.
2. Equal or exceed competitive quality.
3. Conduct programs of improvement throughout the year.
4. Extend to all areas of the business.

For example, a quality policy might be similar to the following:

> *It is the policy of Wild Rover International to grow, to increase market share, to improve our profitability, and to provide our customers with products and services that meet or exceed their expectations in terms of quality and competitive cost.*

At first blush this policy seems to be a mission statement, a reflection of corporate philosophy, and perhaps it is. It is nevertheless a valid policy because, as we shall see, each phrase can lead to a defined, measurable goal.

Goals

A goal is the desired result of the action expressed in a policy. It is specific and measurable. There may be more than one goal per policy. Generally, there is a chain of goals arrayed in a synergistic hierarchy that ensures sequential success. In this book, the word *goal* is interchangeable with the word *objective,* although I confess to sometimes referring to an end as a goal and the intermediate achievements to get there as objectives.

Gibson's approach to goal hierarchy is to first generalize the implementation of the policy. Determining goals is a top-down activity, so you want to proceed from the general to the specific. Thus, your initial cut at creating goals from policy is to start out as general as possible. Do not commit a specific interpretation to a policy right away because the first idea that comes to mind may not be the best, and may even be wrong. The Wild Rover policy statement, for example, includes a policy of increasing market share. One way to increase market share might be to go after a very narrow part of the market, or conversely to take the competition head-on, across the board. Look at the policy as broadly as possible.

Within this broad interpretation, you examine how you are now doing things. This is called developing the *descriptive scenario*. You establish where you are and how you are presently operating with respect to the policy under consideration. Only after you have established where you are do you think about where you want to go—the *normative scenario*. This is where you begin brainstorming and where you will begin to define objectives.

Exhibit 2-1 shows the loop from objectives feeding back to policies. You must validate policies as indicated by the goals, during both planning and execution. One reason why this is necessary was demonstrated in the example of the manufacturer of air conditioners. Perhaps the American automotive industry provides an even better example, with its on-again, off-again policy regarding the manufacture of compact cars during the 1970s and 1980s. In this latter case, a weak commitment failed to win devoted customers. Detroit was not able to compete in the small car market until it developed a policy that it could stick to.

Iteration during the planning phase of goal development refers to a reassurance that the goals derived from various policies will lead to the normative scenario. There are two reasons for this iterative process. The first is a validation effort similar to the policy-goal review. The second, as Gibson puts it, is to allow immense freedom in developing goals by using a closed-loop correction process to reduce error resulting from goals too far from reality. This immense freedom refers to the ability of a corrective process to entertain wildly different goals, and to recover through iterative review if the goals cannot be met or cannot conform to the mission.

A synergistic chain of goals with corrective review is portrayed in Exhibit 2-2. It is organized by level to suggest a deployment of objectives throughout the company. Having arrived at a goal that will satisfy corporate policy, management determines all the levels of achievement required to attain the goal, often by brainstorming. Certain quality goals tend to be universal: product and process performance; quality improvement; and reduction of cost of quality.

Let's use the example of the Wild Rover company to see how this procedure is carried out. The goals are the execution of its policy statement: (1) to grow; (2) to increase market share; (3) to improve profitability; (4) to provide customers with products and services that meet or exceed customer expectations in quality; and (5) to provide customers with products and services that meet or exceed customer expectations in competitive cost. Five goals lie in this single policy statement. Then methods must be determined to achieve these goals, and this is done by generating the necessary sequence of objectives that progress from the general to the specific, and that can be implemented and executed. A valid goal sequence might be thus: to improve profitability → to reduce rework → to begin statistical process control.

Deployment

The deployment of goals identifies resources, responsibilities, integration, and "ownerships" specified for achievement. Put another way, the generation of supporting objectives across the functions of the organization creates quality deployment.

Exhibit 2-2. Chain of related objectives with progress evaluation loops.

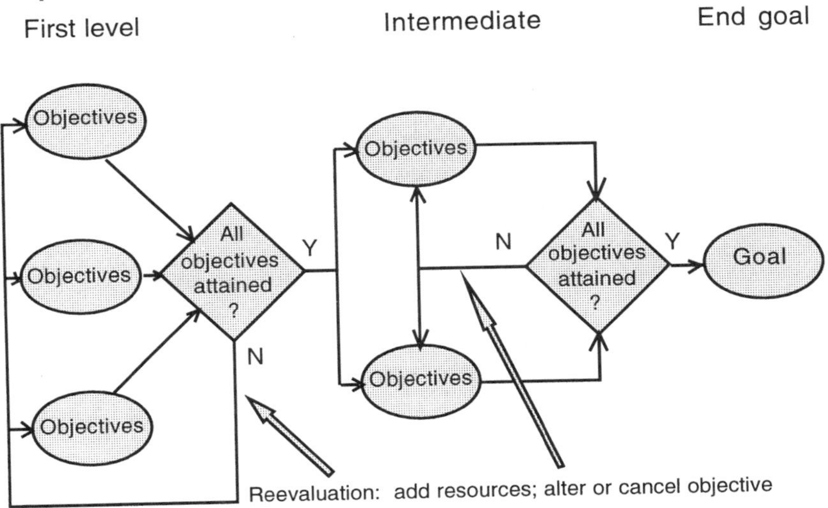

Deployment is a bottom-up activity, which means considerable detail must be provided. How this deployment is achieved will be discussed in Chapter 3. It is sufficient here to say that all actions must be functionally integrated, with an "owner" identified for each objective through its life.

Evaluation

Performance evaluation requires identifying what is to be evaluated, the metric, the methodology, and the feedback for control and improvement. There are two ways to achieve a goal. The first is to simply declare that you have attained it. This strategy has, in fact, been offered relative to certain national objectives, and not entirely facetiously. However, this kind of achievement will likely fail in business, which is subject to the relentless reality of market forces. The second method requires that a true measurement be made, which provides an evaluation of our performance relative to goals. Measurement, though, invokes some questions: "What is measured?" "How is progress recognized?" And very important, "What will be the metric?" An ISO auditor will insist on knowing the metric. I once worked for a government agency that changed its metric from time to time according to whichever index yielded the best numbers. Presumably, you can't do that in the ISO world.

Sometimes the metric is obvious, sometimes not. For example, Wild Rover can evaluate its policy of increasing market share by one of two metrics: sales in dollars, or sales volume. The company also wants to exceed customer expectations in terms of quality. What, then, is the metric? This general policy can be applied company-wide because each function serves the customer directly or indirectly. Then each department implements this policy and determines its own goals and the metrics to measure them by. In every case, identifying indices of performance and metrics takes careful thought in order to achieve improvement and not waste resources.

The best metric will have a double virtue: It will measure progress to the goal and it will validate the policy. For example, Wild Rover wants to exceed customer expectations relative to quality. Suppose the company makes lawn tractors and its designers have developed an engine that can attain greater travel speed while retaining cutting ability. Travel speed is a metric that contributes to quality since most customers would view positively the chance to reduce the time it takes to cut their lawn. Marketing could promote this technical advance, choosing as a metric sales dollars relative to the model. Customer Service would measure reduced backlog of orders or reduction in delivery time.

The methodology of measurement must be appropriate, also. The greatest factor of adversity in production is variance of some quality characteristic. The ISO standards recognize the randomness of most industrial processes and the adverse impact of variation, and as a result, impose certain requirements concerning them. A manufacturer or provider of a service is free to determine appropriate statistical methods to measure variation of a product, depending on the objective of the measurement. For example, there are design methods aimed at prevention of variance. On-line feedback of key parameters can contribute to design improvements. Stability analysis and measurement of process capability during operations can detect variance. Ishikawa diagrams and Pareto charts are used to identify the special causes of variance. Reliability and maintainability measurements are used to determine the effectiveness of a design in terms of common causes of variance. And finally, an audit provides an effective evaluation of processes. The implementation of statistical methods of evaluation will be discussed in detail in Part Four, concerning the quality requirements under engineering purview.

Controls

A dynamic operation requires the attributes of stability, capability, and improvability, and the controls to achieve and sustain them. The control systems may be hardware, software, or managerial. To the extent that humans exercise these controls, we can think of them as responsibility, authority, and accountability. The latter are associated with management and are not usually thought of as controls, but that is effectively what they are. Although it might sound awkward to do so, responsibility, authority, and accountability can be used as universal terms for every control—human, hardware, or software—but I won't press the point.

Exhibit 2-3 depicts the basic relationship of attributes and controls as interrelated properties of a dynamic organization. Attributes will be addressed in Chapter 4, but now let's focus attention on what it means to think of responsibility, authority, and accountability as controls, a notion that might make people uneasy. We have put paternalism and authoritarian management behind and have moved into notions of empowerment, so what is this control business?

Control is strictly a technical term to describe how an operation achieves both stability and some optimal target. Controls are designed into the system, and humans are usually included in the loop. Thus, a function (human and/or machine) must do its job. This is akin to responsibility. Even though we don't think of responsibility when we think of machines, it is nevertheless valid to say that an entity performs the task for which it is responsible. The responsibility defines the task. Moreover, the entity must have the authority to do its job. Again, we do not

Exhibit 2-3. Attributes and controls of a dynamic organization.

think of machines as having authority, but if we consider authority as the provision of necessary resources, then the notion is applicable to human or machine. When a process has humans in the loop, they are part of the system. They always have an assigned responsibility, but they do not always have authority or accountability, as outside auditors often discover. A dynamic quality plan will have well-defined designations of these controls.

Control is achieved through responsibility by precisely defining and assigning the task and metric of the performance function. *Defining and assigning the task* precisely refers to the congruity of job requirements and performer's qualifications, and unambiguity of task and interfaces. *Metric* refers to the index of performance used to measure the achievement of quality.

Control is achieved through authority by the availability and provision of the resources required to achieve the task. These include human, material, and capital resources, as well as time. We usually think of authority as a spoken mandate bestowed by a superior, but the mandate is worthless without accompanying resources, so that the resources are the real authority. One of the major criticisms of matrix management is that the project manager depends on line managers to provide resources. They in turn operate on their schedule, not the project manager's. Thus, the project often suffers from want of resources and we simply say that the project manager lacks the authority to do her job.

Control is achieved through accountability by recognition for achievement and by imposition of a penalty for off-target performance. That means you must account for failure to achieve or maintain the task in the required way. Thus, accountability is the control used to attain improvability. The imposed penalty is usually nonlinear, being greater in proportion to the deviation from the target objective.

Accountability is quite different from responsibility or even authority, and because of a possible penalty, most of us try to escape or minimize it. Few want it. Judges have great authority but very little accountability. Whom do they account to? Politicians are accountable, but only periodically and only if we can remember what it is that they should have done that they did not do, or conversely. You might say that politics is the art of avoiding accountability. On the other hand, Horton says that leaders are distinguished by their desire for accountability. They do not fear penalty but, rather, use the concept to drive themselves. Because it is a control, accountability must be properly assigned in a dynamic quality plan. The production manager who is accountable for a schedule but only responsible for quality will let the lesser burden slide.

Leadership Through Motivation

The relationship between leadership and motivation is as old as history and has been raised to the status of lore. We define a leader as one who has followers; presumably they follow the leader for some reason. Some of the leaders in history, such as Robert E. Lee, enjoy mystical status. And yet we know that Lee sometimes threw lives away and was so accused, acrimoniously, by another member of the Confederate pantheon, George Edward Pickett. Did Lee's troops follow him because they loved him, as folklore tells us? Did they follow him because they thought he provided their best chance to stay alive? Or did they love him in later years, when the pain of war faded and they looked for a remnant of greatness to associate with their lives?

It is not difficult to generate leaders in adverse times; in free societies they seem to appear on the scene when needed. But it is difficult to guess who the leaders might be. For example, based on their earlier careers, who could have predicted the rise and performance of Lincoln or Grant? In adverse times, the preordained often fall and the unrecognized rise to the top. Business faces the problem of finding leaders who can motivate their workforce, not for two hours or two months but for twenty years, in good times and bad, and cannot afford destiny's random selection. Leaders can motivate followers over the long haul by showing that the "team" has a common purpose and benefit that is ongoing. Peter Drucker, in *The Frontiers of Management* (1986), described it best when speaking of the founder of IBM, Tom Watson: "He believed in a worker who saw his interests as identical to those of the company. He wanted above all a worker who used his own mind and his own experience to improve his own job, the product, the process, and the quality."

It seems intuitive that if a person's interests are identical to the company's, then motivation will be maximized. We can count on someone pursuing self-interest. One of the best means of achieving this identity of interests is through empowerment. Empowerment is much the rage these days; the literature is filled with this notion, and includes analyses and data in support of this strategy. Some companies have bet their money on it, becoming employee owned.

Empowerment is a natural step along the evolution of the manager-employee relationship described by Hersey and Blanchard (1996). In Hersey's Situational Leadership® model, he defines various modes that trace out this evolution. Exhibit 2-4 shows how this relationship has grown over the years, corresponding to a parallel development in job complexity. As work shifted from a task to a process orientation, the workforce assumed increasing authority for achieving the objectives of production. In the early days in American industry, when the workforce was largely immigrant and uneducated, the manager was authoritarian and organized work along rigid and simple lines in a style that Hersey and Blanchard call the Tell mode. In the Sell mode, management sought to "sell" the workforce on its responsibility, but never relinquished authority. The Participate mode is the most commonly used today; the workforce is considered skilled and its opinion is sought on the production line. The highest mode defined by Hersey and Blanchard is that of Delegate and corresponds to what we might call empowerment: The workforce determines its own readiness to assume a given level of responsibility and authority, with management playing a consulting role.

Exhibit 2-4 demonstrates that empowerment is not born of benevolence; it is born of necessity. The transition from task to process as the basis of modern industry may well be the driving force. Achievement of large-scale economy and quality require an able workforce at both production and system levels. Empowerment is therefore keyed to training, including systems training. When workers understand the systems within their purview, with its inputs and sources, its outputs and destinations, and its environment, they are capable of their best efforts, have attained their highest level of mutual interest, and, we suppose, their highest motivation.

Exhibit 2-4. View of the Hersey modes of employee empowerment.

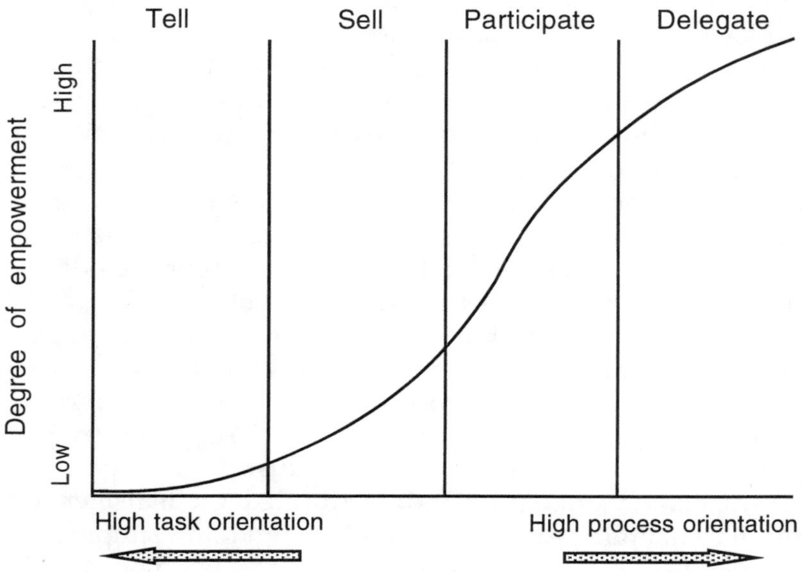

(Adapted from Hersey's Situational Leadership® model, with permission of the Center for Leadership Studies.)

If this sounds to you like motherhood, read it again. Most companies have quite limited training budgets and few of them train at the systems level, with the possible exception of management training itself. We are not talking about training a lathe operator. We are talking about training this operator in both lathe operation and how that task fits into company operations. The idea of ownership is often bandied about in the quality literature, and refers to a continuum of responsibility for each task and product as the unit crosses functional lines. The concept of ownership is crucial to quality deployment, and is best achieved when employees have a systems view of their role in the company.

Summary

Leadership is an essential component of sustainability. It is the process of influencing others to accomplish the mission by providing purpose, direction, and motivation. The leader builds a visionary company with a core philosophy and mission. Policies are derived from this mission. Both top-down and bottom-up planning are used to attain objectives, and a process of validation and verification is employed at all times during the pursuit of these goals. All processes use a control structure of well-defined responsibility, authority, and accountability. The company becomes a unity when all participants, from the CEO to the workers on the floor, perceive a common interest and challenge in the achievement of objectives.

References

Abell, D. F. *Managing with Dual Strategies*. New York: Free Press, 1993.

Blanding, Warren. *Customer Service Operations*. New York: AMACOM, 1991.

Byrne, J. A. "The New Strategic Planning." *Business Week*, August 26, 1996, pp. 46–52.

Champy, James. *Reengineering Management*. New York: Harper Business, 1995.

Collins, J. C., and J. I. Porras. *Built to Last: Successful Habits of Visionary Companies*. New York: Harper Business, 1994.

Cupello, J. M. "A New Paradigm for Measuring TQM Progress." *Quality Progress*, May 1994, pp. 79–82.

Deming, W. E. *Out of the Crisis*. Cambridge: Center for Advanced Engineering Study, Massachusetts Institute of Technology, 1986.

Department of the Army Pamphlet 350-58, "Leader Development for America's Army." *Department of the Army*, October 13, 1994.

Drucker, P. F. *The Frontiers of Management*. New York: E.P. Dutton, 1986.

Flanagan, Thomas. *The Tenants of Time*. New York: E.P. Dutton, 1988.

Gibson, J. E. *How to do Systems Analysis*. Workbook. Charlottesville: School of Engineering, University of Virginia, 1990.

Goldratt, E. M., and J. Cox. *The Goal: A Process of Continuous Improvement*. New York: North River Press, 1986.

Hayes, R. H., and S. C. Wheelwright. *Restoring Our Competitive Edge*. New York: John Wiley, 1984.

Hersey, P., and K. Blanchard. *Management of Organizational Behavior*. Englewood Cliffs, N.J.: Prentice Hall, 1996.

Hewitt, Steven. "Strategic Advantages Emerge from Tactical Tools." *Quality Progress*, October 1994, pp. 57–59.

Horton, T. R. *The CEO Paradox*. New York: AMACOM, 1992.

Juran, J. M. *Juran on Quality by Design*. New York: Free Press, 1992.

Laudon, K. C., and J. P. Laudon. *Management Information Systems*. New York: Macmillan, 1991.

Monk, Nina. "Real fish don't eat pellets." *Forbes*, January 30, 1995, pp. 70–71.

Stahl, M. J., and D. W. Grigsby. *Strategic Management for Decision Making*. Boston: PWS-Kent Publishing, 1992.

Stimson, W. A. *The Robust Organization*. Chicago: Irwin Professional Publishing, 1996.

Tomasko, R. *Downsizing: Reshaping the Corporation for the Future*. New York: AMACOM, 1987.

Chapter 3

Marketing ISO

If you drive from Montreal to the city of Quebec along the Saint-Laurent River, you will pass through the lower part of an area known as La Mauricie. It is so indescribably beautiful in the fall that you may be tempted to leave the autoroute and drive north along the St. Maurice River. Your extra time will be well rewarded, for entering the foothills of the Laurentide Mountains you will come upon hardwood forests ablaze in reds and oranges, golds and greens, of colors so wild that only nature can get away with it—no one would believe an artist's rendition.

Alone among His wonders, you twist through the narrow mountain passes through which the river flows and come upon the bay of Shawinigan. Turning around a mountainside you break into another small valley and suddenly fall upon a clearing on the right, on which is sited a brick building of no identity, but with a huge green and gold banner hung along its width, proclaiming

ISO 9002

Looking closer, you see a posted sign announcing the building's owner as Stone Consolidated Corporation, Belgo Division. You have witnessed a small but very effective case of marketing quality. Those who have never heard of ISO 9000 will remember that sign, and when they hear of ISO influence on quality will say to themselves, "Why, I know a company with that quality—it's Stone Consolidated."

Marketing quality is voluntary; quality marketing is not. ISO 9004, the document of guidelines for certification, includes a company's marketing function within those operations that should conform to ISO requirements. Just how this is done is left to the company, but we shall spend some time with it because of the influence of the marketing function on sustainability. First, though, I shall discuss the value and technique of marketing the ISO certification itself.

The Strategy of Marketing Quality

A company makes a product or provides a service it is interested in marketing. Let's loosely define *marketing* as the interchange of ideas between producer and customer relative to a product or service that leads to attainment of customer and producer objectives. Generally, a company develops a marketing strategy that is in conformance to its corporate strategy and that addresses issues such as planning, pricing, promotion, distribution, and evaluation. The evaluation will be of competition, customer preferences, and company capability. Since an ISO 9000 program, properly installed, represents a definable level of capability, it is reasonable to include certification in the marketing strategy.

This assumes two things: The customer cares about quality, and the customer knows what ISO 9000 means in terms of quality. Neither of these assumptions is safe, and each will need to be examined in order to determine a tactical strategy.

The Customer and Quality

Throughout most of our history as an industrial nation, Europe was our greatest competitor. We received a big boost in World War I, which nearly wiped out most of the European production capability. World War II did it again, giving us such an overwhelming dominance in the years 1945 to 1970 that industrial growth just seemed to go on forever. Champy (1995) calls the period "the era of smooth sailing." However, our quality practices couldn't keep up with the sheer volume of production. Harrington (1987) and Garvin (1988) independently describe a similar tale: We were stuck in a philosophy of corrective quality while our competitors, principally Japan, were moving forward with preventive quality methods. *Corrective* quality attempts to rectify the production of bad product by some inspection scheme and simply becomes overwhelmed with massive production scales. *Preventive* quality is not affected by huge production rates because it addresses the productive process itself. The result was a relative but very real decline of quality in the American marketplace in these postwar years. Phrases such as *planned obsolescence* were bandied about. You could buy a new automobile in 1957 and would not be surprised to find that supporting systems such as battery, tires, muffler, and exhaust pipes might well need to be replaced within the first year and a half.

As the years went by, a generation of Americans began to accept this state of affairs. Weitz and Wensley (1984) present the results of a poll taken about the time of the book's printing that showed the ranking of factors in the selection of a manufacturer. The poll was taken of customers, company salespeople, and company personnel who were not in sales. Customers chose technical support services as the number-one factor in their selection of a manufacturer, with product quality ranking only fourth. This ranking order implies that by 1984 the American consumer was so used to poor quality that the most important factor in buying a product was how fast he could get it fixed after it broke down! (As an interesting observation of the thinking within an organization, company nonsales personnel ranked product quality second only to price; sales personnel ranked quality eighth in eleven categories.)

Today's customer is much more demanding of quality. Champy describes the new world order as the "dictatorship of the customariat" and "the market democracy." Both terms imply the same thing—the customer decides what the product's characteristics will be. Companies that recognize this new order should be motivated to add quality to their marketing efforts. It is a marketable commodity at least on a par with any other.

The Customer and ISO 9000

Whether your customer is familiar with ISO 9000 depends largely on who your customer is. If your customers are other businesses, you can be sure that they know about it. You may even have already received notice from some of your customers that they are moving to a policy of ISO 9000 suppliers only. If your customers are the citizenry, then they probably are not informed about ISO 9000 standards and your marketing strategy should include an education program.

Exhibit 3-1 summarizes some ideas on the strategy of marketing the quality inherent in an ISO 9000 standard. The standards are not too complicated for citizens to understand. Perry Johnson (1993) reports that governments in Europe and in the United Kingdom expend a great deal of effort to enlighten the population on the benefits of the international standards. Unfortunately, the American government has shown no leadership on this issue. Our marketplace policy has always been one of caveat emptor, and this is not likely to change. Nevertheless, the public is educable and interested. For example, many people look for an Underwriters tag on electrical appliances or for a Good Housekeeping seal on household goods. If you are ISO certified, then you want them to look for this endorsement also. Education will do it.

Exhibit 3-1. Formulation of marketing strategy.

The Tactics of Marketing Quality

Quality is a way of doing business, but in a sense it is a product too, the most important product in your repertory. Marketing quality requires an innovative approach, particularly in educating your customers about it. Hills (1994) defines innovation as successfully taking an idea to market. The idea that you want to take to market is that ISO 9000 certification represents a guarantee of quality and that this level of quality is established by an objective observer. Thus, you really have *two* ideas to teach your customers because everyone claims quality, but often the basis of those claims is a sales pitch. The poll discussed earlier by Weitz and Wensley indicates that salespersons really do not hold quality in great esteem but will say whatever they believe the customer wants to hear. The customer knows this, and the sales pitch is often heavily discounted. It is to your advantage to treat customers with respect because they will appreciate this approach and because you really do have quality to offer.

Your approach to educating the public should be founded on a few notions that are simple yet important to the consumer. An ISO 9000 certification represents a level of management of quality that is recognized worldwide. It is like a college degree. It represents a level of achievement of process and assurance that the company's production is consistent. Certification is awarded by registries that are not affiliated with the company and therefore are objective. These registries are supported by the integrity of professional organizations and governments. Where written, these ideas should be accompanied by the registry logo, usually a rather imposing symbol, and by the company logo, in order to make the association. The education program should be ongoing because it requires creating and maintaining a change in consumer perception.

As previously mentioned, the market is in two segments: those customers who are themselves producers and will likely have an awareness of the ISO standards, and the general public, which will not. Both should be targets of your education efforts, so you will need two programs. The program directed to producers should show how your quality system is implemented vertically from subcontractors to distributors and customers and horizontally within the company structure. Some companies even submit copies of their quality manual to prospective customers. These "advertising" copies may be more prettily bound, and of course they are uncontrolled. But otherwise they are the same as the quality manuals within the plant. In this way, if the customer decides to visit the plant, she will find the same situation the registrar auditor finds, that the company does indeed "walk the talk," and that is good marketing.

The education program directed to the public should focus on general ideas of quality, explaining in straightforward terms how and why consistency of quality is enhanced by an ISO standard and how the integrity of the process is ensured. The public is not interested in whether you evaluate your subcontractors. The details of how you arrive at quality is your problem. The public *is* very interested in a standard of quality—for example, the Good Housekeeping seal of approval enjoys public confidence. An effective education program will explain how ISO integrity is similar to this known reference. Both education programs should be channeled through distributors, wholesalers, and large retailers. They are part of the system.

Some of your competitors will be ISO certified also. If this is the case, you don't want to spend a great effort in a "me too" program but must delineate yourself somehow. This is why capability is so important. If you have integrated stability, capability, and improvability structures into your organization, you have a new twist to add to the program. This information should be used with care. You don't want to say that your competitors' ISO programs are not good but that yours is, because this generates the idea that there are really two (or more) ISO 9000 standards. Faced with this complexity, the consumer may well declare a pox on both houses. The trick is to establish belief in the ISO program, including the competitions', while delineating your own in some positive way.

The overall process for marketing the quality within an ISO program is summarized in Exhibit 3-2, using the four steps suggested by Hills (1994). You identify the segments of the market, develop an education program for each, determine how to help the customer delineate you from the competition (both those certified and those not), then estimate the expected effect as a function of time, reviewing your progress as necessary. Notice that

Exhibit 3-2. Process for marketing quality.

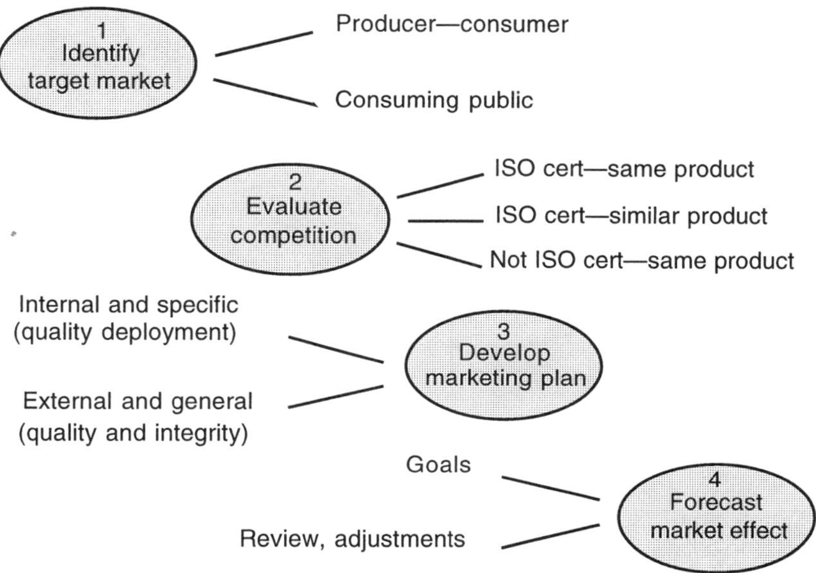

this process conforms to a general marketing analysis; you simply add quality as an additional member of your product line and conduct your usual marketing effort.

The Strategy of Quality Marketing

How does quality marketing differ from the marketing of quality? As I previously discussed, the latter treats quality as one of the company products and markets it as it would any of its products. Quality marketing is a different notion. Here, *quality* is an adjective and it means that the company's marketing function is conducted in conformance to an ISO standard, as are all the other of its functions.

Companies that are already certified under an ISO 9000 standard will have met its criteria in marketing. Nevertheless, it is worthwhile to review these requirements and expand upon them as necessary to effect sustainability. As with all ISO standards, the fundamental requirement is whether the supplier says what he does, then does what he says. This prescription ensures neither capability nor sustainability and is a subject of considerable criticism of the ISO standards. The issue can not be resolved here, and we shall simply go on with the basic objective: to move beyond ISO 9000 to where we want to go.

The ISO marketing function will determine the need for a product; establish market demand and sector relative to grade, price, quantity, and timing; determine customer preferences and trends; and establish good external (customer to company) and internal (customer through company) communications. In other words, a company aspiring to ISO certification will utilize a modern, acceptable marketing function.

Although this requirement is conventional, this does not mean that it is routine or simple. Many companies stress promotion and external communications, but the voice of the customer is not heard within the interior functions of the company: design, manufacturing, and production. Internal communication is so difficult that the Japanese have developed an entire methodology, quality function deployment, in order to achieve it. I recently had the roof of my home reshingled. The salesman and I sat down and had an extensive discussion of what I wanted and what he could provide. We drew up a contract listing all of the requirements. Several weeks went by, then the roofing crew showed up on the appointed morning, just as I was going into town. On the spur of the moment, I asked the supervisor if I might see his job order. Sure enough, the specifications of the job order differed substantially from the requirements of the contract. Big company or small, a good marketing function is hard to sustain.

In order to establish a marketing strategy you need to have some sort of model in mind. The model shown in Exhibit 3-1 is valid for both marketing of quality and quality marketing, but let's look at it from another viewpoint. Consider the arrangement of Exhibit 3-3, in which the function of marketing is displayed as a system within an environment. The competition and the customer are regarded as part of the environment because the company has no control of them, although it may have influence with the customer. The process is dynamic because it is measuring inputs from the environment as well as outputs from the system itself, and using the information in order to conduct and maintain an evaluation program of strengths and weak-

Exhibit 3-3. Dynamic marketing system.

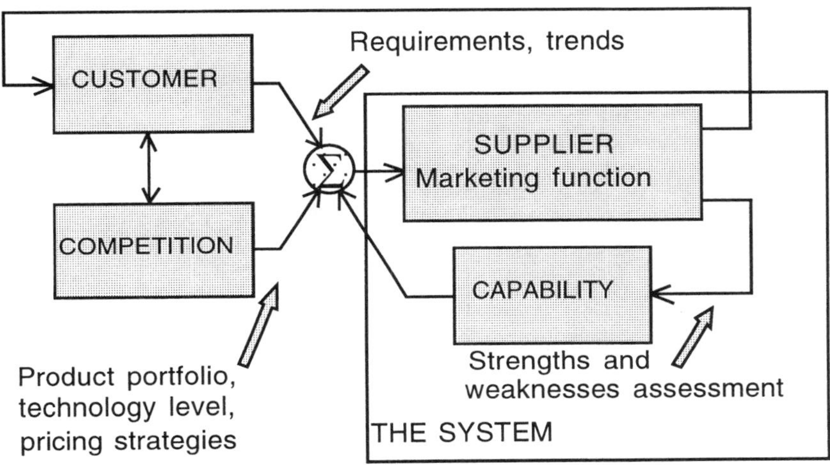

nesses. The summing point is the sensor and intelligence system the company maintains for marketing input.

We portray the marketing function as a closed-loop process to suggest not that marketing functions are usually organized this way but that they *should* be so organized. There are two reasons for doing so. The first is that closed-loop systems can respond in a timely way to changes in the environment and within the system itself. This reactability is what makes them dynamic—they respond to time-driven events. The second reason is that, as Wiener (1954) pointed out, when feedback is used as a control for evaluating past performance and improvement, the structure is effectively a learning process. In this case the evaluation is made against a moving target, the changing environment. The system is no better than the sensors that it uses, so both the structure and active, intelligent sensing must be employed. By "sensing" we mean sampling of customer and competitor dynamics.

Weitz and Wensley (1984) report widespread disaffection among analysts with the notion of strength and weakness assessments. They found that company personnel simply could not perform an objective self-assessment usable for marketing.

People tend to evaluate company strengths in the light of past accomplishments (descriptive scenarios) and weaknesses in the light of where they would like to be (normative scenarios). Thus, strengths tend to look better than they are and weaknesses tend to look worse than they are. Since these assessments are viewed with respect to the environment, they can be disastrous if wrong. The solution is not to abandon the strategy, for what good does it do to sample the environment if you do not use the information for improvement? We won't solve this problem here because it is complex and because it is not a marketing problem but a human and organizational one. Just recognize that it exists and that a company must strive for critical judgment in its process of self-assessment.

The Tactics of Quality Marketing

Whether or not to conduct self-evaluations is a strategic decision; their conduct is a tactical one. We have already discussed the pros and cons of this issue and now go on to some other ideas. I briefly mentioned channeling in the discussion on the tactics of marketing quality, and the issue is also appropriate here. If you are already ISO certified, then you have conformed to the minimum requirements of the Standard vis-à-vis your contractors and intermediate customers. You want to go beyond the minimum and consider your suppliers (sources), distributors, and wholesale and retail agents as part of the system depicted in Exhibit 3-3. Some of them may themselves have ISO 9000 certificates, some not, but the objective is to get them excited about yours. Getting these associates to perform to your ISO program is as much a marketing function as any other. At one time or another they will attend your meetings for planning, production, design and development, and even marketing. In every case, your marketing people should be at these meetings also. Marketing serves as one of the main points of contact between the environment and the system, and between the company and system components outside the plant. Kern (1993) discusses the marketing function at Digital Equipment Corporation (DEC), which utilizes a multidimensioned customer structure: end users, sales, service, engineering, and third party. Third-party customers are those providers that complement Digital's products and services. This notion represents an interpretation of the channeling idea. Perhaps you cannot quickly identify DEC's third parties; a more obvious example is the automobile industry and its relation to the rubber and steel industries.

Kern also points out that at DEC the first initiative of marketing is the voice of the customer. Many companies say this, few would deny it, nevertheless it can be either a rule or a motherhood statement. I'm sure that the roofing company that resurfaced my roof proclaims its belief in this axiom, but somehow my voice was not heard where it counted, down where the performance takes place. This point is discussed in more detail in Chapter 25, but at the moment you should recognize that the fundamental role of the marketing function includes bringing together the customer and the performers.

Summary

The customer in the modern era cares about quality and considers quality endorsements in her prospective purchases. An ISO 9000 certification represents a level of capability of the company and is therefore a marketable commodity. A company should pursue the marketing of quality and the quality of its marketing. The primary strategy for marketing of quality is educating your customers to the benefits they receive through your ISO capability. The primary strategy for quality marketing is to utilize a closed-loop structure as shown in Exhibit 3-3.

References

ANSI/ISO/ASQC. *Q9004-1-1994. American National Standard: Quality Management and Quality System Elements and Guidelines*. American Society for Quality Control, 1994.

Champy, J. *Reengineering Management*. New York: HarperCollins, 1995.

Garvin, D. A. *Managing Quality*. New York: Free Press, 1988.

Harrington, H. J. *The Improvement Process*. New York: McGraw-Hill, 1987.

Hills, G. E. *Marketing and Entrepreneurship*.Westport, Conn.: Quorum Books, 1994.

Johnson, P. *ISO 9000: Meeting the New International Standards*. New York: McGraw-Hill, 1993.

Kern, J. P. "Toward Total Quality Marketing." *Quality Progress*, January 1993, pp. 39–41.

Weitz, B. A., and R. Wensley. *Strategic Marketing: Planning, Implementation, and Control*. Boston: Kent Publishing, 1984.

Wiener, N. *The Human Use of Human Beings: Cybernetics and Society*. Garden City, N.Y.: Doubleday, 1954.

Chapter 4

The Dynamics of Quality

Up to now we have discussed the big picture—the view from the top. We saw that compliance to ISO 9000 is necessary but not sufficient for sustainability, and so we have covered topics such as strategic and tactical planning, marketing, and leadership, all of which you had some notion about to begin with. Thus far, sustainability has been discussed in easy-to-understand, everyday terms.

But this chapter is about stability, capability, and improvability, which cannot be discussed so informally. They must be defined in sufficient detail to be able to build something with them. Bottom-up concepts that make things work, they are at the same time dynamic properties and indices of system performance that require metrics. You cannot measure something exactly until you know what it is exactly, and you must be able to identify these dynamics exactly.

Why bother? Isn't sustainability about management after all? Why do we need this detail? The reason is that all of the high-level thinking, executive decisions, and best intentions must inevitably be put into action, which means that systems must be designed and built to carry them out. When the rubber meets the road, planning reduces to stability, capability, and improvability. Perhaps the best explanation is provided by Drucker's (1992) first law: "Sooner or later strategy and the big picture must degenerate into work." In this chapter, we go to work.

Dynamic Quality Properties

Industry and commerce make products and provide services. A product or service may have certain characteristics that we particularly care about, that seem to express the quality of the item. We call these aspects *quality characteristics*, reasonably enough. For example, a production system may provide a blue automobile that seats six easily and that can accelerate to a given speed in a desirable time. If we care about this, then color, passenger comfort, and acceleration are quality characteristics. Thus, when we refer to the quality of a thing, we mean that we care about, and are pleased by, certain characteristics of it. Without defining quality, we know it when we see it. Clearly, quality is subjective.

But manufacturers and providers of services cannot produce subjectivity. The quality of a knife may be its sharpness. But what is sharp? It depends on the job for which the knife is used, of course. The challenge to industry is to identify the characteristics of a product or service that customers care about, then attempt to define them in ways that can be measured. These measurements are then translated into specifications that can be used to make the product or to provide the service. The specifications are target values for production and, taken together, define the quality of the product. The companies then establish some scheme of production that can meet these target values and produce this same quality over and over again.

The quality process is shown in Exhibit 4-1, and is one of translating the customer requirements into a finished product or service. This process is generally done in this way: Marketing and customer service people talk to the customer and arrive at a conceptual product; then they join with design engineers who design the product, and with manufacturing engineers who design the system that makes the product, in order to arrive at sufficient detail for production. Product characteristics are determined, as are the metrics needed to describe them. Target values are calculated for each of the characteristics, together with the associated tolerances that demark acceptable deviation.

If the customer is important or if the project is long, the customer will have a monitoring role in this process, and should anyway because the process is dynamic. Not only is it hard to exactly determine the requirements of the customer, but these

Exhibit 4-1. The quality process.

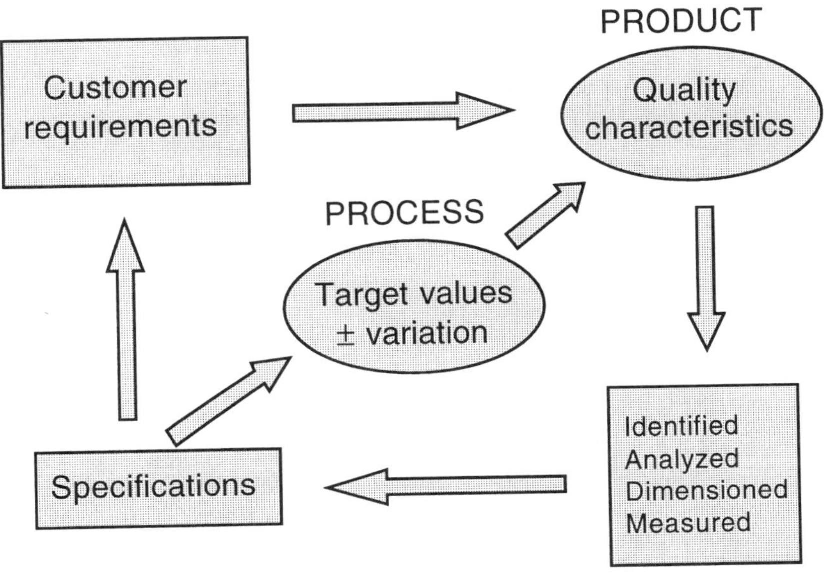

requirements are themselves subject to change. They are based on expectations that respond to real or imagined perceptions of the possible. Customer expectations can be established by education, which may be provided by an external source, but may also be provided by the producer. In fact, it is in the producer's interest to do so. This means that the process in Exhibit 4-1 is iterative from first approach of the customer through product delivery, with the customer in the loop so that there can be a maturity of expectations. To do otherwise is to risk customer disappointment. This risk is the greater in a long-term performance, such as building a house or airport, and in design and development of complex products such as computer systems.

During the production of goods and services there occurs variation in the quality as a result of chance. Shewhart (1931) said that there is a stable and inevitable system of "chance causes" inherent in any scheme of production. Since the variation is off target value by definition, then variation is the enemy of quality.

The variation that is inherent in a given industrial system uniquely characterizes that system. It is arguably the most important and least appreciated aspect of the system. Quality gurus such as Bhote (1991), Deming (1986), and Juran (1992), to name a few, have identified variation as a major responsibility of management, yet one that is most often neglected. Quality auditors and consultants see this neglect manifested in various ways, but mostly in the failure of management to measure the variation in their processes.

The variation in an industrial process can be measured in terms of three properties that derive from that variation. We can think of them as quality properties of the system, analogous to the quality characteristics of its product or service, because they are measures of effectiveness (MOE) of that system to produce quality. This is an important idea: *The inherent dynamic quality properties of a system are the best MOE of its quality.*

The first of these properties is *stability*. Stability is absolutely essential to dynamic processes and has long been a main concern in both systems theory and quality theory. The second dynamic property is that of *capability*, uniquely a quality concern. Capability must be considered in the light of stability; an unstable system has no capability. The third dynamic is that of *improvability*, normally associated with quality, but a concern of systems theory also, under another name (optimality). Improvability is usually defined in terms of capability.

Since these properties exactly describe the variation in a system, why is it that their measurement is so often neglected? The problem is that stability and capability are too narrowly and rigorously defined in quality theory. Quality engineers and technicians understand them quite well, but management deals in general language and rules of thumb. A discourse on statistical capability, for example, may well fall on uncomprehending ears, leaving the issue to the technical people and the production line, provided it doesn't cost too much to measure. At the other extreme, almost all manufacturers talk of being capable. "Continuous improvement" finds itself in every mission statement. Yet if the companies do not measure their capability, then they cannot know what it is, mission statement or not.

In the following paragraphs we will discuss these properties in great detail, beginning with fairly rigorous definitions of what they are, then generalizing the definitions in simple terms that can be applied to any industrial or commercial process without losing the essence of the property. Nevertheless, we shall retain the mathematical rigor of the formal definitions in our everyday language because this rigor is the difference between measures of effectiveness and motherhood statements.

System State

Every dynamic system has a property that we may call its state. State is different from condition. Condition refers to whether the system is functioning well or not, much as we might say that a person's condition is poor so he requires hospitalization. State, however, refers to what a process does, its motion or position as described by attributes such as on or off, high or low, few or many, attitude, speed, or acceleration. The state of a dynamic system represents its instantaneous motion. Over time the state may change and this motion is called the *state trajectory*. For example, if a force disturbs the system its state will change—that is, a state trajectory will occur.

The parameters that describe a system state are called its state variables. If the system produces things, then it has state variables that describe its state and quality variables that describe the quality of the product produced by the system. Sometimes the two kinds of variables are one and the same, but not usually. Nevertheless, quality managers must be aware of the state variables because it is the system state that changes. The variation in quality of product is always due to random changes in system state. It is the system state that must be controlled.

The relationship between state variables and quality variables can be appreciated by studying Exhibit 4-2. For the sake of simplicity we assume that each workstation performs a task with a single dynamic described by one state variable, X, and yields one quality characteristic described by a single variable, Q. The input is F, sometimes regarded as a force, but in our case it is simply the raw materials or purchased products needed to make the end product.

Let us assume that the system makes tape rewinders for video cassettes, and does so in three stages. Workstation 1 is the mounting of components; workstation 2 is the installation of a drive motor; workstation 3 is a torque test. It seems reasonable to consider the torque that the unit is capable of delivering as the state variable, X_3. But since the torque is the primary reason for the

Exhibit 4-2. General industrial process of three state variables that makes a product with three quality characteristics.

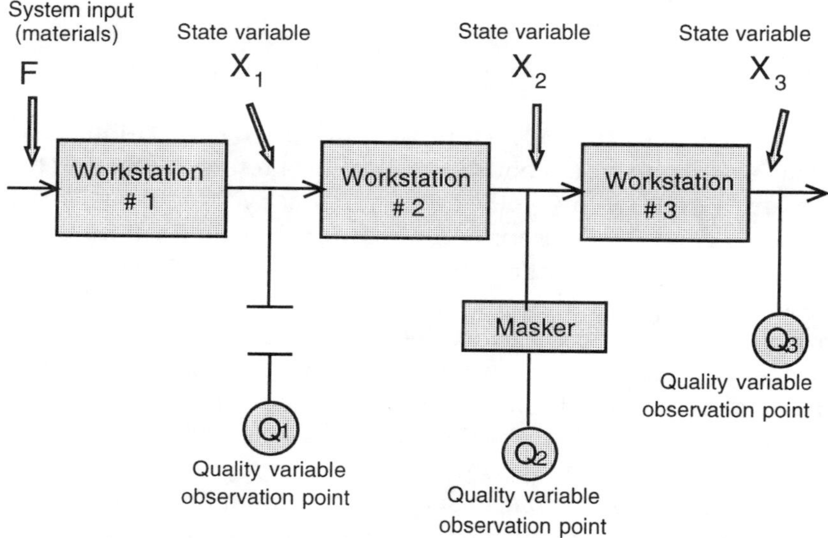

William A. Stimson, *The Robust Organization* (Burr Ridge, Ill.: Irwin, 1996). Adapted with permission.

product, it is also the quality variable, Q_3. Hence we have a happy coincidence where the state variable and the quality variable are the same thing. We can adjust the state variable to the desired torque, exactly and simultaneously measuring the quality.

We have installed a motor at workstation 2. The speed of the motor is the state variable, X_2, but we cannot measure it because of the masker. A masker is any process or device that obscures the relationship between the state variable and the process output. We don't care, though, because the motor manufacturer has provided us with a speed/torque calibration curve. So if we know the torque, we know the speed. However, the motor generates noise in proportion to its speed, and noise is the quality variable, Q_2. People do not like noise. However, we can adjust motor speed to an acceptable noise level, thus controlling the state of workstation 2 by "observing" the quality variable Q_2. Of course, the adjustment must result in an acceptable torque, for the whole purpose of the unit is to rewind tapes.

At workstation 1 we mount components, one of them a voltage rectifier that will provide the appropriate voltage to the drive motor. The obvious choice for state variable X_1 is the output voltage of the rectifier. As customers we don't care what it is, but we do care that the device is safe. Let the quality variable be stray voltage, Q_1, and it should be zero. Q_1 cannot be used as a control variable because we cannot relate it to the state X_1.

Clearly, the more closely related state variables are to quality variables the easier it is to control the process to provide quality. The good news is that state variables are not unique; we can choose whichever parameters we wish that describe what a machine or process is doing. The best choice optimizes the relationship between process state and product quality.

Let's look at a few examples of state and state variables, to clarify the concept. Suppose that you run a delivery service. Then the state of that service might be the number of pieces lost and the average time of delivery. It seems that only these two variables are needed to describe the state of the system. Arbitrarily then, X_1 would be the number of pieces lost and X_2 would represent the average delivery time. Hopefully, $X_1 = 0$, and X_2 is a small amount of time, but in any case you can now measure the state of your system at any time. You could pick any variables you want to be your state variables; the ones chosen in our example are useful and also have the advantage that they are simultaneously quality variables. In deciding upon state variables, the rule of thumb is to choose no more than you need.

Suppose that you work for a company and are responsible for inventory. Then you might describe the state of the inventory by two variables: the number of pieces on hand and the number on order. Are these quality variables too? They could be if their value reflected the effectiveness of your operation.

Suppose that you run a punch machine. Then the state of the machine might be expressed by three variables: the size of the punch, the position of the sheet metal against the stops, and the position of the stops with respect to the turret. These parameters are fixed for a specific product, but over time they vary according to the job and so represent true state variables. They describe the dynamic operation of the machine. This example shows a mixed relationship of the state variables to quality. It is clear that the quality variables would be the size of the hole and its position relative to where it should be. Thus, the first state variable is also a quality variable; the next two state variables establish the location of the hole, but are not themselves quality variables.

Exhibit 4-3 shows how the notion of state space is realized. We form an n-dimensional coordinate system with the state variables serving as axes. There are three axes in this figure; each is called an *attribute* because a state variable is an attribute of the process. Then we measure along each axis the value of the attribute. The state of the system, X, is a point located in state space at the intersection of all the values of the state variables. In Exhibit 4-3, $n = 3$—that is, there are three dimensions. We have given examples of states expressed in two dimensions. According to Lovelock (1990), Federal Express uses twelve variables to measure the quality of its service. Expressed as state variables, the quality state space of twelve dimensions cannot be pictured, but the utility of the concept remains. The notion of state space brings with it the discipline needed to identify parameters that indicate quality and those that indicate what the system is doing dynamically.

Exhibit 4-3. State space defined by three variables.

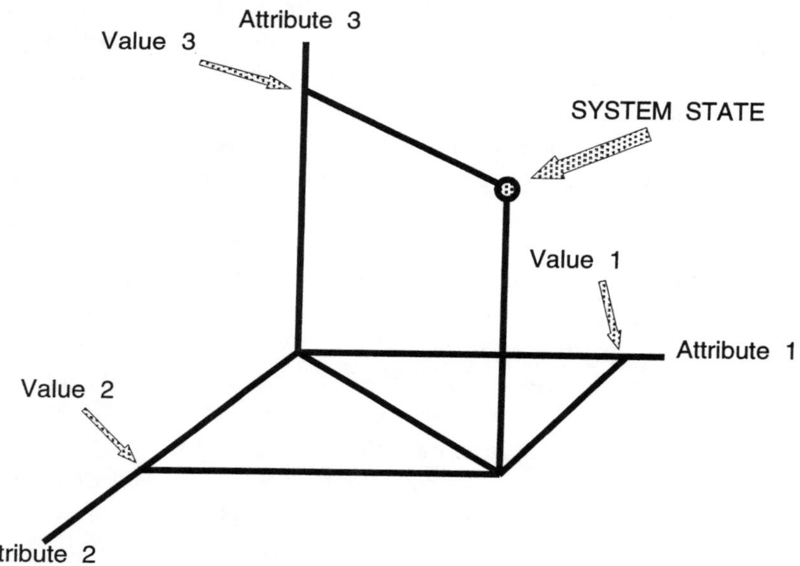

William A. Stimson, *The Robust Organization* (Burr Ridge, Ill.: Irwin, 1996). Adapted with permission.

By calling the axes of Exhibit 4-3 attributes rather than state variables, we deliberately introduce an ambiguity. If we choose state variables as the attributes, then the coordinate system is a state space. If, however, we choose quality variables as attributes, then we have a quality space, which is useful if the quality variables can be used to control the system. As our examples show, quality variables can be used to control the system only if they can be related directly to state variables. It is the system state that changes.

A final but simple example will clarify the issue of control with state or quality variables. When cooking in the oven, a chef controls the process by means of setting the oven temperature and the timer. This is cooking with control by state variables: oven heat and cooking time. When cooking on the range, however, the chef very often controls the process by observing the product's quality characteristics, adjusting the heat and cooking time accordingly. This is cooking with control by quality variables.

MOE 1: Stability

People who design systems spend a great deal of time thinking about stability. It is the first property that every system must have. Systems are built to do something, but if they are not stable that something cannot be done consistently, if at all. Airplanes, production lines, monetary systems, social systems—all must be stable. Unstable airplanes crash, production lines halt, monetary systems inflate, social systems revolt. Instability sooner or later results in the pathological behavior of the system. An unstable system introduces variation into whatever it is supposed to do, and we have already identified variation as the enemy of quality. Therefore, stability is a dynamic property of a system that relates to its ability to achieve quality.

The stability of a system is always considered relative to its state. It is the state that is stable or not. Many industrial systems are not inherently stable, being subject to a wide variety of external and internal forces, so we are concerned with their stability relative to equilibrium states that they may have. An equilibrium state, as its name suggests, is one in which the forces acting on the system are in balance.

Equilibrium is not often thought of relative to industrial processes, but a moment's reflection reveals how important it is. Production lines, inventory levels, monetary systems—all should be in dynamic equilibrium. You might argue that the job of management is to create conditions of short- and long-term equilibrium.

Liapunov's Stability

The definition of system stability used universally today comes from the classical work of Liapunov (1907). In its original form the definition is quite formal (and formidable). Fortunately, we can express it in words and still retain the necessary rigor:

> *The equilibrium state of a dynamic system is stable if and only if for every bounded input there is a bounded response.*

In other words, a process is stable in the sense of Liapunov if its state trajectory remains bounded for a bounded input (driving force). I shall show by some examples that the Liapunov definition of stability put in this form is directly applicable to industrial and commercial systems.

Stable Neighborhoods

Linear systems, according to system theory, are either stable or they are not. Their stability is intrinsic. Nonlinear systems are not intrinsically stable, but may have stable equilibrium states. Liapunov defined stability in terms of equilibrium states in order to address the most general case because few natural systems are linear. At any rate, the definition applies to linear systems also, which may be regarded as systems in which all states are either in stable equilibrium or not.

Exhibit 4-4 presents a visual notion of the Liapunov definition of stability. We shall assume a system with equilibrium states. Let a disturbance move the system from a given state at some instant in time; we shall call that the initial moment and initial state. The system may go to an equilibrium state or wander. As long as the wandering of the state trajectory is bounded

Exhibit 4-4. Bounded state trajectory.

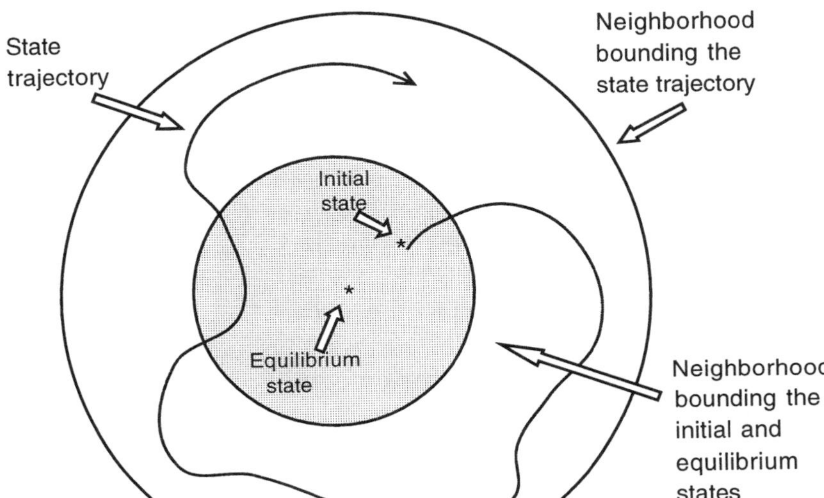

about an equilibrium state, we regard the state as stable. Obviously, the greater the disturbance, the further the system may be driven from the equilibrium state. In the figure we call this the neighborhood bounding the equilibrium and initial states. There may be a corresponding neighborhood that bounds the wandering of the state trajectory. If the state trajectory is not bounded, then the equilibrium state is unstable. We see that there is an exact correspondence to the Liapunov notion of stability and that of Shewhart.

Natural systems tend to be nonlinear. Some authors have written that the natural order is chaos, defined as a nonlinear environment with stable equilibria that permit life and evolution. The purpose in considering this idea is not to expound on philosophy but to recognize that many, if not most, natural and human processes are nonlinear. This includes business and industrial processes. The job of management is to determine the operational regions of a process that can be maintained in stable equilibrium by means of some sort of control system.

This is no trivial task. An aerospace engineer once told me that, given enough money, he could put the Empire State Building on the moon. Governments can afford attempting this sort of extravagance and do it all the time. For example, we see governments in never-ending battle against the forces of nature, dredging against the tide or damming against undammable flood. But business cannot afford extravagance. Businesses must maintain stable processes at reasonable cost. In general they do not exist in the absence of control, and a control system is needed that can maintain a process in a stable operational range at acceptable cost.

Thus the challenge is framed. We need a definition of stability that satisfies the rigor of the classical notion but contains sufficient flexibility to be useful to business. Many industrial and commercial processes cannot be continually operated at a single point in their state space, and a true equilibrium state may not exist in the strict definition of the term. But the idea of a stable neighborhood is useful and can be adapted to process stability. The following definitions conform to the classical one in terms of specifying a particular state, a state neighborhood, and a period in which the state trajectory must remain in the neighborhood.

- An equilibrium state of an industrial or commercial process is stable if an operational range about it can be maintained for a desired period of time and at acceptable cost.
- Stability is the measure of the ability of a process to bound variation.

Those definitions conform to business requirements because they are flexible:

1. They respond to a range of states rather than a specific, perhaps infeasible state.
2. They provide a window of time for stability. The more rigorous definition of Liapunov requires maintaining stable equilibrium for an infinite period.
3. They tacitly accept controlled equilibrium. There is no implied requirement for naturally stable states.
4. They provide cost as the unit of measurement of the balance of forces defining the equilibrium. The challenge to management is to identify the equilibrium states of its processes. Some examples are provided in the next section.

Examples of Industrial Stability

Exhibit 4-5 shows a characteristic curve that, in one form or another, has become well known. Inventory people will recognize it as the curve representing economic order quantity (EOQ), where the parameter of quantity to order is plotted along the abscissa, and the starred value is the optimum order quantity. The preventive cost curve is the cost of holding inventory; the corrective cost curve is the cost of ordering inventory. All curves are determined by treating key parameters as constants. In general they are not, so that a certain area about the optimum value should be examined for cost sensitivity.

Production managers will recognize Exhibit 4-5 as a preventive maintenance characteristic, with the amount of preventive maintenance plotted on the abscissa. The preventive cost curve increases with the amount used; corrective maintenance costs decrease accordingly. It may be feasible to combine maintainability and reliability data to exactly determine the optimum, but in general that optimum is soft, partly because we are dealing in probabilities and partly because of scheduling constraints

Exhibit 4-5. The preventive-corrective characteristic curve.

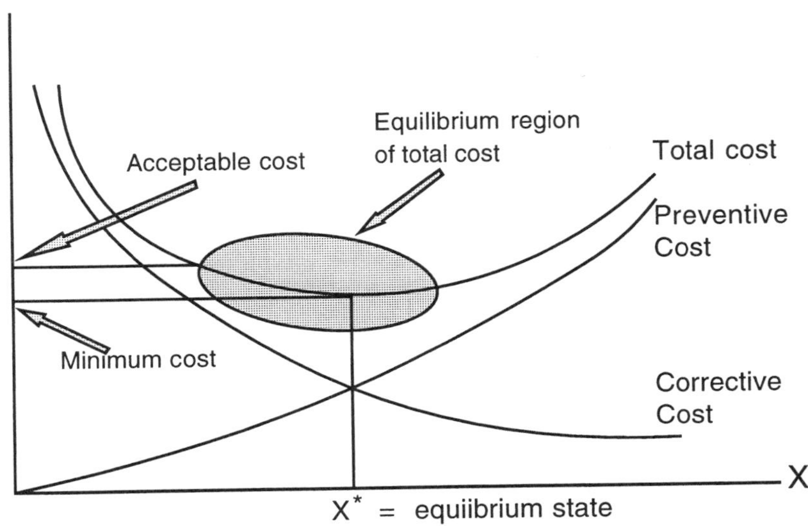

of maintenance against production. Again, an area of maintenance requirements should be managed.

Quality engineers will recognize Exhibit 4-5 as a cost of quality curve, where conformance to target value is plotted along the abscissa. The corrective cost of quality includes rework, but in a sense it includes scrap and regrade. Preventive costs are those actions that a company might take to reduce nonconformance, such as control charting or failure analysis. Relative to quality, this curve can be extremely useful in determining the cost trade-offs for a given failure rate, in order to establish intelligent consumer and producer risks. Irrespective of type of industry or business, processes that can be described by the preventive-corrective characteristic curve can be made stable by defining the equilibrium area of Exhibit 4-5 according to our definition of stability.

Luenberger (1979), among others, has described a process that increases exponentially at a low level of operation and saturates at the high end. This sort of behavior results in an S-shaped curve as shown in Exhibit 4-6 and is often called a logistic curve. In this case, consider a bank, retail store, or other

Exhibit 4-6. The logistic curve as a model for balking.

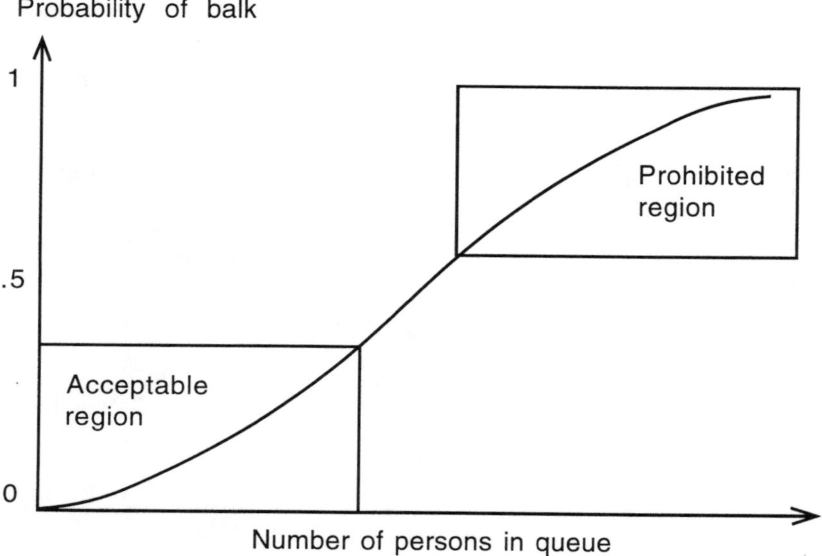

business in which customers must stand in line. At some point new arrivals will look at the length of the line, estimate waiting time, and leave rather than queue up. This is called "balking" and reasonably enough: The longer the line, the more probable the balk. Balking represents lost business. The management solution is to consider service times per station and busy client periods, and open more stations as necessary to arrive at an acceptable waiting period. Moreover, by all means establish a policy of prohibited queue length. Wal-Mart maintains a Speedy Checkout policy that opens a new checkout station if more than three persons are in line. Contrary to many grocery stores that make a similar claim but fail to back it up, Wal-Mart's policy is enforced by a supervisory station overviewing the checkout positions.

Exhibit 4-7 shows another type of characteristic curve for queuing systems. In this case the accumulation of backlog parts at a workstation is shown with a given utilization rate (busy factor). One might suppose that it is worthwhile to keep a workstation 100 percent busy in order to maximize the investment in it. But the figure shows that maximum use implies high prob-

Exhibit 4-7. Workstation activity curve.

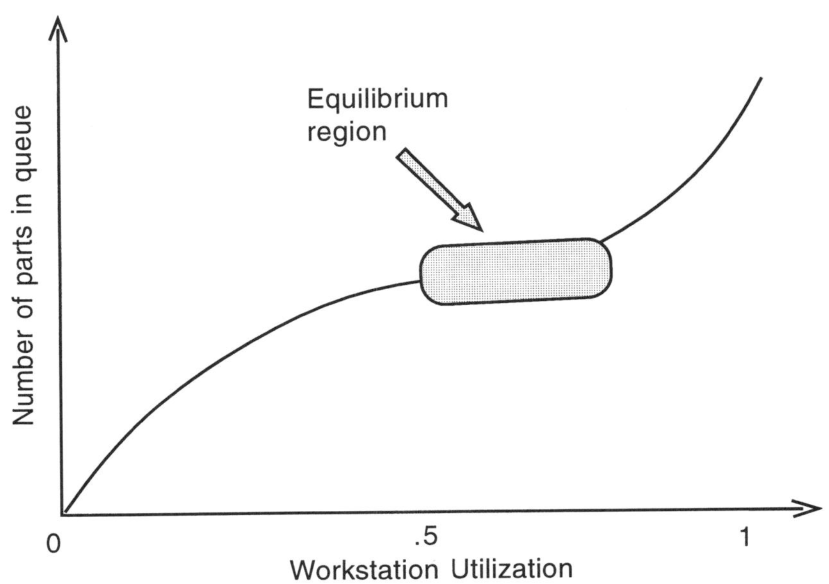

ability of bottlenecks. In their fascinating book *The Goal* (1986), Goldratt and Cox told of the consternation with which traditionalist managers accepted the idea of idleness at workstations on the factory floor. Still, as the figure indicates, the best strategy is to identify a sustainable utilization region, then adopt a control system to maintain it.

These examples are given in order to demonstrate the idea that stability of process can be achieved by a range of states about an equilibrium state, providing economic feasibility and relative ease to maintain.

Stochastic Stability

A dynamic system may have random variation in what it does. If this random variation is related to time, the system is called a *stochastic process*. The stock market is an example of a stochastic process. Most production lines are also stochastic because of variation in quality characteristics. Stability is an important property of stochastic systems too, but is defined differently. Stochastic systems are stable if they are stationary. Stationarity is beyond the scope of this book, but it means, roughly, that a system is stable if its distribution has a constant mean and variance. This notion accords that of Liapunov, and so also with the derived definition, which is therefore the only one needed.

Before going on with the analysis of stochastic stability, let's first look at the normal distribution, the well-known bell curve. This distribution occurs commonly in nature and even when it doesn't, it is still a useful model for other kinds of variability that are often robust—that is, they are approximately normal. A normal distribution is shown in Exhibit 4-8. Values of the random variable lie along the abscissa and the probabilities of those values lie along the ordinate. The normal distribution has the important property that it is symmetrical with respect to its mean, μ; its spread is measured by its standard deviation, σ; and an area under the curve defined in terms of σ corresponds to the probability of the value of variable.

The standard deviation, σ, is the basic unit of area under the curve because it defines the inflection points on the bell, for all normal distributions no matter their mean or dispersion. The area between $\pm 1\sigma$ is 0.6827 of the total area. This means that

Exhibit 4-8. The normal distribution curve.

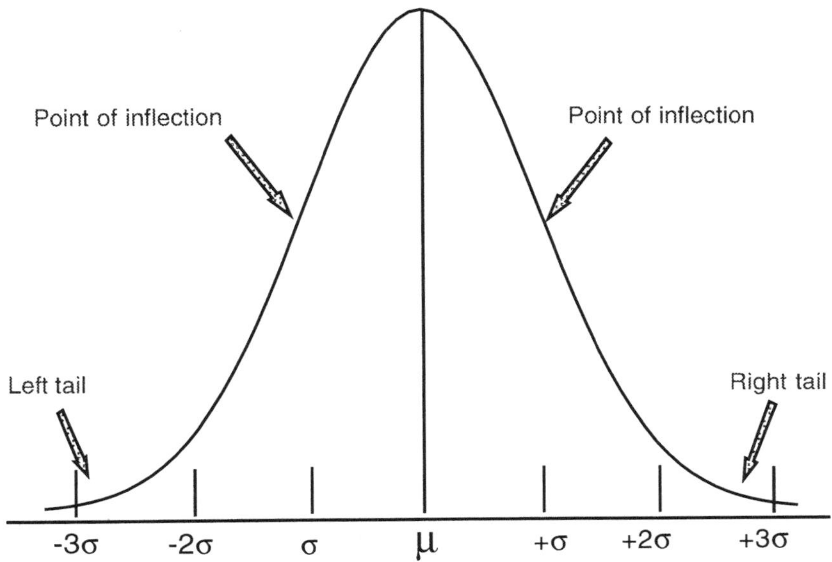

there is a 68.27 percent chance that a value of the variable will occur within these limits. The area between $\pm 2\sigma$ is 0.9545 of the total area, so that there is a 95.45 percent chance that a value of the variable will occur within these limits. The area between $\pm 3\sigma$ is 0.9973 of the total area, and so on. The "tails" of the curve are that part of the bell that extends beyond whatever limits we are concerned with and go on forever because they approach the base asymptotically. Notice that if there is a 0.9973 probability that a value of the variable will occur within the $\pm 3\sigma$ limits, then there is a 0.0027 probability that the value will occur beyond these limits.

The normal curve is a mathematical model. Nevertheless, it is extremely useful as a description of many random processes, both continuous and discrete. Empirical distributions that approximate the normal curve are called robust.

Now let's return to the stability of stochastic processes and how it might be determined. One way of doing so is by the use of control charts derived by Walter Shewhart. Exhibit 4-9 shows a rather typical control chart. The basis of this chart is that during production a pattern of variation will occur in some quality characteristic. This pattern is called a probability distribution or,

Exhibit 4-9. Example of a Shewhart control chart of product sampled periodically.

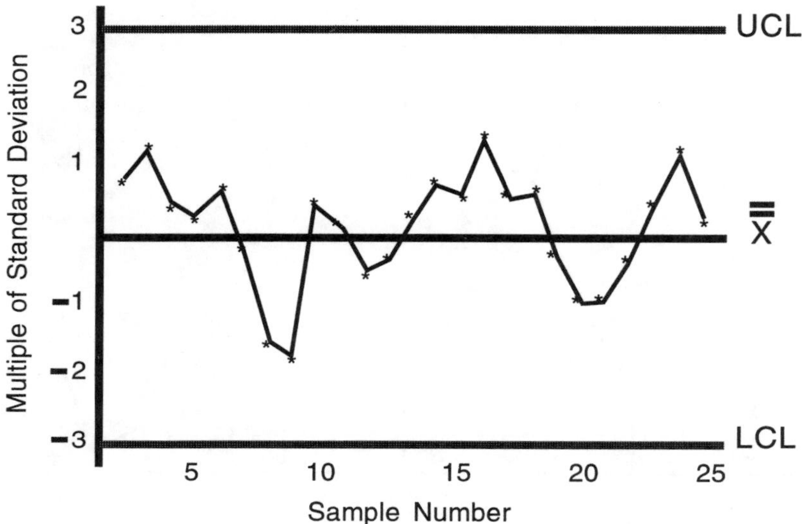

more often, simply a distribution. It will have an average value and a variation. In general, the distribution will not be normal, but if we take a small group of units in our sample, then the average of the group will be normally distributed, according to the central limit theorem.

Exhibit 4-9 shows the variance of the samples taken of an arbitrary production process in terms of one, two, and three standard deviations. The upper and lower control limits are plotted as constant lines on a chart, marked UCL and LCL, respectively, and are traditionally placed at the $\pm 3\sigma$ limits because 0.9973 is usually an acceptable success ratio for production. These limits are determined, of course, from the statistics of periodic samples of the value of a quality characteristic made by the process. They are inherent to the system. The values of the quality characteristic itself are then plotted as dots on the chart corresponding to the time that the sample was taken. The center line represents the average value of samples and is indicated here with the symbol x.[5] In fact, this center line is really an average of averages because each dot represents an average of the handful of samples taken at that time.

Hence, a stochastic process is stable in the sense of Shewhart if its product variability is bounded within probability limits. Random forces acting upon the system cause variation in the quality characteristic and are called common causes. However, this variation is bounded. The boundedness within an equilibrium operating range agrees with the Liapunov definition. The $\pm 3\sigma$ limits represent the bounded neighborhood of equilibrium. Of course, the center line is the mean value of a quality variable and not a state variable, but it represents the equilibrium state of the system that maintains that quality.

Shewhart control charts were developed specifically for manufactured product, but Deming and others have found wide application for the method. Some form of control charting can be used in any function or operation in a company. It is particularly important to do so if the system is nonstationary, which is often the case. In sum, whether a dynamic process is deterministic or stochastic, the property of stability is defined in a similar way: Its state trajectory must be bounded in some sense if the process is disturbed by a finite force. Stability is the first measure of effectiveness of the dynamic quality of a system, and it must be established before capability can be considered.

MOE 2: Capability

You have seen that the stability of a system is a measure of its ability to bound the variation of a product quality characteristic. This is equivalent to saying that the system state trajectory remains in a neighborhood of an equilibrium state. The classical definition of stability was modified slightly in order to meet the flexibility needed by business and industrial systems, but it retained the important Liapunov elements. We concluded that the system is stable if the state trajectory can be maintained in an equilibrium neighborhood for a desired period at an acceptable cost. The notion of stability in terms of system state is important because it is the change in state that causes variation in quality characteristics. It is the state that is controlled.

But stability does not indicate how good the product quality is. You need a measure of the capability of a system to produce quality itself and you can start with the definition of quality from Chapter 1: Quality is conformance to specifications. It seems reasonable to use product specifications in some way as a measure of the ability of a process to make quality product. In fact, this is exactly how the notion of capability is used.

Capability Defined

A process is capable in a stochastic sense if its product variability is bounded within the product specifications. Usually, this means that 99.73 percent ($\pm 3\sigma$) of the product variation is within the limits of the product specification. This idea is shown in Exhibit 4-10, where for purposes of illustration a normally distributed quality characteristic is centered between two sets of specification limits. Assume for the moment that the solid line limits marked *A* are the specifications ("specs"). Clearly all the variability of the product is contained within these limits, indicating a very capable system. On the other hand, if the dotted line limits *B* pertained, then this would mean that only about $\pm 2\sigma$ of the variation was contained within the specs. This corresponds to 95.45 percent of the area under the curve and means that 95.45 percent of the product is good; conversely, about 4.5 percent of the product is bad. This is an unacceptably high defect rate, and a manufacturing process that produced 4.5 percent defects would not be considered very capable.

The example of Exhibit 4-10 makes an important point: A process can be stable and not be capable. The variability of the process may well be bounded, but if that variability exceeds the specification, then the process is not capable. You must either slacken the specs or design a new process. These alternatives are not facetious. Sometimes initial specifications are "soft"—that is, they are based on optimistic expectations that can be redefined somewhat without yielding to the competition or disappointing the customer. If the specs are hard, then the process itself is the only thing left to change and a significant effort must go into reducing its variation.

Capability, then, is a measure of how much of a product is within specifications. It is apparent from the example of Exhibit 4-10 that a quantitative index of capability can be derived. One, two, three, or more standard deviations might be contained

Exhibit 4-10. Normally distributed quality characteristic centered between specification limits.

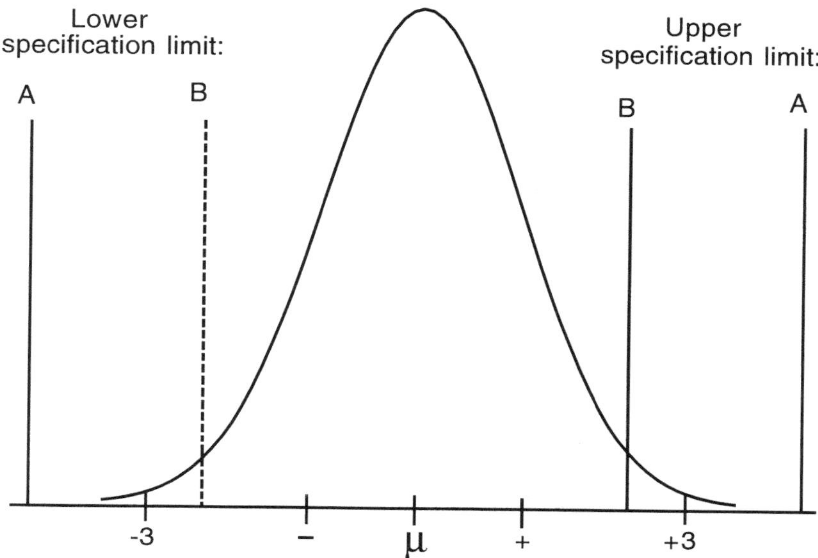

within the specs. In fact, this is exactly how capability is measured. The index can be written as

$$C_p = \frac{(L - \mu)}{3\sigma},$$

where L is either the upper or lower limit value. If the distribution is centered, either limit can be used. The symbol, Cp, is used to represent the index of capability. If the distribution is not centered within the specs, then two capability calculations are needed, one with respect to each limit, as they will produce different results depending upon whether L is the lower or upper limit. Just as a chain is no stronger than its weakest link, so also a capability is no better than the nearest limit. Therefore, if the distribution is not centered, the capability of the system is defined as the lower value of the two calculations, and is usually called *Cpk*.

The equation shows that if a limit is 3σ from the mean value, then $Cp = 1$. This means that 99.73 percent of the product is good, so that there is a 0.27 percent failure rate. Is this any good? Many

American companies, such as Federal Express and Motorola, which produce very high volumes of product or service, are not satisfied with a 3σ capability because a 0.27 percent failure rate still leaves thousands of unhappy customers.

Bhote (1991) gives us some idea of capability, pointing out that most U.S. companies have not reached a capability of unity, whereas most Japanese firms were at $Cp = 1.33$ fifteen years ago. American companies are not standing still, however. Motorola, for example, has put in place an initiative to achieve a 6σ capability ($Cp = 2$) in all its products and services (Bemowski, 1995). This translates to about four defects per million.

I reiterate that a process must be stable before its capability can be determined. It is possible, even probable, that an unstable process can turn out quality product. However, it cannot do it consistently. So you take a few measurements and they appear good. You claim acceptable capability, then begin mass production. But if the process is unstable, an unacceptable number of products have inferior quality and your customers are disturbed indeed. So first you establish stability of process, then you go after quality of product.

A Reluctance to Measure

Companies in business often advertise their expertise and the quality of their product. They might say that they are focused on their "core competencies." We suppose that these claims are based on more than assumptions, that the companies know their capabilities because they are measuring their performance. Auditors are surprised, however, to find how few companies actually measure their capability. Considering what is at stake, we must wonder why.

As we shall see later in this book, neither the 1987 nor 1994 version of ISO 9000 requires that capability be measured. Any standard represents an agreement by participants to adhere to it, so that the strictness of the standard is limited by compromise. Since ISO 9000 does not require a measurement of capability, we can assume that there may have been considerable resistance to doing so. Why?

I suspect that there are three reasons. The first is psychological. Companies are, after all, groups of humans and manifest both the strengths and weaknesses of humans. One weakness is a fear of failure, and a good way to avoid failure is to avoid the measurement. A current apologia encourages this view. Consider that a corporation is simply an extension of its community and is subject to the same forces. There is an increasing movement in society in general, and in our schools in particular, to reduce or eliminate the measurement of individual performance on the grounds that this results in competition and the outcome may be demeaning to participants. This philosophy is manifested in the world of quality by exploiting Deming's Point 8: Drive out fear. Psychologists and sociologists say, "See, even Deming recognizes that performance measurement is bad for quality." In fact, Deming recognized that *bad* performance measurement was bad for quality. His faith in good measurements of every type was shown by his devotion to the Shewhart cycle: Plan, do, observe, study.

The second reluctance to measuring capability is based on its proletarian status. It is considered a manufacturing activity and is best left at that place and in those hands. Most senior management has little to do with it, regarding measurement as a bottom-up activity. The best-selling quality literature is directed at the strategic level of management, which indicates the focus of many CEOs. As discussed in Chapter 2, leaders must be concerned with both top-down and bottom-up approaches. For example, one of the disciples of the top-down view is Tom Peters (1995), who talks of "going from a narrow, technical engineering idea of quality to a much larger idea of things that are new and exciting." The problem is that this notion is only half right, as you can see by considering the words of yet another respected expert, Peter Drucker: Sooner or later strategy and the big picture must degenerate to work. This applies to all the work of the company: planning, designing, financing, training, marketing, administrating, purchasing, manufacturing, handling, shipping, and servicing. There is variation in every one of them.

That brings us to the third, and perhaps main, reason: management's innocence of variation. This incomprehension is compounded by another—that capability is so difficult to understand.

It is couched in statistical terms. Large manufacturing companies with engineers or a few statisticians aboard are liable to measure capability, at least on the factory floor. Small companies of any type or even large service companies often do not employ statisticians. Even in the case of the large manufacturer, capability is often limited to the production process only. Other departments and functions may be turned off by the statistical terms, which is too bad because money can be lost in many operations, not just on the factory floor.

Quality is inversely related to variation. If you do not measure variation with respect to some objective, you cannot know if you are capable or not. Managers who want to know how well their systems are performing need to come to grips with both concepts: the variation in the value of their service or product, and the capability of the processes within their purview.

A General Idea of Capability

The notion of capability is so important that it ought to be expressible in plain language to encourage its use. A simple, general definition is this:

- An industrial or commercial process is capable if it is stable and if it can deliver quality.
- Capability is the measure of the ability of a process to bound variation within desired limits.

These definitions conform to the statistical one. The requirement of stability is explicit rather than implicit; the target value or goal is the mean value; an acceptable bound is the specification if there is one, or a management criterion of some kind. The advantage to these definitions is that they provide an intuitive notion of the meaning of capability. They allow the manager of any sort of function or operation to think of that process in terms of how well it does compared to some designated criterion. The definition also delineates the fundamental difference between stability and capability. Stability is in reference to a system state. Capability is in reference to a quality characteristic. But they are both measures of the process.

Managers should bear in mind Goldratt's (1990) theory of constraints when measuring capability. According to Goldratt, if all the parts of a system are performing as well as they can, then the system will not be doing so. This notion may overstate the case, but it is true that optimizing all parts *may* result in a system that is off target in some sense. Thus, individual departments within a company may optimize their own capability, yet not benefit the company. A simple example will demonstrate this point. Suppose that a materials manager defines "available when needed" as the metric of inventory capability, then overstocks in order to maximize availability. This might well conflict with the comptroller's view of funds capability! Or consider the maintenance manager who schedules equipment maintenance without discussing that schedule with the production manager. The measurement of capability throughout the company can be an effective MOE when the metrics selected for the measurements are coherent to overall goals.

The basic idea for any manager is, first, to define the "product" or "service" of the process under her purview. Second is to determine a metric that expresses the quality of that product or service. Third, then, is to establish bounds within which the quality remains acceptable. And fourth is to determine an evaluation scheme based upon the definition of capability. Rose (1995) lists a few characteristics of a good metric. It benefits the customer. (This may be an internal customer.) It measures performance over time. It is coherent to the company's mission and overall goals. It is developed in collaboration with those who provide the data.

Once the metric is determined, the manager is ready to take data to determine both stability and capability. An introductory knowledge of statistics is absolutely necessary in order to do this, for the purpose of statistics is to make sense out of data. However, the principal idea is that of understanding variation; both stability and capability are defined within this context. Introductory courses in variation are offered through both community colleges and training consultancies.

To iterate, the capability of any function or operation in a company should be known. Its determination is a group effort and has both strategic and tactical implementation. The first group is facility-wide, and is used to establish a cohesion of capabilities relative to the company objectives. The second group is within the function or operation itself, and is used to determine what data are necessary and how and when they will be gathered.

In sum, whether a dynamic process is deterministic or stochastic, the property of capability is defined in a similar way: The value of a quality characteristic must be bounded within some limit about a desired norm. Capability is the second measure of effectiveness of the dynamic quality of a system and it should be established before improvability can be considered.

MOE 3: Improvability

Stability is a measure of a system's ability to bound the variation of a product quality characteristic, and capability is the measure of its ability to bound that variation to a desired level of quality. All this is well and good, but a fundamental characteristic of dynamic systems remains unaccounted for—change. Dynamic systems are subject to internal and external changes. For the sake of argument, let's define internal changes as those that occur within the system itself; external changes are those that act upon the system. Internal changes are manifested by a drift of the system from its target values or goals. External changes are represented by new target values or goals. In either case, it must be possible to improve in some sense the system from its status quo performance. This frames the notion of an improvable system.

Improvability Defined

The notion of improvement presents a semantic problem. Continuous improvement is sometimes criticized on the grounds that it leads only to incremental improvement and impedes breakthrough improvement. Critics recommend reengineering or organizational transformation—that is, abrupt change in the way of doing something that needs improvement. But there is nothing inherently incremental about the notion of continuous improvement. I am not talking about continuity in the mathematical sense. In any case, Deming used the phrase *continual improvement,* meaning constancy of improvement, incremental or otherwise. His ideas are not limited to small increments in any way. In this book I use the words *continual* and *continuous* interchangeably, always with the Deming meaning in mind. You can choose the techniques you want, incremental or breakthrough. The objective is constancy of improvement.

Consider the deviation in the value of an arbitrary quality characteristic or goal shown in Exhibit 4-11. The evaluation of this deviation is nonjudgmental—as long as the value remains within specs, the quality loss is considered constant. First, let's identify what it is that we are looking at. The abscissa indicates values of a parameter. It could be the deviation in the diameter of a manufactured product, say an engine valve. It could be the deviation in the delivery time of a parcel service. It could be the sales goal of a company. In other words, the notions of variation and improvability are treated the same way in any type of company, within any operation, and relative to any quality objective or target.

Exhibit 4-11. Quality variation uniformly distributed within specifications.

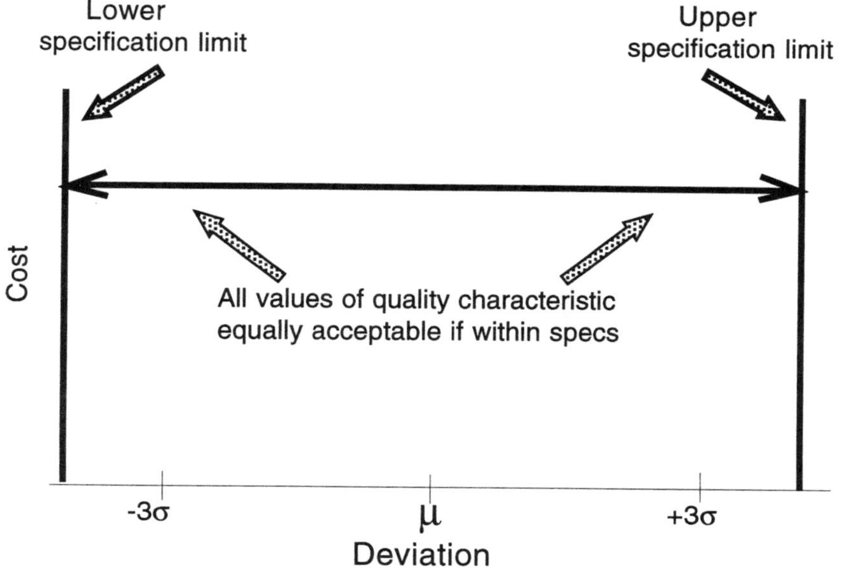

Genichi Taguchi had a great deal of trouble accepting the idea portrayed in Exhibit 4-11—that there is a range of values of a characteristic that have equal quality, and therefore the variation can be treated uncritically as long as it remains within specified limits. An engineer, Taguchi also understood that the errors in complex products accumulate in effect. Moreover, he could not accept that values just within the limits are acceptable, whereas those just outside are not. He wrote (Taguchi et al. 1989) that loss is always incurred when a product's functional characteristic deviates even slightly from its nominal value. Moreover, the loss increases in proportion to the deviation. Taguchi refers to loss of this type as a quality loss, or as a loss to society. The latter term is effective in demonstrating the breadth of application of the idea. The ordinate of Exhibit 4-11 is plotted in terms of cost because it is a universally recognized parameter. Cost catches everyone's attention.

Exhibit 4-12 shows a variation in the value of a quality characteristic or objective that is evaluated critically with respect to cost. For very small changes from the target there is not much

Exhibit 4-12. Quality variation increasing nonlinearly within specifications.

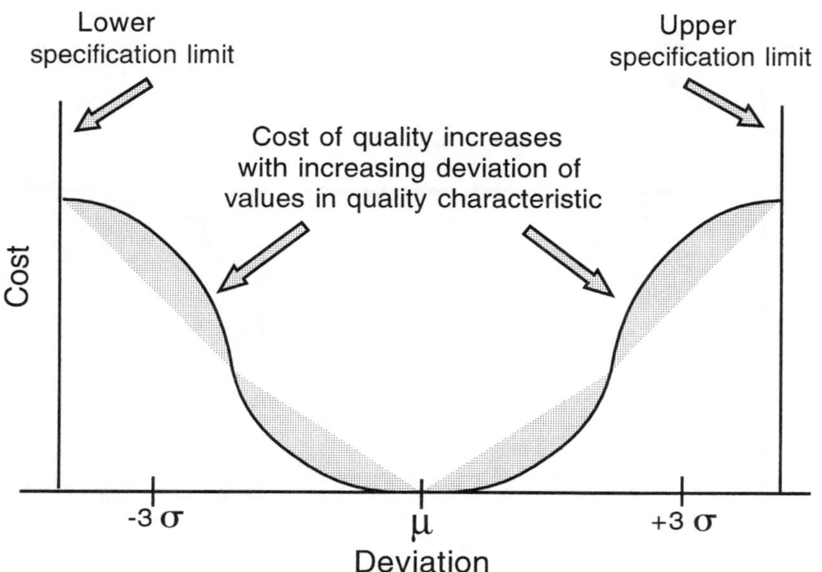

penalty to be paid. As the deviation from target increases, however, the cost also increases exponentially until it begins to level off at some maximum value.

A system is improvable in the sense of Taguchi if incremental product variation is measured and can be reduced. For example, the deviation shown in Exhibit 4-11 is not improvable because as long as degradation is within the limits it is not evaluated. The deviation shown in Exhibit 4-12 is improvable because a cost or penalty function evaluates the amount of variation.

A system is improvable in the sense of Deming if the customer appeal of its output can be increased. Exhibit 4-13 shows this idea. An improvement function of some sort is inserted in the system as one of its subsystems. The position of this function must be as shown in order to be most effective. The customer-driven feedback ensures that the process tracks customer satisfaction and brings about improvement as customer requirements

Exhibit 4-13. Improvement function properly inserted within a system structure.

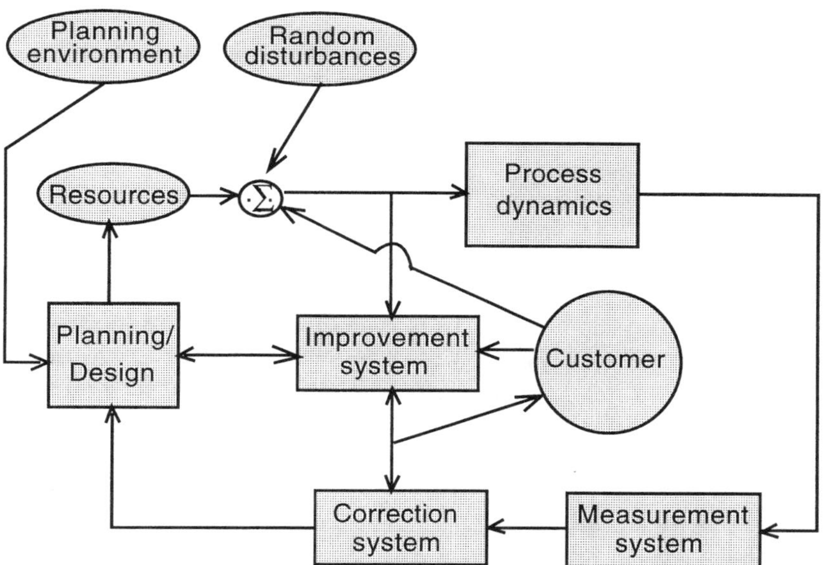

William A. Stimson, *The Robust Organization* (Burr Ridge, Ill.: Irwin, 1996). Adapted with permission.

dictate. Exhibit 4-13 represents a stable, capable, and improvable structure. The system can be considered a prototype for any kind of process: hardware, software, organizational, social, economic, or what have you. The improvement function is completely general and can be anything from an automatic lathe speed controller to a regularly scheduled executive council meeting.

The structure accommodates random disturbances as well as predicted and unforeseen external forces acting upon the planning function or directly upon the process, respectively. In this context, the "planning environment" refers to the environment in which the system operates, and thus is used in the sense of systems theory. It does not refer to the popular notion of environment—that is, the natural world. For example, market, competition, customer, and governmental forces are part of the planning environment. The random disturbances, on the other hand, are those unforeseen or unpredictable forces, internal or external, that act upon the system. They might be caused by changes in the external world or they might be, say, machinery breakdown, parts delivery failures, or internal labor strife.

- An industrial or commercial process is improvable if it can reduce variation.
- Improvability is the measure of the ability of a process to attain and maintain a value or goal.

Summary

It was noted in the beginning of the book that an ISO 9000 quality standard was necessary but not sufficient for sustainability. The critics are correct: ISO standards do not provide quality per se; they simply lock in whatever level of quality the company may have. This "stability of form" is not to be taken lightly, however. It is a significant improvement from the widespread problem of inconsistent product quality. The solution to sustainability is to proceed through ISO 9000, then go beyond, to stability, capability, and improvability.

Stability, capability, and improvability are effective MOE of operations and systems, and as defined in this chapter, they (1) provide the flexibility needed by line managers to reduce variation in quality; and (2) accommodate the realities of time and cost, thus sustainability.

References

Bemowski, K. "Motorola's Fountain of Youth." *Quality Progress*, October 1995, pp. 29–31.

Bhote, K. R. *World Class Quality*. New York: AMACOM, 1991.

Deming, W. E. *Out of the Crisis*. Cambridge: The Center for Advanced Engineering Study, Massachusetts Institute of Technology, 1986.

Drucker, P. F. *Managing for the Future*. New York: Dutton, 1992.

Goldratt, E. M. *What Is This Thing Called Theory of Constraints and How Should It Be Implemented?* New York: North River Press, 1990.

Goldratt, E. M., and J. Cox. *The Goal: A Process of Continuous Improvement*. New York: North River Press, 1986.

Juran, J. M. *Juran on Quality by Design*. New York: Simon and Schuster, 1992.

Liapunov, M. A. "Problème Général de la Stabilité du Movement." *Annals of the faculty of science*, Université de Toulouse, 9 (1907), pp. 203–274.

Lovelock, C. H. "Federal Express Quality Improvement Program." Case study of the *Sloan School of Management*, Massachusetts Institute of Technology. Lausanne, Switzerland: International Institute for Management Development, 1990.

Luenberger, D. G. *Introduction to Dynamic Systems*. New York: Wiley, 1979.

Peters, T. "The New Gurus." *Quality Digest*, March, 1995. p. 39.

Rose, K. H. "A Performance Measurement Model." *Quality Progress*, February 1995, pp. 63–66.

Shewhart, W. A. *Economic Control of Quality of Manufactured Product*. Princeton, N.J.: Van Nostrand, 1931.

Taguchi, G., E. A. Elsayed, and T. Hsiang. *Quality Engineering in Production Systems*. New York: McGraw-Hill, 1989.

Chapter 5

Organizing for Sustainability

Fundamentally, an ISO standard requires that the factors governing quality of product be under control and that the process be documented. This idea is illustrated in Exhibit 5-1. It sounds and looks simple. It is not. ISO states the requirements, but leaves their implementation to individual suppliers on the grounds that each company has its own way of doing business. It is nevertheless true that control is achieved in one way only: through a feedback system that senses variation from target value and corrects for it. All functions must be organized in this way.

Therefore, Exhibit 5-1 goes beyond the letter of the Standard because it shows you how to meet the requirements throughout the company through organization. In each function the customer will be involved in its structure in some way to ensure an agreement of expectations. Both productive and corrective processes will be documented. The elemental form of Exhibit 5-1 should be realized at every level of aggregation in the company. It is so arranged that the customer is at once the driver and the corrector, first defining the initial requirements, then participating appropriately during the performance phase. This basic form does not mean that the customer is required access to the factory floor. Just as the Standard leaves implementation to the individual company, so does this author. The *form* of Exhibit 5-1 is essential to sustainability, but implementation depends on circumstances. Also, appropriate participation means that the customer has access to company records on its inspection and test

Exhibit 5-1. Elemental industrial process showing the unifying structure of production, correction, documentation, and customer that enhances sustainability.

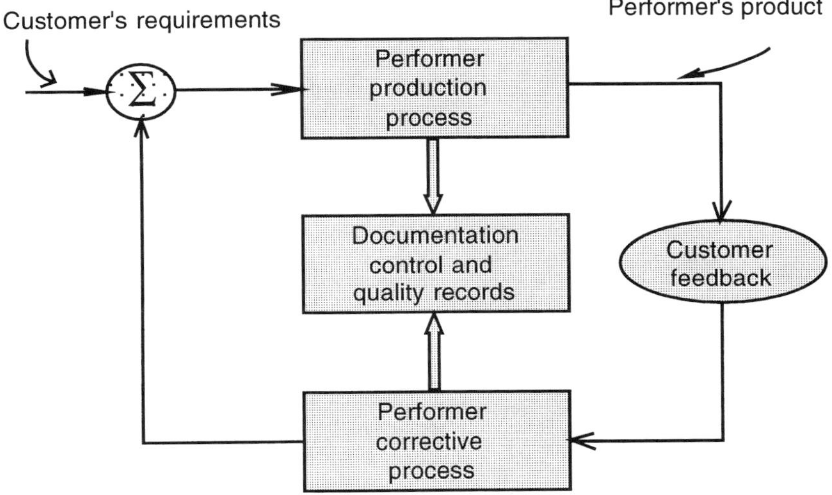

William A. Stimson, *The Robust Organization* (Burr Ridge, Ill.: Irwin, 1996). Reprinted with permission.

results, is involved in review of the accord of specifications to requirements, and participates in a contract review process.

Reach and Range

The scope of an ISO standard can be conveniently described by the notions of reach and range. We arbitrarily define the reach of the standard as the breadth of company operations within its purview. Similarly, the range is defined by the clauses of Paragraph 4 of the standard that are applicable to the particular company, and so depends upon the breadth of operations of the company. For example, a company that provides no service or does no design will have less breadth of operations than one that does, and will have fewer ISO requirements upon it. These ideas are clarified by Exhibits 5-2 and 5-4.

As seen in Exhibit 5-2, all company operations that may affect quality of product or process come under the *reach* of an

Exhibit 5-2. The reach of ISO 9000 expressed as a continuum of functions.

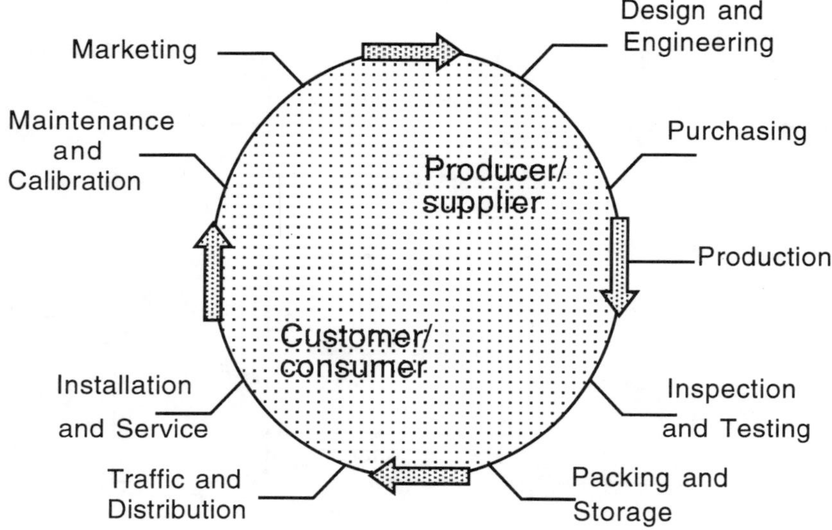

ISO 9000 standard. The symbology of the circle represents a continuum of interest between customer and performer through the various operations. This idea reinforces the basic ISO structure of Exhibit 5-1, and supports a correspondence of logic between functional flow and company organization. The functional flow is clockwise around the circle. As in a Deming cycle, there is neither beginning nor end; all functions operate all the time. There is a rough, per contract, logical order to the functions if one starts at Marketing and continues around through to Installation and Service, but the illustration is meant to be interpreted as a cycle continuous in time. For example, Maintenance and Calibration represent a microcycle within the contract cycle. Design and Engineering imply both product and process—that is, initial design, development, and manufacturing engineering.

The requirements of ISO 9001, the most comprehensive management standard, are provided in Paragraph 4 as twenty clauses pertaining to the various processes of a company that may affect quality. These clauses are listed in Exhibit 5-3, by clause number. They may be considered as the *range* of interest that ISO 9001 has in company operations. Basically, the reach of an ISO standard is concerned with the functions of a company—that is, *what* the compa-

Exhibit 5-3. Clauses of paragraph 4 of ISO 9001.

4.1	Management responsibility	4.12	Inspection & test status
4.2	Quality system	4.13	Control of nonconforming product
4.3	Contract review	4.14	Corrective and preventive action
4.4	Design control	4.15	Handling, storage, packaging, preservation, & delivery
4.5	Document & data control	4.16	Control of quality records
4.6	Purchasing	4.17	Internal quality audits
4.7	Control of customer-supplied product	4.18	Training
4.8	Product identification & traceability	4.19	Servicing
4.9	Process control	4.20	Statistical techniques
4.10	Inspection & testing		
4.11	Control of inspection, measuring, and test equipment		

ny does. The range of the standard is concerned with the processes of a company—that is, *how* the company does what it does.

Exhibit 5-4 displays these requirements in the form of a graph to show how the clauses are connected. The graph is

Exhibit 5-4. The range of ISO 9001 expressed as a graph of clauses of the Standard. An arrow indicates that the clause is connected to Clause 4.16.

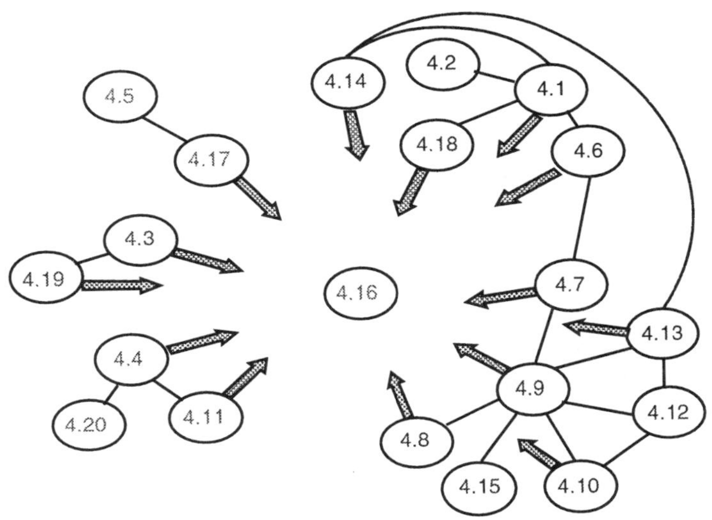

formed as a cluster of subgraphs that associate those activities that are closely related. For example, it is quickly apparent that Clauses 4.5 and 4.17 are closely related and represent a small cluster connected to the whole through Clause 4.16. Similarly, Clause 4.9 is the center of a large cluster, and is related to the whole through Clause 4.16. So also, Clause 4.1 is the center of a third rather large cluster of clauses.

The exhibit indicates the importance that ISO 9000 places on Clause 4.16, the maintenance of quality records. Clause 4.16 is the center of the graph because it is the repository of quality history. Everything that the company does that affects quality is traceable because of Clause 4.16.

The purpose of clustering to portray the clauses is to form associations of logically related requirements. Characterizing the individual requirements in this way will create an integration of reach and range through the assignment of ownership.

Clusters and the Functional Organization

A successful business will have many tasks to achieve on a continual basis. Companies create an organization of distinct functions to achieve the tasks, implicitly creating groups of tasks that are similar in some sense. For example, some tasks belong to production, others to purchasing. Most people imagine that there is no difficulty in determining which tasks belong where; in fact, there is. The division of labor often fails to prevent things from falling between the cracks. The litany of criticisms about the effectiveness of functional organizations and task achievement is too long to repeat here. MacKenzie (1986) estimates that this effectiveness is usually no better than 50 percent and that a well-organized company might achieve 60 percent. Pascarella and Frohman (1989) state that functional organization develops layers of hierarchy over time that interfere with rather than expedite the completion of tasks.

We are concerned with sustaining quality throughout the organization and cannot accept an organization where things fall between the cracks. ISO 9000 is supposed to help here, isn't it? Not necessarily. The concept of reach and range explains the breadth and depth of the ISO Standard purview, but companies are still left with the task of integrating, or matching, them. In order to prevent things not happening that should happen, or conversely, you can call upon a principle of total quality management called *ownership* to ensure that there is continuity in product across process. A sustainable ISO organization will distribute its range across the reach of company operations in a way to assign ownership. The decision of who is the owner of a group of tasks is made easier by using the technique of clustering.

Clustering for Ownership

The technique of clustering measures the degree of homogeneity among members of a given population. There are qualitative differences between groups of functions and tasks within a company so that they might be perceived to cluster into related groups. You don't really need to measure the homogeneity of your functions, but you want to use the notion of clustering to assign ownership to them. You can rely on qualitative business reasoning to do this. Mills (1991) has shown the validity of the clustering concept to organizational management, forming small sets of business units and teams into larger groups of subcontractors and internal and external customers.

Consider Exhibit 5-5. This distribution is somewhat arbitrary, of course, but in general accountability it makes sense. For example, the quality assurance (QA) manager is the owner of internal audit and quality documentation and records. Who better? Engineering is responsible for product and process design, which implies a corresponding responsibility for measurement of quality variance and the equipment with which measurements are made. Operations is responsible for all functions and activities on the floor. Executive management is responsible for those areas for which it usually has sole decision-making authority. This includes specific responsibilities assigned by the ISO program, the quality system, training, and purchasing. Most companies have a purchasing officer, and this is usually an executive-level responsibility because the person has the authority to spend significant amounts of the company's money.

Clustering helps to clarify the principal owners of a task. The purpose of ownership is to ensure that a task that transits from one process to another is achieved in its entirety.

Exhibit 5-5. The distribution of range over reach, arranged in homogeneous clusters.

Quality Assurance	Engineer'g	Operations	Management	Sales & Service
4.5 Document control	4.4 Design control	4.7 Customer supplies	4.1 Management responsibility	4.3 Contract review
4.16 Quality records	4.11 Test equipment	4.8 I.D. and traceability	4.2 Quality system	4.19 Service
4.17 Internal quality audits	4.20 Statistical techniques	4.9 Process control	4.6 Purchasing	
		4.10 Inspect & test	4.14 Correction & prevention	
		4.12 Test status	4.18 Training	
		4.13 Nonconform product		
		4.15 Handling & delivery		

Ownership is not a responsibility. All the responsibilities have been designated in the functional organization of the company. Ownership is accountability. The tasks can be clustered in some other way. We admit that the proposed clustering is qualitative; other variants may seem more reasonable to the reader. Some readers might assign Clause 4.14 to operations, for example. The important thing is that ownership be established for every task.

Management's Role in Nonconformance

The problems of corrective and preventive actions may seem to be a responsibility of operations. However, there are important issues of policy and resources inherent in this clause, requiring management decision. Therefore we *arbitrarily* assign Clause 4.14 to management rather than to operations in order to stress its importance as an executive management concern.

In its most narrow sense, corrective action is taken to resolve nonconformances that occur in production. Defined in this way, Clause 4.14 is closely related to Clause 4.13, nonconforming product. This view is too narrow on three counts. First, the cause of nonconformance may be systematic. Systematic problems often, indeed usually, require management review and decision for correction. By definition, the system must be changed in some way. Second, Clause 4.14 governs corrective and *preventive* actions. Prevention requires a systematic approach, including training to improve cognitive skills. Sometimes, new or upgraded equipment is required also. Third, in the broad sense, Clause 4.14 does not apply solely to production, but applies to all company functions that affect quality.

One of the explicit requirements of Clause 4.1, management responsibility, is that a company conduct management reviews of its quality system. In order that these reviews have meaning, corrective and preventive actions must be on the agenda. Thus, Clause 4.14 is a managerial responsibility, in both policy and implementation.

The issue of corrective and preventive action is so important that some registrars focus major attention on Clause 4.14. Every audit is done by a sampling technique. Auditors do not have time to examine a company's quality system in minute detail—the audit would be prohibitively expensive. The usual audit is an arbitrary mix of random and selective sampling, the selective part being in those areas with which the registrar is particularly concerned. Some registrars focus on Clause 4.1, management's responsibility. Others might focus on Clause 4.5, document control. Many of them focus on Clause 4.14, on the premise that a quality system is no better than its efforts to reduce nonconformance.

The Sustaining Structure

We have acknowledged earlier that an ISO 9000 standard does not, of itself, ensure capability. It will lock the property in for you if you implement capable processes, but it does not require it. That property is left to the discretion of the marketplace, in the sense that the large production of inferior quality owing to incapable processes will result in dissatisfied customers or higher costs. However, you do not want to leave the capability decision to the marketplace because to do so is to risk failure in business, and then what good is your pretty blue banner? You are going to build capable systems into your ISO organization because to do so doesn't cost any more, and because capability is an essential element to sustaining your quality program.

You build capability into a process solely through the way it is organized. Exhibit 5-1 depicted the basic structure of a sustaining organization. Every process and subprocess must be organized in this way. You will see this structure over and over again throughout this book, applied to every function or operation subject to ISO 9000 scrutiny, and at every level of aggregation in a service or manufacturing company. Each function is, of course, distinct, but the fundamental structure remains the same. It is very general and so is applicable throughout the company. Exhibit 5-6 indicates this idea. It is a closed-loop control system in which each block represents a process that can represent any one of many different functions. Some functions are listed adjacent to each block and others may come to mind. Companies that have been successful for a long period of time are organized this way, whether they set out to do so deliberately or not. In the passage of time, and seeking efficiency, a company will evolve to this organization or it will go out of business.

Exhibit 5-6. Dynamic industrial process in stable configuration.

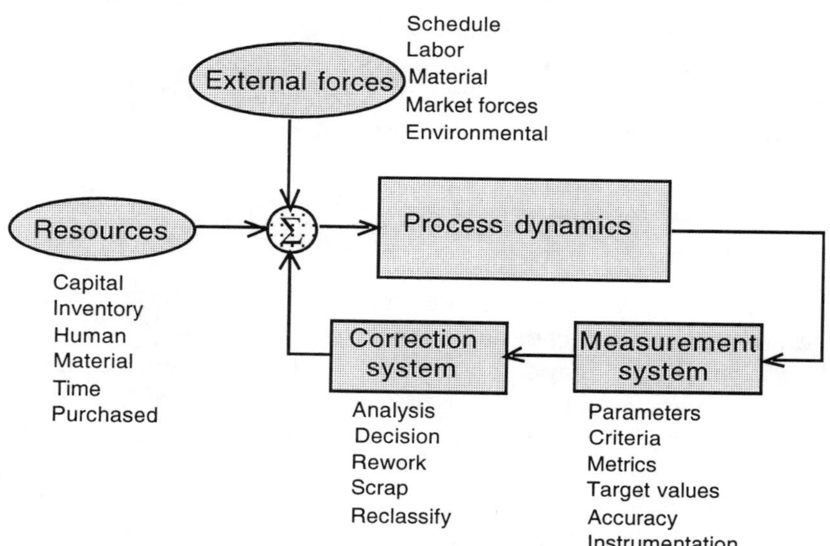

William A. Stimson, *The Robust Organization* (Burr Ridge, Ill.: Irwin, 1996). Adapted with permission.

But why wait for evolution? There are two reasons why this structure leads to success. The first is that it provides adaptability. If the output changes beyond an acceptable value, some corrective action is fed back through the closed loop in order to maintain the desired output; thus stability is achieved. If the environment changes, target values and nominal reaction times change also; thus you achieve adaptability. You can make the operational range whatever the system can technically support; thus you achieve capability.

The second reason, as discussed in Chapter 3, is that the structure provides learning. Wiener (1954) stated that feedback was simply a way of controlling a system by reinserting into it the results of past performance. In this case you are feeding back information. If this information can change system response, the process may well be called learning.

In sum, this book shows how to achieve sustainability in an ISO program. Sustainability is possible only if you have achieved stability and capability of all processes. The remainder of the book shows how to do this through process structure, and this task is approached in chapters arranged according to the divisions of Exhibit 5-5. Each division, or cluster, represents a purview of accountability—that is, ownership. For example, one cluster concerns the purview of management. It discusses the ISO requirements within that purview and how to organize the appropriate processes according to Exhibit 5-1 to achieve a stable and capable operation. Another cluster concerns the purview of operations and so on, always showing how the appropriate processes are effectively organized.

Summary

The *reach* of an ISO standard is the breadth of operations of a company that are subject to the quality system. The *range* of an ISO standard are its requirements that apply to the quality system. Sustainability is achieved by integrating reach and range with organizational and functional structures that are stable, capable, and improvable. These structures are demonstrated in Exhibits 5-1 and 5-6, and should be implemented at every level within the company.

References

MacKenzie, K. D. *Organizational Design: The Organizational Audit and Analysis Technology*. Norwood, N.J.: Ablex Publishing, 1986.

Mills, D. Q. *Rebirth of the Corporation*. New York: Wiley, 1991.

Pascarella, P., and M. A. Frohman. *The Purpose-Driven Organization*. San Francisco: Jossey-Bass, 1989.

Wiener, N. *The Human Use of Human Beings: Cybernetics and Society*. Garden City, N.Y.: Doubleday, 1954.

Part Two

Quality System Requirements: Management Purview

Chapter 6

Clause 4.1: Management Responsibility

Brief: Clause 4.1 concerns the responsibility of executive-level management in regard to quality policy, goals, commitment, and implementation of the company quality system.

In years past, I used to lead a team of engineers and technicians aboard fighting ships of the U.S. Navy to conduct ship qualification trials. These trials preceded deployment of the ships and went on for a month or more. The purpose of the trials was to verify and validate computer, surveillance, and weapons systems repairs, installations, and upgrades, and to train the crew in their use. The trials were mandatory but were not graded. Other evolutions, such as the propulsion examining board, were graded and enjoyed a certain priority because of this.

Ships readying for deployment face a variety of evolutions and activities so that all of them must be well integrated if the deployment schedule is to be maintained. It was customary to visit a ship several months before the trials to explain the requirements and objectives, and to plan for integration with other activities competing for the ship's time. I found that if the commanding officer could be convinced of the utility of our service, then the trials would enjoy the full support of ship's force, from the commanding officer himself down to the lowest ranks. But if I could not "sell the trials" for one reason or another, then ship support would be meager, other evolutions would get priority, and many of our objectives would not be attained.

And so it is with quality. The notion of quality has taken on a motherhood persona in many quarters. Managers speak well of it, but many do not want to be bothered. They believe that Americans have seldom demanded quality per se, that quality is what the company says it is. Why change now? True believers of quality are very often challenged by management to show how quality decreases costs and increases profits, and if that demonstration cannot be made then they cannot make the sale.

The ISO standards recognize the essential role of management in the achievement of product quality and the very first requirement of the Standard pertains to this responsibility. Certain actions are defined as pertinent to management: establishing policies and responsibilities, allocating resources, assigning a central accountability, conducting reviews, and so on. Exactly how these things are done is left to the individual, but we shall discuss the implementation because how a thing is done determines its sustainability.

On the first level, management must take an active leadership role in the processes of quality in order to satisfy the requirements of the Standard and attain certification. If this active role is ingrained into the quality processes by structure of commitment and activity so that it is inherent and fundamental, then a sustainable level is achieved. This general structure is indicated in Exhibit 6-1 in terms of its essential components of policy, organization, and quality system. This task begins at the highest level and carries all the way through the ranks. Everyone must get on board if ISO certification is to be achieved and sustained.

Quality Policy

In French, the management of a business is called *la direction*. I have always liked this name because it reflects very accurately what it is that management is supposed to do. You can control day-to-day affairs and therefore, perhaps, call yourself a manager, but that is not direction; it is supervision. Sustainability carries with it a notion of the future. The job of management is to lead the company into the future, and that task begins with thinking about where you want to go and how best to get there.

Exhibit 6-1. The scope of management responsibility: structure of the quality program around the customer.

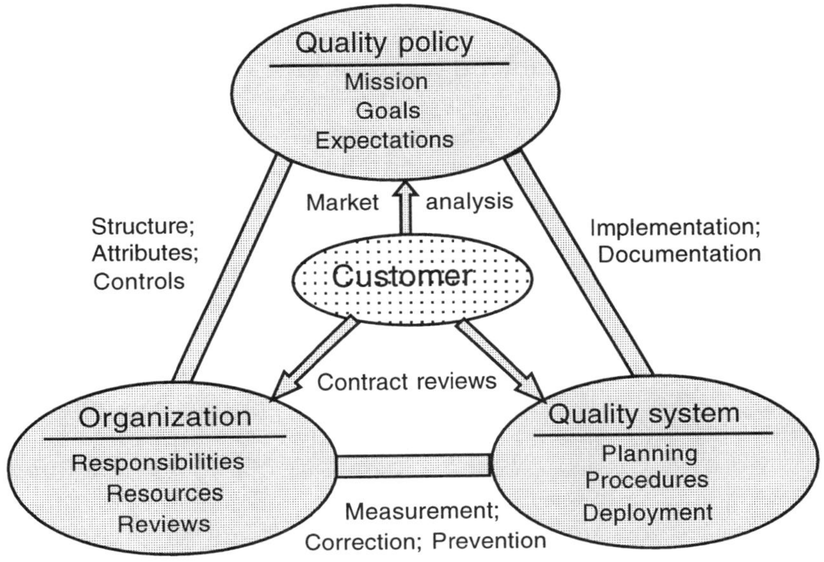

William A. Stimson, *The Robust Organization* (Burr Ridge, Ill.: Irwin, 1996). Reprinted with permission.

These decisions culminate in policies from which goals can be derived. Thus, we begin a discussion of management responsibility with a consideration of policy.

Special and General Policies

Executive management is responsible for developing and implementing quality policy. We talked about the nature and function of policies in Chapter 2, and traced their relation to goals and objectives. In this chapter we get into applications, pursuing the idea of both specific and general policies that support the requirements of the ISO 9000 standards.

There are twenty clauses of requirements to ISO 9001. Every one of them will require some sort of policy, and we call these policies specific, as they directly address a given clause. In fact, it is wise to begin the consideration of each clause by first determining the policies that must govern its achievement. For example, *4.6: Purchasing* will require a policy of contractor evaluation;

4.9: Process Control will require policies on equipment maintenance and on parametric measurements; *4.15: Handling and Storage* will require a policy of zoning for the various kinds of storage that product and inventory will undergo. The methods of dynamic quality planning will prove most effective in implementing quality policies because it calls for thinking about what you want to do and how, before you begin.

This is no mean achievement. The tendency to jump in and do something when confronted with a task is overwhelming to many people. Gibson (1990) talks of the tendency of programmers to "throw together a few lines of code, just to get started." If you begin things in this way, invariably you will be faced with having to undo or redo them, as developments reveal impasses, disconnects, and just plain bad ideas. Starting out by determining the policies appropriate to an effort forces you to understand the nature of the task and associated constraints up front.

We have defined a specific policy as one that is identified with a given clause of ISO 9000. The set of specific policies form a cadre, but this framework should not be limiting. There are also policies whose nature contributes to all the clauses, or to company operations in general. Let's call them general policies. For example, it is worthwhile to develop policies relative to continuous improvement. ISO 9000 does not directly require continuously improving systems. Perhaps it assumes that you recognize that it is in your own best interest to do so. Clause *4.14: Corrective and Preventive Action* does enhance improvement through its requirements related to prevention, but clearly, a policy encouraging continuous improvement is a robust factor. Consider the Japanese concept of *kaizen*. *Kaizen* is a process that becomes a policy when it is applied as standard operating procedure throughout the company. It is established at that status by executive management or it doesn't happen. This simple policy identifies a three step-effort:

1. Identify problems.
2. Develop several solutions.
3. Implement the solutions.

Kaizen can be used to advantage directly in making the company robust and indirectly in satisfying the requirements of ISO

9000. For example, ISO 9004 suggests that the company consider risk and cost in its operations. Cheser (1995) shows how *kaizen* can be used to determine optimum values of the cost of capital. All ISO standards require that resource allocations be considered in process control. Kinni (1995) shows how *kaizen* can be used to achieve incremental improvements at the worker-machine level, using bottom-up expertise. Thus, a company using *kaizen* policies throughout its organization has a head start in demonstrating to ISO auditors that its capability is well defined and current.

Exhibit 6-2 provides some suggestions for general policy. Although not directly related to the clauses of ISO 9000, many of these issues are concerns of ISO 9004. Note that statistical quality control (SQC) is a much more broad concept than statistical process control (SPC), which is the concern of Clause 4.20. SPC has come to refer to methods of reduction of variation in manufactured product. But in fact, variation occurs in all corporate activity; methods to reduce company-wide variation are often called SQC. In this sense, SPC is a subset of SQC.

Both general and specific policies are formulated through an identical process. The process is easier to understand for specific policies, so let's start there. Suppose that you want to organize your shipping and handling processes in accordance with ISO requirements. You need to consider objectives, forces, and constraints associated with shipping and handling in view of the goal, and determine policies that reflect these considerations. You will go nowhere without the participation of management, because only management can establish company

Exhibit 6-2. Some suggested subjects for general policy.

Subject	*Brief Description*
Benchmarking	Self-assessment against a standard
Continuous improvement	Systematic *kaizen* iteration
Empowerment	Participation of bottom-up expertise
Environmental issues	ISO 14000 purview
Market research	Anticipation of customer requirements
Quality costs	Prevention and failure cost analysis
Safety	Healthful working environment
Statistical quality control	Capability analysis throughout the company

policy. And you will go nowhere without the participation of the people who actually *do* the shipping and handling, the experts. Thus, formulation of specific policies requires a simultaneous top-down and bottom-up approach, a view shared by the ISO guidelines. Brainstorming techniques conducted by this varied talent are extremely useful to policy development, providing the widest approach to both participation of players and view of alternatives. There are always nuances in forces and constraints. Brainstorming offers the best way of identifying them. Participants should include production control, purchasing, and customer service because shipping and handling covers the transition from receipt of purchased parts to delivery of final product.

There are two kinds of constraints to every system. One is inherent to the system—that is, there are things that it cannot do well or at all. The turning speed and radius of an automobile are inherent constraints. The other kind is a constraint that is imposed on a system that is, of itself, not so constrained. Speed limits imposed on automobiles are external constraints. Import and export quotas, labor rates, and market sectors are all external constraints.

There is a theory of constraints advanced by Goldratt (1990). This subject will be discussed in some detail when we discuss process control, but with respect to policy, we can summarize just a few points. According to the theory, a system has both subsystem and total system constraints and they are usually not the same. Management must make policy while acknowledging intrinsic and imposing external constraints, and needs the expertise of the workforce to do this effectively—thus the recommendation for wide participation and brainstorming in order to determine specific policies. Similar reasoning pertains to general policies.

Corporate Commitment

We discussed the Hayes and Wheelwright (1984) definition of corporate philosophy in Chapter 2: "A set of guiding principles, driving forces, and ingrained attitudes . . . reinforced through conscious and subconscious behavior at all levels of the organization." This definition ideally suits the concept of sustainability because it goes quality policy a step further—it includes commitment, reflected by management recognition of its responsibilities to quality in both definition and active participation. These responsibilities will be spelled out in the company's quality manual by position title for all management including the CEO. Although commitment may be hard to define, its absence is easily recognized in disarray and unaccountability in a quality program.

My opening tale suggested the need for the commitment of the ship's commanding officer in carrying out shipboard evolutions. It was pointed out that without this commitment at the highest level, achievement of objectives was at risk. So also, the commitment of the CEO is essential to the achievement of quality within the company and carries with it certain responsibilities that are identified in the ISO literature. This role is not rigorously or explicitly defined, but is nuanced in a policy statement written by the CEO, in prose, and includes an assumption on the part of the CEO of certain responsibilities. A mission or policy statement should include the responsibilities shown in Exhibit 6-3.

Organization

ISO 9000 does not dictate organizational structures, recognizing that each company must be free to organize in whichever way it deems most effective. Within that latitude, the organization must maintain under control those technical, administrative, and human factors that affect quality of a product or service. In particular, the basis of effective organization is the integration of two factors: the internal processes of the company and the

Exhibit 6-3. The quality role of the CEO.

State the quality policy.

Confirm own commitment to quality.

Ensure the understanding and implementation of policy at all levels.

Encourage management participation in the quality system.

Ensure enforcement of quality procedures.

requirements of the customer. Integration never happens haphazardly, but is the result of systematic structure, assignment of responsibility and authority, use of resources, and active management participation in process operations.

Responsibility and Authority

We defined responsibility and authority in general terms in Chapter 2. The Standard has specific requirements, however, concerning the direction of this responsibility and authority. These terms must be defined and documented in terms of product, process, and system relative to the following activities:

1. Prevention and detection of nonconformances
2. Problem identification, solution and records
3. Control of processes

We shall discuss items 1 and 2 in other sections of the ISO requirements. In regard to item 3, we said in Chapter 2 that responsibility and authority are controls. This control is achieved through responsibility by precisely defining and assigning the task and metric of the performance function. Control is achieved through authority by the availability and provision of the resources required to achieve the task. These controls have an inherent shortcoming that can be compensated by organization. When you define a task precisely, and then another, also precisely, there is almost always a gap in between. Even if there is not, one will develop. The reason for this is the "rice bowl" syndrome of human behavior—the tendency to establish exclusive domains. Consider the functional layout of Exhibit 6-4, a simple but rather common schematic of some arbitrary manufacturing facility. The functions are strictly defined. Customer service has its set of responsibilities. Engineering has a different and distinct set. But we all know, as does the ISO auditor, that there must be some integrated interface between them. In fact, as the exhibit shows, there are at least four departments that need to be involved in the transition from requirements to delivered product. Organization must be structured to support this reality.

I once witnessed an assembly-line worker drilling holes in a steel cabinet, which had already been accomplished by a computer-controlled drilling machine. Her reason for doing the ad hoc drilling was that the holes drilled by computer did not match those of the panels to be mounted. Did she complain about this? Yes. On several occasions she had filled out feedback reports of nonconformance, but no corrective action was ever taken.

The concept of ownership can be used to ensure continuity of responsibility through the functional divisions of a company. Ownership can be assigned several ways. One way is to assign a single person as owner of a task from its beginning as a customer requirement to final delivery. This person acts as a sort of project manager or coordinator for task integration over line organization. The arrangement avoids the shortcomings of matrix management because the person does not need authority over the task when it is solely within the boundaries of a defined function, but is responsible to ensure its integrity as the task transits from process to process.

The single-owner concept can work well in a job shop facility or custom-made production scheme, but it requires the cost of a dedicated position. Moreover, it would be inefficient in

Exhibit 6-4. Strictly defined functional layout.

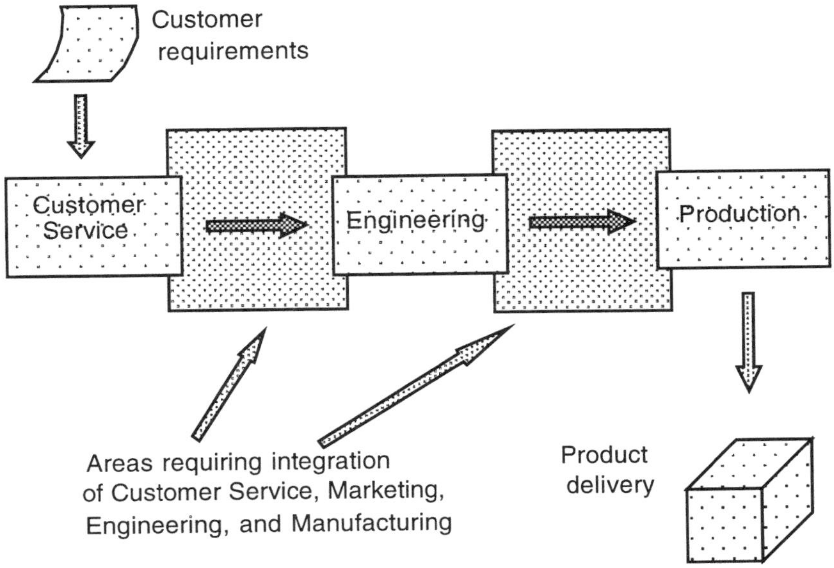

mass production. Alternatively, a multiple-owner concept can be used in which line managers are responsible for a task during its transition through their process and through the interface regions indicated in Exhibit 6-4, transition regions that always exist.

This means that the transition regions must be acknowledged and identified, and one good way of doing this is through the creation of flowcharts and process layout charts. Flowcharts establish process flow logic. Process layout charts indicate spatial or functional logic. The two logics must be consistent, or at least not in opposition. Moreover, the flowchart must be compatible with the organization chart. Then line managers from the various functional units work together to assign continuous ownership of responsibility through the flowcharts.

Process organization is effective when put in terms of inputs, outputs, and management control systems. This should be done at all levels. At the top level there are two distinct functions—one for strategy and one for operations. The company should be organized to facilitate efficient operations, to allow rapid response to changing conditions, and to clearly define accountability and responsibility. The organization should provide for policy setting at the top and decision making at the lowest possible level.

Consider Exhibit 6-5 (repeated from Exhibit 4-13 of Chapter 4 for ease of reference), showing a closed loop of connected functions. Each function is itself a closed-loop system. It is possible, even desirable, to have a number of nested closed loops. Every process should be closed, as should every subprocess. Control engineers call this an arrangement of minor loops, and sometimes equalization. When the principle is applied to organizational structure, we call it control of levels of aggregation. A robust system doesn't need an infinitude of closed loops, but every process must be closed. For example, Exhibit 6-5 portrays a closed-loop system within the company. Each block within this system represents a subsystem, but may itself be a closed-loop system of its own subprocesses. For example, the correction subsystem will have a closed-loop structure of evaluation, analysis, and amendment. Imagine that you are viewing Exhibit 6-5 through a microscope with discrete power settings. At each level of magnification, you can focus on another level of aggregation.

Exhibit 6-5. The continuous improvement process.

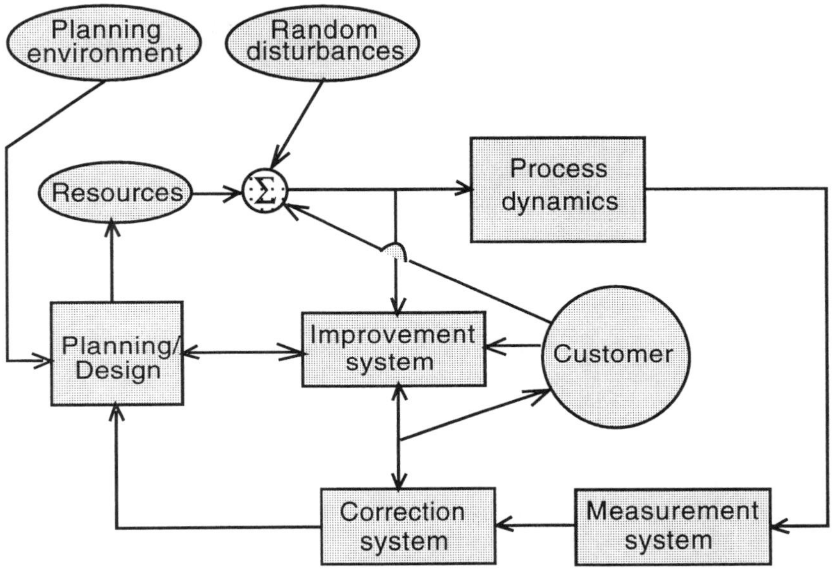

With robust systems, at each level you will see the structure of Exhibit 6-5.

Let's see how the concerns of the preceding paragraphs are addressed by this structure. Unforseen external problems are inputted at the random disturbances block of Exhibit 6-5, and detected and addressed by the improvement system and planning and design. Similarly, nonconformances and internal problems are detected and addressed by the corrective system and planning and design. Organizational complexity is reduced by the simplicity of this layout, whose fundamental structure never varies no matter the process being implemented. You have created a basic unit of organization for each key process that produces a result for a customer. You have structured the organization in terms of inputs, outputs, and management control systems. Finally, with traceable documents, you can determine the congruency and redundancy of the organized processes. Exhibit 6-5 represents any arbitrary aggregate level. It can be blown up to discretely higher detail; variance from this ideal form will be immediately obvious. Redundancy may not be obvious, but that is one of the reasons for documentation control and quality records.

Resources

Few would argue the importance of resource utilization in manufacturing or service. This disposition is even more critical because of the way authority has been defined here. Authority is a control only if resources are available to the task. ISO 9000 is concerned in particular with human resources and specialized skills, design and development equipment, manufacturing equipment, inspection and test equipment, and instrumentation and software. The use and availability of these resources are noted by auditors in their routine examination of the various ISO requirements. For example, human resources and specialized skills are examined under Clause *4.1: Management Responsibility*, and Clause *4.18: Training*. Resource utilization in general may be examined by the in-house audit team under the authority of Clause *4.17: Internal Quality Audits*. An important aspect of Clause 4.17 in regard to resources is the requirement to verify quality of product with verification activities of trained, independent personnel. Independence refers to inspection, test, and audit activities. Irrespective of the clauses used in auditing, resource utilization is a management organizational responsibility.

In general, resource utilization is optimized in an organization where all levels communicate. Communication top-down tends to define general resource requirements through corporate direction, whereas communication bottom-up tends to define specific resource requirements as the job boundaries are understood. As a simple example, suppose that an instrument of insufficient bandwidth is used to measure the bandwidth of a signal generator being custom-made for a client. The purchase of a new instrument with the required bandwidth is ruled out by management, as its cost would exceed the profit in the contract. Instead, the employee making the measurement is instructed to "extrapolate" the probable bandwidth of the generator based on boundary measurements made by the old instrument. If this measurement were witnessed by an ISO auditor, it would be regarded as one major nonconformance, and possibly two: the first against the measurement under the jurisdiction of Clause *4.9: Process Control*, and the second under Clause *4.1: Management Responsibility*, in this case bad policy.

Management Representative

The company quality system is the responsibility of executive management. Beyond the participation of management at all levels in the operation of this system, the company is explicitly required to designate an ISO management representative (MR) from among its management ranks. This person is responsible for the day-to-day management and operation of the company's quality system, and to verify its adherence to the appropriate ISO standard. The MR will have sufficient authority to be able to change or modify the system as necessary.

The company quality assurance officer is usually assigned as MR—indeed, for a company with a quality assurance (QA) department it would be quite awkward if the MR were anyone else. On the other hand, the Standard is flexible about this; the MR responsibility can be a corollary duty, as long as the requisite authority obtains. Smaller companies often have no QA department, assigning quality control responsibility to the employees themselves and assigning QA overview as a corollary duty to one of its executive management.

Whether or not the MR is a full-time job, the task will be heavy during the period of preparation for certification. This means that the MR must have at least one full-time assistant, if only to install and track the documentation and quality records systems. This task won't go away after certification, nor will it diminish. Therefore, when all is said and done, an ISO-certified company will have a full-time QA operation, however small. A company can finesse the issue of full-time management, assigning this task as a corollary duty, but this person must have full-time assistance, best provided by an exempt "key person."

Let's talk about this key person a moment, as it might apply to a company that chooses to keep its QA function lean and mean, assigning the MR responsibility to a line manager as a corollary duty. In a study of corporate organizations, MacKenzie (1986) identified the "virtual position"—one that does not appear on organizational charts but nevertheless exists because the job must be done. The key person in QA is similar to, but not quite, a virtual position. The job will be on the organization charts; the task will not. We all know that management embodies a wide range of activities: doing things, making decisions, and providing leadership. Corollary duties require all these things too, but don't get them to the same degree. This means that someone else will attempt to provide them. In our hypothetical company, the key person will be that provider. In my experience this person is often a woman, so I shall use the feminine gender.

By force of her responsibilities vis-à-vis documentation, she will know more about the de facto and de jure quality systems than anyone in the company. She will be everywhere on the floor several times a day and will often recognize which systems are underperforming and how to improve them. Not being a manager, she will not have the authority to make changes. Nevertheless, using willpower, common sense, and suggestion, she will contribute as much or more than anyone in getting the system to work.

This is why I refer to this position as a key person. Neither manager nor supervisor, she is absolutely essential to the operation of the quality system and the first person that I seek out when visiting a plant where the MR is a corollary duty. This does not mean that such MRs are irrelevant or lacking in some way; on the contrary, most are as conscientious as they can be. But the QA role is a tandem in such companies, and it takes both the MR and the key person to provide the complete picture. Several of the quality system tasks belong explicitly to the MR, however, among them management of the internal quality audit program, reporting to executive management on the state of the system, and representing the system to external parties.

Management Review

Every ISO standard requires periodic review of the company's quality system by executive-level management. This review always includes the results of an internal quality audit, which indicates the minimum frequency with which this review should take place. The review should also include the effectiveness of the system in achieving objectives, the systematic handling of problems, and the impact of new technology or new persons in the system. Moreover, ISO 9000 considers the results of management review a quality record, which must be retained. Frequent executive review of the quality system adds dynamism and ensures that the quality manual will be a living, utilized document.

Although ISO 9000 does not specify the attendance at management review meetings, it is easy to determine whom they should include. The MR will be concerned with improvement of the quality system, which means change. Change in an organization requires the concurrence of the affected line managers if it is to be effective. Apprehensive line managers require a referee. In short, for most medium-size companies, an appropriate representation at the quality system management review would include the MR, department heads, and the general manager or president. And the key person. It never hurts to have bottom-up input as a reality check.

Implementation

The company should begin its quality system with a stated quality policy and objectives that are in accord with its mission statement. Quality policy and strategic policy must be coherent. Once defined, the policy and objectives can be written into a tier 1 manual serving as a definition of principles and control of the quality system. This manual is the apex of the collective manuals of the quality system.

Quality objectives in this case are ongoing goals concerning safety, training, performance, reliability, maintenance, and other factors that pertain to the ISO range described in Chapter 5. They should be stated in the appropriate sections of the quality manual. There would be no point in putting short- or near-term objectives in the manual, for this would necessitate its rewrite. An auditor, finding an outdated objective in the quality manual, might suspect the document itself as outdated, an ISO nonconformance.

As suggested by ISO 9004, management should conduct periodic analyses of cost of quality. The categories of cost of quality have been well established by Juran (1992) and others, and are, roughly, costs of failure, costs of appraisals, and costs of prevention. Because cost analysis is suggested by the ISO guidelines but is not stressed in ISO 9001 itself, the factor is sometimes overlooked by ISO auditors. It should not be overlooked by management. Management often worries about the cost of appraisal (inspections and testing) but is nonchalant about the cost of failure. I have witnessed companies that do not discriminate between predelivery and postdelivery failures, even though the cost of repair is often many times greater in the latter case. Other companies regrade nonconforming product without evaluating the opportunity loss in the lesser market. Cost-of-quality analyses not only favorably impress ISO auditors as an indication of competence but are plain good business.

Responsibility, authority, and accountability of the management representative must be determined and agreed to at all levels of the company. This may take some wrangling, but should be done up front. The MR is the personification of the company's quality system, whose relations to the other company managers indicate the relationship of the quality system to operations. Basically, the company quality system starts here, at Clause 4.1. Policy, objectives, and the individual quality responsibility of all management must be defined and recorded first.

Performance measurement programs should be implemented across the board. Parameters, metrics, and performance goals should be established for every process and function. These measurements needn't be—indeed, shouldn't be—complicated. As in the measurement of state, you want to monitor the necessary indicators and no more. We shall talk more about this in the discussion on inspection and testing, but the issue needs to be raised here because every process within the company should be measured, not just the product. Rose (1995) describes the attributes of good performance metrics. They are customer oriented and reflect added value, reliability, timeliness, and quality. They measure cost and waste reduction, innovation, integration, and customer satisfaction. These attributes are clearly not confined to the factory floor, but can be applied to the entire reach and range of ISO requirements.

Summary

Sustainability in Clause 4.1 requires management to take an active role of leadership in the company quality system, as indicated in Exhibit 6-1. The exhibit does not represent a structure that can be implemented. It represents a philosophy that can be implemented in many ways, so that it is adaptable to each company. The implementation includes quality policies and integration of quality initiatives into the company's processes. It includes the deployment of quality functions horizontally and vertically within the organization in such way as to ensure continuous ownership of responsibility from receipt of purchased parts through delivery of final product.

References

ANSI/ISO/ASQC. *Q9001-1994. Quality Systems—Model for Quality Assurance in Design, Development, Production, Installation, and Servicing*. Milwaukee: American Society for Quality Control, 1994.

ANSI/ISO/ASQC. *Q9004-1-1994. American National Standard: Quality Management and Quality System Elements and Guidelines.* Milwaukee: American Society for Quality Control, 1994.

Cheser, Raymond. "Financial Kaizen: Lowering Hurdles to Long Term Investments." *Quality Progress*, April 1995, pp. 57–61.

Gibson, J. E. *How to Do Systems Analysis*. Workbook. Charlottesville: University of Virginia School of Engineering, 1990.

Goldratt, E. M. *What Is This Thing Called Theory of Constraints and How Can It Be Implemented?* New York: North River Press, 1990.

Hayes, R. H., and S. C. Wheelwright. *Restoring Our Competitive Edge: Competing Through Manufacturing*. New York: Wiley, 1984.

Juran, J. M. *Juran on Quality by Design*. New York: Free Press, 1992.

Kinni, T. B. "Process Improvement." *Industry Week*, January 23, 1995, pp. 52–58.

MacKenzie, K. D. *Organizational Design: The Organizational Audit and Analysis Technology*." Norwood, N.J.: Ablex Publishing, 1986.

Rose, K. H. "A Performance Measurement Model." *Quality Progress*, February 1995, pp. 63-66.

Chapter 7

Clause 4.2: Quality System

Brief. Clause 4.2 requires a quality system that ensures that product conforms to specifications. The system will be described in documentation of sufficient detail to include structure, processes, and procedures that ensure product quality.

ISO 9004 defines a quality system as the organizational structure, procedures, and resources needed to implement quality management. This definition is deliberately general in order to accomplish two things: to make the definition applicable to any company in manufacturing or service, and to make it applicable to any operation, process, or function within that company. It is a good definition, but as with any terminology, you can read into it what you will. Two persons building a quality system based on their interpretation of a definition may very well arrive at distinct implementations, one good and one not. The guidelines do not effect stability and capability.

Several companies have complained to me of a decrease in quality of purchased product, where the supplier (subcontractor) had recently received its ISO 9000 certification. How can this be? Surely such a development represents the very minimum in sustainability. It is possible to attain certification through a Herculean effort with a quality system built as a house of cards. The sheer willpower of a few individuals might do it. Then with the banner on the wall, things begin to unravel. Left to its own devices, the system falters. The quest for certification overwhelms the goal of unceasing quality, eventually itself becoming the objective.

A Strategic Quality System

The objective is to build an effective and enduring quality system. Let's begin with the definition provided by the ISO, but interpret it in the most broad sense. Don't limit your purview to the structures, processes, and procedures that ensure quality of product. *All* processes within the company ensure quality of product directly or indirectly, or they are not needed. For example, in manufacturing, the production line is where the rubber meets the road, so to speak. Quality is put into the product at that point. Most executive management will think of the production line when the subject of quality comes up. But many other processes within the company enable this quality, too. For example, just as a chef cannot make a great meal from inferior ingredients, quality cannot be created from poor purchased parts. Clearly then, the purchasing department contributes directly to a quality product. So does Engineering. Throughout this book the broad view of systems is maintained to include all subsystems and processes within the company. In principle, the quality system comprises all company operations, from accounting to verification and validation.

The chief executive officer is the owner of the quality system of the company. This accountability cannot be delegated. However, the responsibilities of the system can and must be delegated because they are so extensive. The breadth of the quality system is clearly established by the reach and range of an ISO standard as presented in Chapter 5. The company's quality system is effectively described by how it implements all the requirements of the appropriate ISO standard. Each of these clauses is discussed in detail in dedicated sections of this book, so that only general considerations are addressed in this chapter.

The company's quality system must be dynamic, consisting of a comprehensive set of activities that are, in effect, a systematic program to ensure quality of product by achieving quality of process. An example configuration is shown in Exhibit 7-1. When integrated into *all* processes at all aggregations of the organization, the result is a dynamic total quality management (TQM) program. This program of quality is manifested in company operations, but should be defined and described in written documents and should be the basis of all planning.

Documentation

The ISO requirement for documentation meets a great deal of resistance in the workplace, particularly in small and middle-sized companies. This is partly because the requirement is misunderstood, and partly because paperwork itself suffers a bad reputation among achievers. While working for the government, I remember having to fill out a chit every time I made a telephone call. I remember, too, having to make four copies of everything in order to satisfy government contractual requirements, even though I knew that

Exhibit 7-1. Robust quality system with feedback loops of customer, documentation, and management overview.

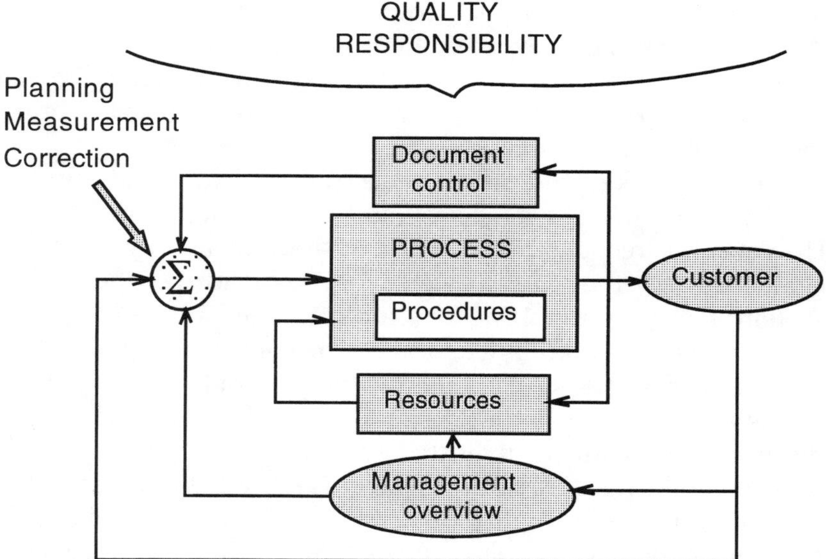

William A. Stimson, *The Robust Organization* (Burr Ridge, Ill.: Irwin, 1996). Reprinted with permission.

few people would read any of them and that all four would wind up in a storage vault at the end of the contract. Still another government agency required that its travelers fill out forms designating how much they spent for each meal. Furthermore, although the traveler was allowed a certain amount per diem, it had to be spent in the correct ratio, say 20 percent for breakfast, 30 percent for lunch, and 50 percent for supper. There was no spillover. If you spent 30 percent for breakfast, then 10 percent of the compensation was lost; it would not do to simply spend less for a later meal.

Things are not much better in the private sector, particularly in large companies. One purchasing manager complained that he had heard that an ISO program introduced hundreds of new documents that had to be maintained. There is some justification for this complaint if a company is using very little documentation, or if the forms being used do not meet the ISO criteria. The truth is that an ISO-capable quality system is dual in nature, part of it being the physical system, part of it being the paper system.

It need not be a Jekyll-Hyde relationship, though. Castor and Pollux might be a better analogy. Twins, each system is useful and necessary. A reasonable amount of the right kind of documentation provides consistency of process and therefore makes a major contribution to the stability of the quality system. The task is to determine what is reasonable and right.

A Stable Structure

The ISO Standards require documented procedures for all operations within the quality system. The major document will be a quality manual that describes how the company will conduct its operations in conformance to ISO 9000. The quality manual is so important and fundamental to the quality system that an entire chapter of this book is devoted to it. Although the manual is a key element of the quality system, and therefore within the management purview, it is a living document. This means that it drives the actual quality function, and is therefore the responsibility of the person charged with this function. For practical reasons, then, the quality manual is discussed in detail in Part Three, pertaining to the purview of quality assurance.

The quality manual is just one of the documents required by the Standard. All operations and activities used to effect the quality system must be documented in a systematic way in the form of policies and procedures. Moreover, these documents must be controlled. Typically, it is convenient to use a three-tier system of controlled documents, such as:

Tier 1. Quality manual
Tier 2. Departmental procedures
Tier 3. Work instructions and standard operating procedures (SOP)

Early versions of the ISO 9000 requirements listed a fourth tier consisting of standard forms, but the 1994 revision has reduced the documentation system to that shown above. Even here there is some room for disagreement. Some quality experts say that work instructions have been replaced by standard operating procedures (SOP). However, many companies use the terms interchangeably. Others use work instructions to document production line operations and SOP to document office operations. Personally, I believe this to be a bad idea, especially in small to mid-size companies. It sets up a class system between the different kinds of employees, all of whom are equally important in achieving quality. But rather than argue it, let's agree to the convention that work instructions and standard operating procedures are at the same document level. They describe tasks and activities of individuals and teams.

Documents need to be controlled for several reasons. The first is to ensure the availability of current documents where and when they are needed. The second is to keep documentation from getting out of hand. Configuration management entails documentation. This means that there must be procedures to change procedures. When you combine this magnifying effect with a tendency to bureaucracy or pedantry, it is easy to imagine that documentation can far exceed that required by ISO 9000 itself, and can become a driving force of its own. The Standard requires the minimum documentation to enhance quality of product and no more. Control serves to bound the enterprise because each document must be justified, preferably by a quality committee of peers of the person wanting to create it.

Boundary conditions are easy to establish if you keep your focus on the customer. The first is the record of the initial contact with customer requirements. The last is the signed receipt for the product following delivery. If there is a service requirement to the contract, then the last will be a written acknowledgment by the customer of satisfactory service. All the activities in between require a procedure and a record if the quality of product is affected by that activity. The documents must include associated policies if the activities are repetitive and it is desired to conduct them a certain way, consistently. The Standard does not rely on habit or good intentions. Beyond this minimum paper trail, documentation is unnecessary.

Quality Planning

Let's approach the subject of quality planning by the book. Having identified what that planning is, we will throw the book out and do it over in a different way. The reason for this strategy is that satisfying the guidelines of quality planning per ISO 9004 will get you certified but it won't make you capable. This book is about capability.

Within the context of ISO 9000, a quality plan is a plan about quality, narrowly defined. ISO 9004 says that a quality plan "may be a part of an overall plan." The implication of this statement is that a quality plan may be filed with every plan as a distinct adjunct. This distinct plan is particularly necessary for a new or updated product or process.

Continuing with this strict definition, quality plans should define quality objectives such as specifications, a description of the organization and functions to be used in the process (with use of flowcharts), the allocation of responsibilities and resources during the project, the specified procedures, an effective test program, change procedures, and measures of performance.

Now let's raise our sights a little. There is at least an ambiguity in "quality planning" that should be resolved to the company's advantage. Quality planning as defined in an ISO standard refers to plans used to establish and maintain the quality system. As the previous discussion traces it, examples are calibration, equipment maintenance, and training programs. Upon further thought, financial planning or strategic planning is also quality planning if it focuses somehow on customer satisfaction. Usually, it does. The point is that quality planning should be integrated with any other planning. It is advantageous to do so and indicates a more profound understanding of quality management than the alternative of creating a "quality plan" as distinct from the nitty-gritty of company operations.

Now let's break away altogether from the idea that there is somehow a difference between quality planning and any other. There is no advantage to thinking this way. In my own view, quality planning is any planning that is conducted with Deming's (1986) fourteen points in mind. Certainly, a calibration plan for plant equipment is a quality plan. But so is a financial plan, a sales plan, or a production plan if they conform to a Deming philosophy, whether or not the connection to quality of product can be readily identified.

It is cold comfort to fail in business knowing that your product was among the best on the market. I know a winemaker who made consistently good riesling and pinot noir. He failed. The product was quality but the company was not. I suppose that in the interest of purity, you could do an analysis and, perhaps, delineate product quality from cause of failure. It seems meaningless. This is not to say that success equals quality; not at all. Unfortunately, the correlation between the two is not what you might hope for. But it strikes me that a correctly run company is a prerequisite for sustaining both the company and the quality of product.

This generalization of the meaning of quality planning is not counter to the requirements of an ISO standard, but is inherent in it. ISO 9004 says that quality objectives should include specifications, uniformity, effectiveness, cycle time, cost, resource utilization, and yield. Many of these goals are regular business objectives of a competitive company, whether it is interested in ISO 9000 or not. Thus, you can take the broad view of quality planning, gain capability, and remain within the spirit and the letter of the ISO requirements.

ISO 9000 recommends no particular planning methodology. Indeed, Gehani (1994) cites studies showing that there is no conclusive evidence that planning is positively correlated to competitive position. If not, then ISO requirements appear to be out of touch. Not so. The dichotomy is not because planning has become irrelevant in the global marketplace; it is because of the way that planning is often done. Top-down planning is frequently autocratic and is focused on a single metric—financial. Gehani also discusses the shortcomings of bottom-up planning, stressing that results are usually incremental and lay one open to the competitor that adopts radically advanced initiatives.

In sum, the best planning strategy integrates quality initiatives and philosophy into all the company plans, and the best planning methodology is dynamic quality planning—the use of top-down and bottom-up methods concurrently, as discussed in Chapter 2. The idea is not to show the ISO auditors a fancy document entitled "Corporate Strategic Quality Plan for 1997", but to show that quality considerations are an inherent part of all company activity and planning.

Discretion also pays, however. You want to make things as explicit as possible, if only to satisfy ISO auditors. I once spent several weeks studying the operations of a shipyard in which the word *quality* was seldom used. Yet the company was doing everything it should do to satisfy, say, the Malcolm Baldrige criteria, and was doing nothing that it should not do. ISO auditors do not have several weeks to complete their study, so it is astute to make it easy for them. Yes, effective quality measures should be part of all planning to enhance capability and to be in conformance to the appropriate standard, but it is useful to formulate them into a general process and set of policies described in the quality manual. This process should include the consideration in all planning, where appropriate, of the factors shown in Exhibit 7-2.

These elements do not replace the characteristics of dynamic quality planning described in Chapter 2. They are in addition to them, put into quality procedures in order that a certain minimum quality planning be explicit. The problem with the elements of Exhibit 7-2 is that they tend to be narrowly interpreted—that is, their application is often perceived as applying to the production line. Full reading of the Standard enforces that notion. You want to break free of this narrow view in order to achieve broad application of quality principles in all planning.

Consider management information systems as an example. Laudon and Laudon (1991) identify general controls to be used

Exhibit 7-2. Elements of ISO quality planning.

- Identification of controls, processes, and equipment required for quality
- Compatibility of design, implementation, and documentation
- Development and update of techniques for control and measurement
- Identification of measures of effectiveness
- Identification and clarification of standards
- Identification of quality records

for the design and security of data systems, and applications controls for specific processes such as payroll, accounts receivable, and order processing. Managers, supervisors, and workers should identify measures of effectiveness for the various information and data systems. They have the expertise, and by doing so build into their systems both capability and improvability.

Measures of Performance

The link between planning and improvement is measurement of dynamic performance. Cupello (1994) demonstrates the classical model of measurement by posing three questions:

1. Are we achieving our long-term strategic vision and mission?
2. Are the functional areas performing in support of strategic goals?
3. Are employees, processes, products, and services performing in support of functional goals?

Note in passing that these questions clearly apply to every activity in the company. For example, they apply to the planning of the accounting department. They apply to the planning of the personnel department. Thus, it is important to measure performance of every activity, not just those whose connection to quality of product is immediate.

But Cupello also advances an idea that is pertinent to the company pursuing ISO certification. This idea has to do with the maturity of measurement—the notion that measurement should match the degree of development of the quality system. This does not mean that measures of performance should be less strict; it means that they should be different. For example, if you choose to implement a quality system in the purchasing department, you would not say "Let's start out with a measure of effectiveness (MOE) of delivery within a specified time of target date, and within a specified acceptance, then tighten the MOE with maturity. In fact, you might start out with no MOE at all, but simply assess the purchasing process qualitatively. You might then initiate one or two MOE that are meaningful and direct. As the purchasing department matures in its quality system, MOE will be adopted to measure quality function deployment and capability, the two most difficult and most critical of quality indices.

Summary

Sustainability in Clause 4.2 requires a quality system that is documented and implemented throughout the company, with management overview as structured in Exhibit 7-1. The documented system is structured in tiers of responsibility. The implemented system includes planning for quality goals and process measurement to determine achievement of those goals A management representative will be responsible for creating and maintaining the quality system.

References

ANSI/ISO/ASQC. *Q9001-1994. Quality Systems—Model for Quality Assurance in Design, Development, Production, Installation, and Servicing.* Milwaukee: American Society for Quality Control, 1994.

ANSI/ISO/ASQC. *Q9004-1-1994. American National Standard: Quality Management and Quality System Elements and Guidelines.* Milwaukee: American Society for Quality Control, 1994.

Cupello, J. M. "A New Paradigm for Measuring TQM Progress." *Quality Progress*, May 1994, pp. 79–82.

Deming, W. E. *Out of the Crisis*. Cambridge: Center for Advanced Engineering Study, Massachusetts Institute of Technology, 1986.

Gehani, R. R. "The Tortoise and the Hare." *Quality Progress*, May 1994, pp. 99–103.

Laudon, K. C., and J. P. Laudon. *Management Information Systems*. New York: Macmillan, 1991.

Chapter 8

Clause 4.6: Purchasing

Brief. Clause 4.6 requires a purchasing system that ensures the purchased product conforms to specifications and that subcontractors maintain quality criteria.

The secret to haute cuisine, agree the great chefs, is to begin with the best, freshest ingredients. This principle should be taken seriously by those seeking sustainability. You build your products from the basic materials delivered as purchased product. Therefore, Clause 4.6 should include the assurance that purchased products are of the highest quality. This objective is achieved by a network of activities governing the purchasing process: source documents to ensure that the purchase order meets customer requirements, evaluation of suppliers or vendors (called subcontractors in the ISO vernacular), receiving controls, and quality records.

Let's begin with a purchasing organization, and the model is the closed-loop structure shown in Exhibit 8-1. Note that this control loop differs from previous examples in that external activities (vendors) are part of the system. The circuit is closed by receiving verification. From a systems engineering viewpoint, whether all the elements of the system are in-house, distributed, or even composed of other companies is immaterial. The ISO standards take the same view—the company is responsible for the quality of its subcontractors. They are part of the system.

The logic of flow shown in Exhibit 8-1 can be classified in three phases: requisition, receiving, and parts management.

Exhibit 8-1. Flowchart of a dynamic purchasing system.

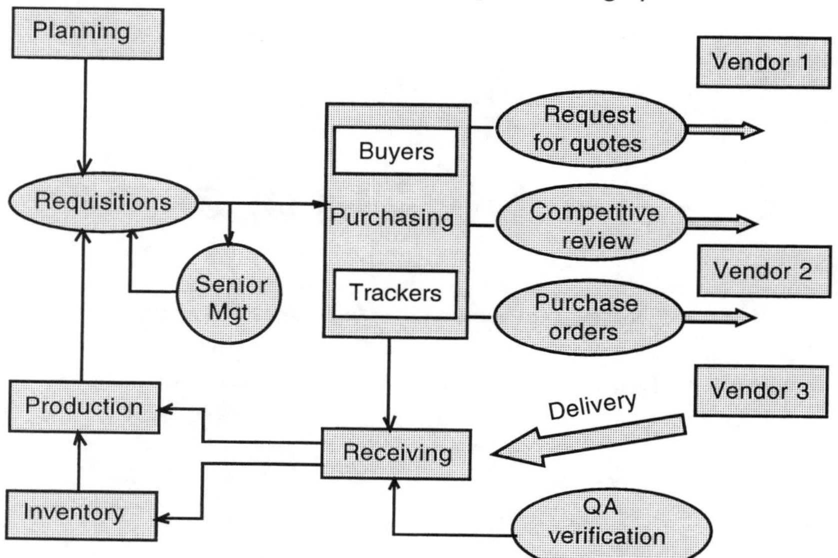

William A. Stimson, *The Robust Organization* (Burr Ridge, Ill.: Irwin, 1996). Reprinted with permission.

Requisitions are driven by the planning and production functions according to future or short-term needs. For example, long lead time material (LLTM) will be ordered by the planning function sufficiently in advance to accommodate projected need dates. Unforeseen needs or material required for growth, new work, or breakage will be expedited by the production function. Senior management often reviews these requisitions because company money is being spent. Buyers conduct the actual purchase process, requesting quotes, reviewing competitive pricing, and issuing the purchase orders. If delivery dates are close to need dates, active tracking of the logistic process may be used. Tracking is particularly important in project management, where delivery dates will often impact the objective if they slip. Upon delivery, there must be a verification of the material against the purchase order. Verification will establish whether the correct material is received, as well as its count and condition. By count, we mean either a literal count of the number of units or a measurement of volume, capacity, weight, or other quantity. Once the verification is satisfied, the appropriate persons are notified of the arrival of the material and the parts go to production or inventory according to need date.

Requisition

The requisition process is easy to describe and difficult to do. Basically, what it amounts to can be expressed with two questions: What do we buy? Who do we buy it from? The ISO 9000 standards are strict on both issues. Material to be purchased must be defined rigorously in accordance with specifications derived from customer requirements. Vendors must be selected from those demonstrated capable of delivering consistently acceptable products. We shall address both issues in great detail in ensuing paragraphs.

Purchasing Data

Documents associated with a purchased product must describe the product and include pertinent technical data. The product description will include an identification of its characteristics such as classification or grade. For example, an order for a metal fitting will specify whether it is to be brass or steel, and if the latter, whether it is to be stainless, galvanized, or some other. The description should be sufficiently detailed that no error can be made in verifying that the physical product is the same as the required product. The technical data establish the correctness of the order relative to customer requirements. Typical technical data are drawings, specifications, process requirements, and inspection instructions. As an example, specifications might exclude the combination of certain materials. Mixed metals in an environment of sea air may decompose quickly by electrolysis, so that if the purchaser is required to find substitute materials, some of which are prohibited, then technical data can provide this information. In brief, those data are required that ensure two things: the purchase order matches the customer requirements and the received purchased product meets the specifications of the purchase order. Thus, there are both outgoing and incoming purchase procedures. And, of course, the purchasing and technical data are provided to the subcontractor so that it, too, can meet the requirements. The company is expected to maintain a close, feedback relationship with its subcontractors.

Evaluation and Selection of Subcontractors

A few years ago, Canon Corporation opened a factory in the Hampton Roads area of Virginia and, in conformance to its practices in Japan, cast about for local suppliers that might provide acceptable service. One of its directors, Mr. Tadao Okabe (1991), tells of a local vendor who agreed to supply a certain product for, say, $1 apiece this year and then $1.10 apiece the following year. The Canon manager replied, "No, you have it wrong. You will supply the part for $1 apiece this year, then for ninety cents apiece the following year. Otherwise, you are not improving your processes. You are learning nothing from your experience."

This story indicates the range of a critical selection process that a company may adopt in selecting and evaluating its suppliers. It might consider a supplier based on the quality of its product or the quality of its processes. In the latter case, it might emulate Canon and insist that the supplier implement continuous improvement.

Most companies maintain a list of suppliers that have been approved in some way. In a few cases, the government requires that certain products be purchased from licensed vendors. Examples might include vendors of powerful drugs or toxic chemicals. ISO 9000 standards do not explicitly require an approved vendor list, but they do require that a vendor selection process be maintained. Henceforth, we shall use the term *subcontractor* in lieu of the more commonly used terms *supplier* and *vendor.*

Subcontractors will be selected based on their ability to meet specifications. The method of evaluation must be documented in a procedure, and records of these evaluations must be retained as quality records. How do you get started? Most companies that apply for certification to an ISO standard have been in business for a substantial period of time and already have preferred subcontractors. You can "grandfather" long-time subcontractors, but they must be, henceforth, continually evaluated. Their retention must be justifiable from a quality viewpoint.

The performance evaluation process need not be burdensome. Only a few metrics are needed, such as on-time delivery, correct product, good condition, correct count, and acceptable quality. Not all these metrics are important to all companies; each company is free to choose the metrics that it deems effective to its business.

Desai (1996) describes an evaluation program in which subcontractors are judged on issues of price, quality, process control, technical support, purchasing support, on-time delivery, product technology, and lead time. The company in question manufactures disk drives and purchases parts that account for 75 percent of the cost of a drive. In other words, subcontractors are responsible for most of the cost. To improve its own price competitiveness, the company has no choice but to maintain strict subcontractor control.

At the other extreme, a single metric may be sufficient—cost, for example. Suppose that you are a small manufacturer of sheet steel products. Your subcontractor is a major producer whose users purchase steel by the boxcar. Your needs are modest; you purchase small lots such that most steel producers won't bother with you. The subcontractor is willing to sell her secondary quality to you in small lots, and you find that about 10 percent is unusable. Her policy is take it or leave it. How do you evaluate this subcontractor, and why should you bother?

You can meet ISO 9000 requirements in this case in one of two ways. The first is to maintain a cost analysis of the material failure rate. If the failure rate increases, you formally notify the subcontractor. This cost is then compared to a worst-case scenario where the quality of the material falls so low that it becomes feasible to purchase a boxcar of sheet steel from some other vendor even if this means that you then have a one-year inventory of the stuff. Such a cost analysis shows that at least you are addressing the cost of quality as well as circumstances permit.

The second way to meet the ISO standard is to maintain rigorous receipt inspection practices. This shows that you are ensuring quality in your end product irrespective of the quality of purchased material. In the end, the ISO standards are meant to provide quality to your customers and that is all you need to prove.

Subcontractor evaluation implies that a receipt inspection process is maintained in order to determine "correct condition." This should be a formal acceptance testing process, and again, the method of inspection is of the company's own choosing as long as there is a procedure for it and as long as the results are retained as quality records. You begin by taking nonconformance data, determining a metric, doing statistical analysis, then evaluating and recording subcontractor performance on the basis of this analysis.

It is probably easier to evaluate all subcontractors than to try to formulate or justify a policy of exceptions. For example, a company may prefer to exempt from evaluation a supplier that is a subsidiary or division of the same company. As a general rule this practice is not acceptable. There are conditions under which purchased parts verification may be relaxed; these conditions are discussed in a later paragraph, but the decision is based on the *how*, not the *who*, of verification. An ISO auditor will expect that all subcontractors are evaluated in an ongoing process.

Receiving

Most of the comments on subcontractor evaluation apply to receiving as well as to requisitioning. You might select your subcontractors based on an initial estimate of their ability to produce quality parts and upon their price competitiveness, but selection is an ongoing process, continually revised by evaluation of service in receiving. The receiving phase of the purchasing process thus includes verification of parts and associated service, and of performance evaluation.

Verification of Purchased Product

Purchased product can be verified either at the subcontractor's facility or upon arrival at the company's facility, or both. The arrangement should be formal, described by the company in its policy and procedures documents, and in the contract or agreement with the subcontractor. Let's consider both alternatives. Verification at the contracting facility places most of the weight of quality on the subcontractor. This itself can be achieved in several ways. Company purchasers or quality experts can visit the subcontracting facility and examine its inspection procedures. Alternatively, the company may accept, with the delivery of the purchased product, associated control chart results, other statistical evidence of product quality, third-party certification of test results, and certifications of conformance from the subcontractor. That is, the company can rely primarily upon the subcontractor's quality control procedures.

However, verification of product quality by the subcontractor does not relieve the company of its responsibility to provide acceptable product to its customers. Nevertheless, the company need not repeat the verification process in its own plant. Major corporations often use subcontractor verification if they have hundreds of subcontractors and the sheer volume of receipt inspection is inefficient or costly.

If, however, the company opts to inspect purchased products in its own facility, the process for conducting these inspections is discussed in great detail in Clause 4.10, under "Receiving Inspection and Testing." There must be a formal procedure to notify the subcontractor of the outcome of such inspections. Collman (1995) describes a company that uses a nonconformance form to report failures to its subcontractors. The form requires the subcontractor to report back to the company whether it has identified the root cause, and any corrective or preventive action that it takes in regard to the failed product.

Some companies may choose to conduct a purchased-part quality control program that uses both subcontractor verification and receipt inspection. Subcontractors are selected on the basis of demonstrated consistency in supplying quality product and are admitted to a qualified vendors list. A close association is formed between these preferred sources and the company, in which technical data are shared, long-term contracts are issued, and assurances of profit are offered. The company then conducts a greatly reduced receipt inspection process, conducted only to enhance the statistical assurance of end-product quality and acknowledge its final responsibility.

Some customers may wish to verify the quality of purchased product themselves, either at the company facility or even at the subcontractor facility. This option will of course be in its contract with the company. The U.S. government is often such a customer. ISO 9000 standards make it clear that inspection of purchased product by the customer absolves neither the subcontractor nor the company of its responsibility to the quality of its products.

Parts Management

The management of purchased parts is an ISO 9000 requirement, but whether it falls under the purview of Clause *4.6: Purchasing*, or Clause *4.9: Process Control*, depends on how the company chooses to define it. One view is that once the parts are received and verified, they are in the process. It is also true that Clause 4.9 requires materials planning. But so does Clause 4.6. And quite often the purchased parts go into inventory at least briefly, and are not immediately "on the floor." We shall arbitrarily take the latter view and classify purchased parts management as one of the purchasing requirements, under the guise of planning and control of purchasing suggested in ISO 9004. The rationale for this decision is that most inventory systems contain purchase triggers, so that inventory is simply one of the phases of the purchasing cycle.

ISO standards do not mandate or recommend any particular inventory method. Just-in-time, economic order quantity (EOQ), material requirements planning (MRP and MRP II), and manufacturing execution systems (MES) are just a few of the dynamic inventory-to-production management tools in common use; the company is free to choose from these or any other, including any of its own invention. However, the more formal and documented the method, the more likely it will satisfy ISO requirements.

And here we detect evidence that ISO 9000 standards are minimum requirements. Inventory must be planned and controlled, but whether or not it is effective is not at issue. If you can locate a part and identify it as appropriate to a specific contract, then you meet ISO requirements. If your inventory costs are too high or inventory does not support production optimally, you will take your hit from the marketplace, not from an ISO auditor. But this book is about capable systems, so you want to go beyond the minimum requirements and address dynamic response requirements that also satisfy the standards.

Stevens (1994) discusses some of the limitations of MRP, pointing out that even MRP II, which provides scheduling capability, does not solve scheduling problems. However, when supplemented with a software capability called finite capacity scheduling (FCS), the dynamics of customer orders can be addressed. Detailed analysis of the strengths and weaknesses of any inventory system is beyond the scope of this book, but Exhibit 8-1 is meant to stimulate the awareness of dynamic purchasing. A purchasing system that tells you what you need and when you need it is necessary but not sufficient. You also need a system that tells you if the item is available, and if not, when it will be. The difference between need date and availability date must be maintained at zero, and since both these dates can change, the problem is a dynamic one. This is what is meant by "tracking" in the exhibit. Obviously, if required parts are described by a vast number of line items or are provided by a large number of subcontractors, then computerized tracking is a must. But even a relatively small logistics system should be supported by tracking, which may be handled by the buyers themselves.

Dynamic tracking is one major factor in a capable system of parts management. Another is the reduction of redundancy. Redundant parts inventory is particularly a problem when it comes to small hardware items or general electronics devices. Stevens (1995) points out, for example, that engineers designing a product may specify a new part rather than cull through the company's approved parts list to see if it is already available. He states that redundant parts are a soft cost in the sense that the time devoted to the underlying support is hard to identify: design time, release, acquisition, and maintenance, as opposed to the actual cost of purchasing the item, which would be the same whether the item were redundant or not.

An ISO standard is specific on one aspect of parts management—quality records. More will be said about this issue in the discussion of traceability in Chapter 19, but here we will define quality records relative to purchasing and exactly what must be maintained. In brief, quality records are any data that describe a characteristic of a product that is taken to represent its quality and that pertains to a specific contract. For example, an inventory of dyes is not necessarily a quality record, but a dye used in a given contract is a component of the quality record of that product. And, of course, subcontractor evaluations are quality records.

Summary

Sustainability in a Clause 4.6 program requires a purchasing system capable of governing and integrating the operations of requisition, receipt, and parts management, as structured in Exhibit 8-1. The requisition process will include provision, maintenance, and tracking of purchasing data; and evaluation and critical selection of subcontractors. The receipt process will include verification of the amount, type, and condition of purchased product. Parts management will consist of the timely delivery of purchased product to the appropriate production points.

References

ANSI/ISO/ASQC. *Q9001-1994. Quality Systems—Model for Quality Assurance in Design, Development, Production, Installation, and Servicing*. Milwaukee: American Society for Quality Control, 1994.

ANSI/ISO/ASQC. *Q9004-1-1994. American National Standard: Quality Management and Quality System Elements and Guidelines.* Milwaukee: American Society for Quality Control, 1994.

Collman, Dave. "The Proper Distribution of TQM." *Quality Progress*, February 1995, pp. 75–77.

Desai, M. P. "Implementing a Supplier Scorecard Program." *Quality Progress*, February 1996, pp. 73–75.

Okabe, Tadao, former director of Finance and Administration, Canon Virginia, Inc. Vendor selection story related to students at the Darden Graduate School of Business Administration, University of Virginia, September 11, 1991.

Stevens, Tim. "Prolific Parts Pilfer Profits." *Industry Week*, June 5, 1995, pp. 59–62.

———. "Success Runs on Schedule." *Industry Week*, August 15, 1994, pp. 83–88.

Chapter 9

Clause 4.14: Corrective and Preventive Action

Brief. Clause 4.14 requires systems to correct and prevent nonconformances. Corrective or preventive actions will be appropriate to the risks.

By the first quarter of the twentieth century scientists knew that particle theory could not explain the behavior of the physical world. They also realized that although wave theory answered many of the questions that the particle approach could not, the converse was also true. The evidence demanded that both theories, totally opposite in their view, were needed to provide a complete understanding of physics. Niels Bohr (1934) called this duality the principle of complementarity. The two models complemented rather than contradicted one another.

Complementarity in Quality

There is a similar phenomenon in the world of quality. You can wait until things go wrong or you can take steps to prevent the errant event before it happens. Both notions have their adherents. For example, the first is described by the old saw "If it ain't broke, don't fix it"; this is more elegantly called a run-to-fail philosophy. But as with the wave-particle approach in physics, quality is not best served with an either-or approach. Correction and prevention are complementary. Together they are necessary and sufficient.

Corrective and preventive actions represent two different philosophies. Corrective actions are those taken to address a problem of variability that exists in the process. This problem may be due to an assignable cause (external disturbance) or to a common cause (a variability inherent in the system). Preventive actions are those taken to address a potential problem of variability that might occur in the process. The problems might be regarded as either potentially assignable or potentially inherent. In sum, corrective actions are remedial. Preventive actions are anticipative.

Problem Solving

There is general agreement on the problem-solving process. Gibson (1990) describes a general approach to problem solving that is virtually identical to the method described by Guffey and Helms (1995) of the Tennessee Valley Authority; by Feinberg (1995) of Plessy Semiconductors; by Bemowski (1994) of Ford Motor Company; and by Shaw et al. (1995) of the Strong Memorial Hospital of Rochester, New York. The basic iteration is to (1) identify a problem; (2) analyze the problem; (3) evaluate alternate solutions; (4) select and implement a solution; (5) evaluate results.

Corrective and preventive measures use the same iteration but use somewhat different strategies in doing so. This difference is indicated in Exhibit 9-1 in terms of problem solving. As a general statement, correction tends to focus on product, or in the small; prevention tends to focus on process, or in the large. The reason is that things break down individually, but when we try to predict something or conceive of a problem, we tend to a broader view. For example, a printed circuit card may malfunction somehow, perhaps owing to overheating. You cannot predict the breakdown of that particular card; nor would anyone try. Instead, you would approach the problem from the other direction. If you were to imagine problems with printed circuit cards, you might think that perhaps heat would be a

Exhibit 9-1. Problem-solving strategies for prevention and correction.

Step	*Prevention*	*Correction*
Identify problem.	Research, surveys, audits Maintenance, training Forecasts	Test, inspect, customer complaint, operator reports
Analyze problem.	Environmental impact Process analysis Modes and interactions	Product analysis Root cause analysis
Evaluate alternate solutions.	Incremental changes Changes in kind	Redesign, repair, replace
Implement solution.	Effect in the large Effect in test case	Effect in the large Effect in test case
Evaluate results.	Evaluate in the large	Evaluate locally

problem because air cooling was not installed in the equipment room.

The difference in strategy is very apparent in the identification of a problem. Correction is reactive. The problem is self-identified, more or less—at least the symptoms are identified. On the other hand, prevention requires predictive strategies, such as surveys and forecasts, or activities that suggest potential problems, such as audits. There is little difference in the implementation of a solution. You are going to resolve the problem either on a large scale or on a test or local basis. Techniques such as failure mode analysis can help to determine the breadth of approach.

Cost of Quality

Contrary to the well-known slogan, quality is not free. Most managers are quick to remind you of that when you request a budget for quality programs. In fact, many managers will require monetary proof of the value of a quality initiative relative to its cost. Yet this is often difficult to demonstrate. For example, control charting has cost associated with it. How do you demonstrate, a priori, that charting will save money?

Preventive and corrective measures have cost to them, and like the activities themselves, the costs are complementary. We saw the nature of this relationship in Chapter 4, but we see it in a different perspective in Exhibit 9-2 in order to understand what is going on. The prevention curve indicates that the cost to achieve specifications increases as you get closer to target. The curve is nonlinear and sooner or later the cost runs into diminishing returns. Every manager knows that, and it explains why compromise on quality may be sought earlier than the customer might wish. On the other hand, the cost of correction is quite high for poor quality, but the closer to target you get, the less the cost of quality because of correction.

A Word About Policies

The quality manual should present policies in regard to both corrective and preventive actions. A corrective policy might concern shutting down the production line in case of special cause.

Exhibit 9-2. Relating the costs of quality, prevention, and correction.

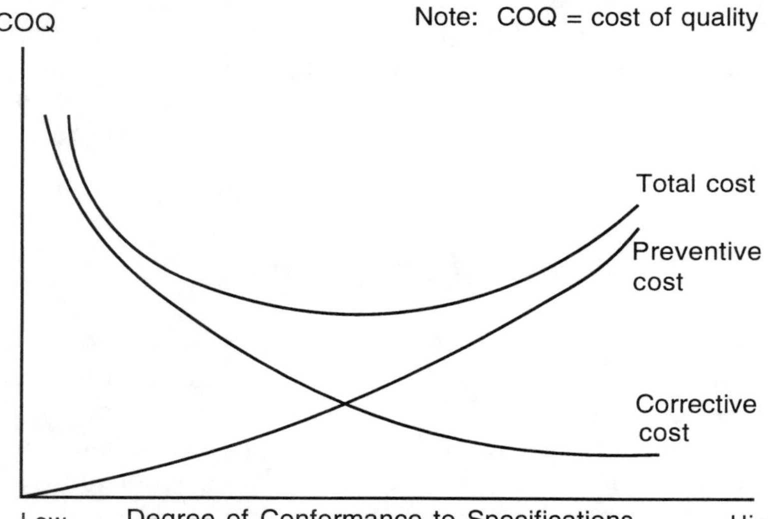

Preventive policy might be the installation of a continuous improvement review committee. The policies are then translated to implementation schemes that are described in the various departmental procedures.

As corrective and preventive actions warrant, these policies and procedures may have to be updated or changed in some way. For example, suppose that you employ control charting in your plant. A corrective procedure might be to consider as a special cause a problem in which sample averages fall on the same side of the process average seven times in a row. This sequence of events is statistically unlikely for a system in control.

If the subsequent operation shows that this policy is not sufficiently sensitive, then the policy might be changed to define as assignable a sequence of five samples in a row on the same side of the process average. Similarly, a preventive maintenance procedure might require that a certain adjustment to an equipment be made daily. Subsequently, operations may reveal that weekly adjustments are satisfactory.

Corrective Action

Corrective action has two aspects. The first refers to detecting, identifying, and correcting causes of nonconformities in product quality. The second refers to the disposition of nonconforming product; this will be discussed in Chapter 23. In this section, we shall focus on the first aspect.

Corrective Action Programs

Before you can take corrective action you need to know that something is wrong. Corrective action begins with detecting variability in product quality. You do this with inspection and test programs, but can also detect problems with on-line monitoring systems such as control charting. Inspections and tests detect problems in product, not in process. Control charting detects problems in the process. An effective detection strategy uses surveillance techniques for both process and product, and is an important part of an overall corrective action program. Detection and correction should be conducted at a program level, complete with policies, procedures, and methods, rather than as a reactive fire drill.

Erin (1993) discusses methods of approaching a problem once it is identified. First, the identity is formalized by an ID number, date of occurrence, description, and symptoms. An owner is assigned who will size the job of solving the problem: estimate the nature of the problem; determine functional contacts, if any; set up a status reporting process; determine appropriate analytical techniques to resolve the problem, then move to solution. The problem report will record these issues through evaluation of the solution. The process is shown in Exhibit 9-3.

Once a problem is detected, corrective action is taken to determine the cause. There are a number of techniques for determining cause, among them Pareto analysis and fish-bone charts. The force behind both of these methods is often collective discussion, using some sort of committee analysis or brainstorming technique. Assuming that the cause is found, Clause 4.14 then requires that investigation include a period of confirmation to verify that, indeed, the corrective action has resolved the issue.

Exhibit 9-3. The flow of a corrective action program.

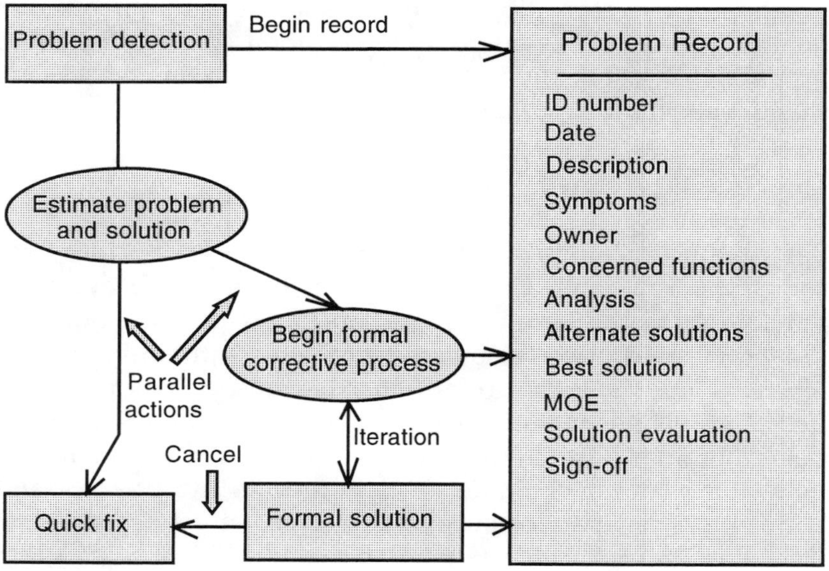

Problem detection
Begin record
Problem Record
ID number
Date
Description
Symptoms
Owner
Concerned functions
Analysis
Alternate solutions
Best solution
MOE
Solution evaluation
Sign-off
Estimate problem and solution
Begin formal corrective process
Parallel actions
Iteration
Cancel
Quick fix
Formal solution

In sum, a program of corrective action will identify four phases: detection, identification, resolution, and verification.

The assurance of problem solving lies in formalizing a corrective action program, but the power lies in the analytical techniques. Both methods and applications are under constant improvement in the industry so that the literature must be read regularly just to keep up. Maul and Gillard (1994) provide an example of the effective use of simple tools, such as histograms, in the difficult analysis of electrostatic coatings. Kenett (1994) shows a test that can be used with Pareto charts to compare presolution and postsolution data to determine the degree of improvement.

The Quick Fix

A formal process may seem too cumbersome to be effective, but it is necessary to ensure a systematic solution. Furthermore, as the figure indicates, a formal process does not preclude a quick fix. A quick fix is an ad hoc, on-the-spot repair or solution to a problem. It can be reasonable, economically necessary, and very often sufficient. Sometimes a problem is simple and its solution obvious—an assembler may notice that some of the cooling fins on an air conditioner may be bent. If they can be straightened out on the spot, why not do so? Should it be reported? Yes, if only to detect a systematic problem. The incident may be a recurring one.

As another example, suppose a test is being conducted of an electronic system and a line breaks. If it is possible to jury-rig a line in order to continue the test, while aborting the test would be costly, then the quick fix is the reasonable thing to do. Eventually, of course, the line must be properly repaired.

There is always a quick fix in the real world. It is best to recognize it and to integrate it as a subprocess of a formal corrective action. An example will show why. I once ran a test of the telemetry package in a guided missile as part of a routine check to verify that the telemetry electronics were in good order. Normally, the telemetry remained off until the missile was launched, at which time it was powered by the missile power system, as was everything else aboard. This particular missile was powered by a gas generator system that, once lit off, ran to expiration. Obviously you do not want to light off the missile power system prior to launch, or you will launch a dead missile. Thus, it was necessary to use an external power source to light off the telemetry package. This was achieved by throwing a switch in the control room, which removed the normal light-off command and applied the external power. Over the years this switch had failed and had been jury-rigged around the failure. The quick fix had been forgotten. Presto, we threw the switch, thinking to remove the regular missile power light-off command, but instead did exactly what we did not want to do: a $150,000 missile was just wasted. Quick fixes by definition are pragmatic, on the spot, often unknown by anyone except the installer, and are prone to be forgotten or come to be accepted as a properly ordered solution.

Corrective Cost of Quality

Exhibit 9-2 showed that, for a given reliability, the corrective cost of quality decreases as the quality of the product gets closer to target value. However, there is another characteristic property of the cost of correction: Early detection reduces the cost of quality. This fact is not fully appreciated in industry. Some companies do not distinguish between nonconformities discovered internally and those discovered after delivery, although clearly the latter can be expensive, in actual cash outlay and in terms of customer dissatisfaction.

I know of one company that maintains a sizable staff of field technicians for warranty work. In a particular problem, the Pareto analysis of failure data revealed that the major contributor to warranty work was wiring failure. The nature of wiring leads me to suspect that the failures existed before the product went out the door, and could have been found by better test procedures. Repairing wiring mistakes is relatively inexpensive if found in the factory, and dirt cheap if found right away. It stands to reason that if the factory is in San Diego and the customer is in Chicago, then the cost of failing to find the defect before delivery is going to be expensive.

Preventive Action

Preventive action implies the ability to see into the future, to conceive the possible. In this sense it differs in no way from strategic thinking. It could be argued that every well-conceived plan is inherently preventive, but we need to narrow the field somewhat or talk forever. So we shall focus the meaning of prevention on the issue of potential failure. Thus, the base of preventive action lies in analysis and the recognition of pervasive and persistent effects, trends, and patterns of failure. We cannot prevent random failure; Shewhart (1931) tells us that it will always be with us. But we can take steps to remove the causes of repetitive failure. How do you know that failure is repetitive? Through a program of study and analysis of your processes. Prevention is the main reason why you take data and keep records—to look for systematic causes.

Preventive Action Programs

As in the case of correction, preventive actions require a formal framework. The purpose of a prevention program is to anticipate and identify systematic problems in product or process. An effective program includes a regular scrutiny of operations, quality records, audit reports, customer complaints, and results of inspection and testing in order to detect, analyze, and remove potential problem areas. Additionally, a well-defined program improves the cognitive skills of employees, establishes organizational motivations, and identifies proactive analytical methods.

Cognitive skills should be improved because the very nature of forecasting potential trouble implies human intellect. The better that people understand the product, process, and environment, the better is their ability to see nuance and to anticipate a problem.

Cognitive Skills

Systems-level training is the best vehicle for broadening the view of an employee vis-à-vis the task at hand. An understanding of system and subsystems, modes and parameters, and interaction with the environment provides the employee with the breadth of view to conceive of what might go wrong or of what can be improved. This is in line with the view, presented in Chapter 2, of IBM's founder, Tom Watson, Sr. He wanted people who could use their minds and their experience to improve their jobs, their products, and their processes.

I once interviewed an assembly-line worker whose job was to install pieces of equipment on a metal panel. He had no idea of the processes before him or after him. He did not care. His ignorance robbed this man of the motivation to improve. It could be argued that the person did not need to know what function that equipment served. Perhaps not. But how about the production system itself? That assembler could make a greater contribution, particularly in prevention, by knowing where the assembly came from, where it was going, and what the thing was supposed to do. Even more important, the assembler should have been taught the big picture—where his operation fit into the grand scheme of things. This knowledge is the beginning of the ability to think of ways of improvement.

Where systems training provides the breadth of view, training in problem formulation and in the scientific method teaches how to use it. This training need not be—indeed, should not be—any more exotic than the situation calls for. Some people have the native skill to formulate problems—the best analyst I ever met had only a high school education. Others should be taught the elements, at least, of how a problem is identified and how the issue is carried through to solution.

Shipyards provide many opportunities for formulating a problem in fundamental ways. Consider this example. One department has checked out hydraulic hoses that it uses sporadically during the day. Another department needs hydraulic hoses and can either go to the other end of the yard to check them out or can "borrow" hoses that they see lying nearby. When the first outfit needs its hoses again, they have disappeared. This is a system problem, the system being one of resource distribution. It was resolved to everyone's amity by an employee who figured out how hoses might be time-shared on an ad hoc basis, yet still identified by the owner. The hose fittings were color coded; you checked them out by color. If another group must borrow your hoses for a while, it and you know where the hoses must be returned.

Organizational Motivations

Employee empowerment can contribute to an overall continuous improvement program in which employees and first-level supervisors are encouraged to use their expertise to identify potential problems. We know that the foundation of preventive action is in analysis, but analysis is done by motivated, qualified people—the ones who do the work. The motivation comes from empowerment, that is, relying on worker insight. As Kinlaw (1992) puts it: "No one can question the importance of executive leadership to focus a total organization on improvement. Nevertheless, improvement, however it is conceived, planned, or initiated, almost invariably comes down to the cooperative actions of teams of people."

Empowerment is controversial in some quarters, resisted by management, held in skeptical regard by employees. We are not exploring the limits of empowerment here, but rather that the notion ought to be considered at least at its minimum level: to recognize that people are usually competent in what they do. Some degree of empowerment can encourage this capability. For example, Masaaki Imai (1997) describes one level of empowerment: Employees have the authority to improve their own work as long as they follow a standardized process. This level of empowerment does *not* include participative management or shared decision making (p. 231).

Proactive Methods

We have not discussed root cause analysis, yet the term is in vogue. However, the bloom is beginning to fade as more and more quality people arrive at the idea that few problems are so simple as to have a single root cause and that proper analysis is done by the systems approach. The difference is that in the root cause view, the relationship of cause and effect is isomorphic. In the systems view, each effect has interactive causes. One does not preclude the other, but some people who use root cause analysis may tend to look for the single cause and may well miss interactive factors.

The issue would be purely semantic if it were not for the human tendency to simplify things and then to cast them in stone. The scientific method that comes to us from the age of reason never made the claim that cause and effect were isomorphic. It is arrogant and wrong to suppose that we have moved beyond Newton. Few people have moved beyond Newton. We could easily call the method "root cause(s) analysis," then put the controversy to rest. Except that the notion of a single cause for a single effect won't go away. Still, root cause(s) analysis remains an effective proactive method because it can be a search for systematic sources of problems.

Similarly, SPC methods are often considered in the light of correction, but they too can be equally useful as preventive measures. Wozniak (1994) identifies several characteristics of an SPC program that will lead to improvement. A proactive SPC program will be customer oriented at all levels in the company, and will provide formal channels for team meetings to discuss quality problems, thus opening the door to imagination.

Summary

Sustainability in Clause 4.14 requires a dual approach to quality. Corrective measures need little explanation in principle because correction is a well-established strategy. Corrective processes should be integrated as shown in Exhibit 9-3. However, correction, although necessary, is not sufficient. Modern quality theory stresses preventive measures also. Prevention depends upon the skills and ingenuity of a well-motivated workforce, and this can be enhanced by training and by management leadership.

References

ANSI/ISO/ASQC. *Q9001-1994. Quality Systems—Model for Quality Assurance in Design, Development, Production, Installation, and Servicing*. Milwaukee: American Society for Quality Control, 1994.

Bemowski, K. "Ford Chairman Was, and Continues to Be, a Progress Chaser." *Quality Progress*, October 1994, pp. 29–32.

Bohr, Niels. *Atomic Theory and the Description of Nature*. Cambridge, England: Cambridge University Press, 1934.

Erin, Tim. "Closed Loop Corrective Action." *Quality Progress*, January 1993, pp. 51–53.

Feinberg, S. "Overcoming the Real Issues of TQM Implementation." *Quality Progress*, July 1995, pp. 79–81.

Gibson, J. E. *How to Do Systems Analysis*. Workbook. Charlottesville: School of Engineering, University of Virginia, 1990.

Guffey, C. J., and M. M. Helms. "The IRS and TVA Are Leading the Way." *Quality Progress*, October 1995, pp. 51–55.

Imai, Masaaki. *Gemba Kaizen*. New York: McGraw-Hill, 1997.

Kenett, R. S. "Making Sense Out of Two Pareto Charts." *Quality Progress*, May 1994, pp. 71–73.

Kinlaw, D. C. *Continuous Improvement and Measurement for Total Quality*. San Diego, Calif.: Pfeiffer & Company, 1992.

Maul, G. P., and J. S. Gillard. "Solving Chronic Problems With Simple Tools." *Quality Progress*, July 1994, pp. 51–55.

Shaw, D. V., D. O. Day, and E. Slavinskas. "Learning from Mistakes." *Quality Progress*, June 1995, pp. 45–48.

Shewhart, W. A. *Economic Control of Quality of Manufactured Product*. Princeton, N.J.: Van Nostrand, 1931.

Wozniak, C. "Proactive vs. Reactive SPC." *Quality Progress*, February 1994, pp. 49–50.

Chapter 10

Clause 4.18: Training

Brief. Clause 4.18 requires a training program that will identify training needs, resources, schedules, and records for all persons whose work affects quality. Personnel will be assigned tasks that are appropriate to their level of training and experience.

Few aspects of business have greater variation than training. The need for training employees has been recognized for a long time; Bigliazzi et al. (1995) discusses the continuous training programs of Roman building yards in the Augustan period. The variation is due to a difference in view on the extent and breadth of training needed. Almost every company will train an employee for a specific skill. Some companies provide career-long training programs that recognize that an employee may change jobs both laterally and vertically. A lateral change might be a shift from typewriters to word processors, or from burning to welding. A vertical change might be from apprentice to journeyman, or from shop worker to supervisor. We can extrapolate from these examples to see that a company providing career-long training programs to hundreds of employees will require a massive training program.

The reason for the great variation in training programs is, without doubt, economic. If you hire someone to throw a switch one way when a given condition exists, and throw it the other way when the condition is absent, why spend money to train that person to do anything else? Breka and Rubach (1995) point out that it is often difficult to show the connection between the cost of training and the gains made. In that sense, training suffers the same dilemma as quality itself—intuitively we tend to believe that it is good, but we cannot directly trace its effect to the bottom line.

Because the relationship of training to profit is not easy to see, many American companies are not very good at providing it. Whereas Japanese firms train their employees more than 300 hours during the first six months of employment, U.S. workers receive less than 50 hours (Lamprecht, 1993). Breka and Rubach report that only 0.5 percent of all U.S. corporations spend 90 percent of the total annual outlay for training. Small firms, which account for 35 percent of American jobs, often have no training budget at all, and many mid-sized firms hire personnel already trained in order to perform a specific contract. Without reinforcement, these skills become dated or obsolete.

Quality standards have not been much help in deciding the issue. On the one hand, the quality standards Mil-I-45208A and Mil-Q-9858A contained no requirement for training. One result of this is that some government contractors have no training program at all and simply hire specific expertise when needed. (And lay them off when not needed.) On the other hand, the ISO quality standards and the Malcolm Baldrige criteria of the U.S. Department of Commerce require extensive training programs. It is enlightening to examine what these agents have to say so as to come to a consensus on the characteristics needed in a training program that will contribute to quality sustainability.

Malcolm Baldrige Training Criteria

The U.S. Congress established the Malcolm Baldrige National Quality Award program in 1987, with Public Law 100-107. The program's purpose is to establish the global leadership of American industry through continuous improvement of quality methods in product and process. The program is a quality award, not a quality standard. An applicant company is free to meet the criteria in any way it chooses, and the annual award goes to the best competitor in one of a few categories. Hence, there can be only a few winners each year.

The criterion of interest to us is that related to training. A Malcolm Baldrige examiner will look to see if the applicant company provides opportunity for training that goes beyond current job assignments and offers chances for developmental assignments. A company with a minimal training program will score poorly in competition with one whose program is extensive. Clearly, the Malcolm Baldrige award encourages a broad training program—the broader the better.

ISO 9000 Training Criteria

Although an ISO 9000 standard does not use the word *program* per se, its requirements amount to nothing less. When you meet the criteria of Clause 4.18 appropriately, you have a training program: policy, objectives, schedules, resources, records. Effectively then, training programs are required for all personnel engaged in work affecting quality. An individual's program will:

1. Define and identify past, present, and future training needs.
2. Provide the training.
3. Ensure that only qualified people perform a given task.
4. Keep training records.

ISO 9000 does not purport to tell the employer what sort of or how much training the employees need. The company is free to determine training policies and procedures according to its own needs, but the training system must be defined and formalized into a program.

Training for Sustainability

We are not going to establish the connection between training and the bottom line in this book. Instead, I shall show justification for the expense of training in two social trends. The first is intuitive. Over the centuries we observe that consumers will buy products of good quality and will ignore products of inferior quality. At the very least then, a training program should ensure that workers can do their job in some minimal sense. The rationale behind this idea is primitive. It cannot be proved but it is accepted as reasonable based on historical observation.

Anderson et al. (1994) report on a study showing that by the end of the millennium, 70 percent of jobs in Europe and 80 percent of jobs in the United States will require cerebral skills. This trend to cerebral jobs provides another rationale. I am not sure what "cerebral" means, but suppose that a cerebral job refers to one that requires thought. This definition bothers me, however, because it implies that there are jobs that do not require thought. Does painting require thought? Playing the piano? Carving a violin? Digging a ditch? Let's agree that all tasks require some combination of thought, intuition, soul, passion, and physical activity.

I once viewed a television documentary of a physicist who was attempting to learn how one plays the piano. The notes are before the eyes of the pianist, the keys at fingertip; presumably there is some instantaneous transfer of thought from one to the other. But the response time from eyes to brain to fingers doesn't correlate with the rate of transmission that a pianist displays. After a great deal of analysis, the physicist tentatively concluded that perhaps human beings had an intermediate thought center located somewhere in the area of the hips!

All jobs require thought, many of them in ways that we do not understand or cannot measure. I do not intend to demean any task in trying to understand what a cerebral job is. Let's begin with a primitive definition of data: facts and figures from which conclusions can be drawn. From this we move to a definition of knowledge: conclusions and understanding from data based upon established theory and principles. To have knowledge, then, we must have data, understand the relevant theories and principles (lore), be able to analyze the data, and be able to draw logical conclusions based upon the established lore.

Data change, often rapidly. Analytical methods change, also rapidly if technology is involved. For example, digital computers have introduced new methods of analysis that were simply too cumbersome to attempt by hand: dynamic and linear programming, spreadsheets, and brain scans, for example. Theory and principles change too, but much more slowly. If the knowledge required for a task changes slowly, then we quickly get up to speed and can perform in proportion to the years of experience.

If the knowledge required for a job changes rapidly, then experience, while still important, is less so, and the ability to keep up with the data and analytic techniques is more important. Let's arbitrarily say that this kind of knowledge is dynamic. Therefore, an intuitive definition of a cerebral job is one in which knowledge is dynamic. Cerebral jobs require almost continuous training.

The Training Process

Training involves learning, of course, but it involves much more, as Exhibit 10-1 indicates. As in every other process, a closed-loop configuration is preferred because the concern is stability and capability. Zaciewski (1993) iterates this theme in different terms, saying that a training process should be predictable (stability) so that students in one season achieve the same objectives as students in another. Furthermore, he asks if the process actually

Exhibit 10-1. The training process as a closed loop.

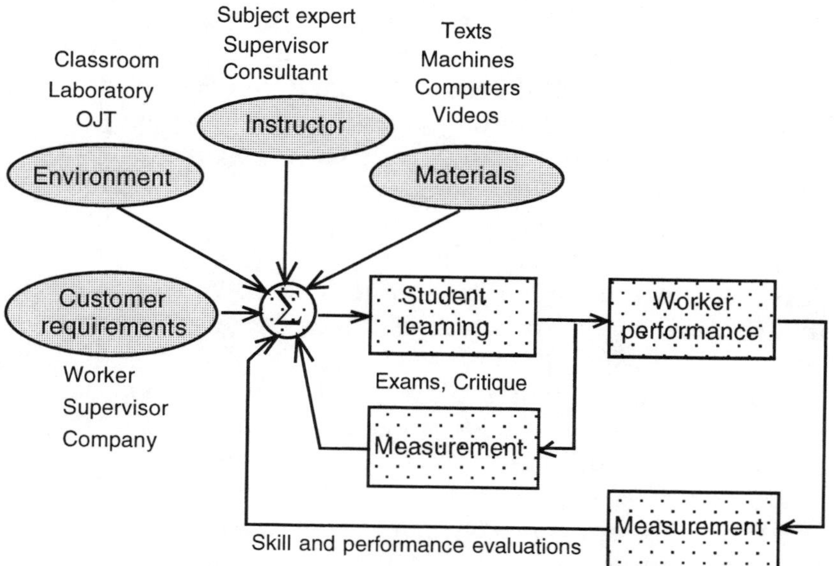

teaches the intended skills and whether these skills are used on the job (capability).

Some of the elements of Exhibit 10-1 are ambiguous. We talk of customer requirements, but just who constitutes the customer is often hotly debated in education, particularly at the university level. On the subject of company training, we must recognize three customers. The student is the most direct, of course, as the user of the learned skills. The company is presumably the beneficiary of the learned skills, and is also the paying customer. However, the supervisor's interest in this training must be recognized also. Tasks are achieved as a team effort at the first level of management more than at any other. As team leader, the supervisor has a comprehensive and unique interest in the depth and scope of the skills of the team.

The environment is often taken for granted in a training process. We assume, without thinking about it, that some appropriate location will be available. However, "appropriate" really does need to be thought out. Some subjects are best taught in a classroom, some in a laboratory, some at the worksite. There are different kinds of classrooms—large, small, amphitheater, and so on. The best environment will have no distractions, sufficient lighting, and a clear view of video matter for all students. This all sounds like motherhood, but from my experience it is not easily arranged. I've had to give classes in airplane hangars, in dark debrief rooms, in engine rooms, and in rooms whose physical dimensions were opposite to the requirements. Imagine making video presentations to a large class that easily fits into a room very wide on one axis but narrow on the axis facing the screen. The reality is that people must work very hard to make *any* process function correctly; nothing worthwhile comes easily.

The effectiveness of the training process can be determined in two ways: one to examine in some fashion whether the student can use the new skills, the other to evaluate the process itself, usually through interviews of the customers. In the first measurement, Zaciewski states the need for an appropriate metric. This metric should be straightforward—can the student do the new task? It should not be based on a vague metric such as understanding. He claims that attempts to measure understanding often lead to inconclusive results.

Cleary (1996) disagrees with this view, stating that learning is composed of information "how" and understanding "why." Tuttle (1993) echoes her view, stating that training should be conducted at an understanding level, not just at a knowledge level. My view is that a person cannot really achieve a systems perspective of a process without asking the why of things, and that this perspective is the key to sustainability. We shall get into the need for systems training in a moment, and for now concede to Zaciewski that testing understanding can be ambiguous. If so, the solution is not to abandon the metric but to determine better ways to test it.

Course evaluation is almost always by means of student critique. It is interesting to reflect that while the private sector evaluates its training programs by the simple expedient of asking its students for critique, the nation's universities rarely do. The result of this policy is that there has been a great shift from teaching to research as the primary objective of our universities. A study by Fairweather and Paulson (1992) shows a strong positive correlation between the research and remuneration of a university professor (as measured by published papers and research dollars), and an equally strong negative correlation between teaching and remuneration (as measured by classroom hours). Does this shift meet customer requirements? It does if we define the government, which pays for most of the research, as the customer. But if we define the student body as the customer, then we have a situation that would be unacceptable in any quality system.

It appears that it is easy to lose sight of the goal, which is another reason to adopt structures such as Exhibit 10-1. The customer is identified up front and asked to evaluate the course. Tuttle provides some sample responses in the form of a Pareto analysis: In his study, the students wanted a more hands-on approach, with better-quality materials and better organization. Thus the loop is closed and improvement is possible.

Training Programs

Parr and Hild (1995) reported on a company that trained all its employees in statistical process control, then found that few of them ever had the occasion to use it. This large block of training was, with 20/20 hindsight, obviously mostly an unnecessary expense that could have been avoided by focusing in advance on just who needed what kind of training. The authors state that the purpose of training is to provide employees with the knowledge and skills necessary to do their job. I find this purpose too constraining, but agree that skills learned and then neglected are wasted. We shall approach the subject of curriculum in a moment and concentrate for now on how training is focused for effectiveness. Training can be made continually effective through a program as structured in Exhibit 10-2.

In this configuration, *training* is an all-encompassing word that includes education, on-the-job training (OJT), symposia, home study, seminars, and any other form of information input that increases one's abilities in a measurable and documented way. The most elemental training is, of course, that required to qualify for the job. This might be as simple as presenting proof of a high school education plus some OJT. From this initiation, the employee's career continues on through advancement or job change. Perhaps the company may change the equipment or system with which the employee works. These changes require additional advanced or upgrade training, with associated record keeping and performance evaluation.

Exhibit 10-2. Dynamic training program structure.

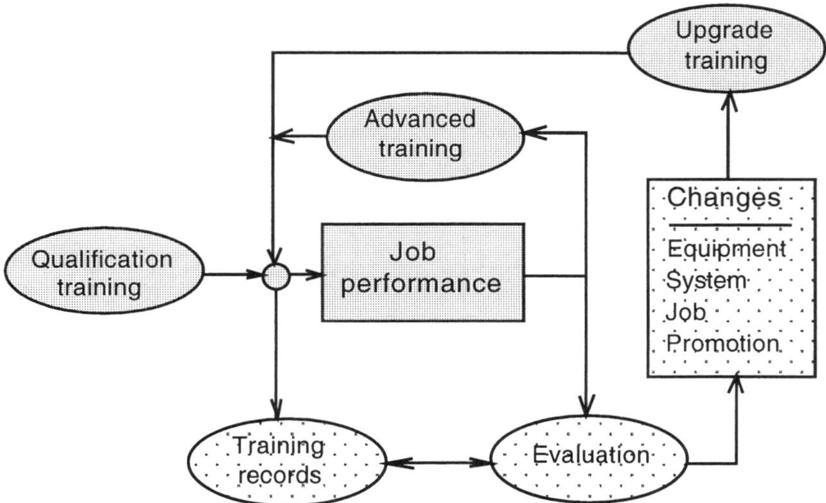

Some companies maintain very large training programs, complete with training departments, an in-house staff of instructors, facility classrooms, and even their own training centers. According to Breka and Rubach, Motorola corporation maintains its own university just to provide quality training to its worldwide workforce of 119,000 employees. Similarly, Ford Motor Company provides training facilities on a university scope.

Such luxury is fine if you can afford it, but it is not necessary. An effective training program can be maintained on a very modest scale. Let's consider just how simple such a program can be. First, it does not require that a company maintain a training department or hire an in-house lecturer or even a full-time training program manager. Requirements for training are identified and agreed upon in a joint employee-supervisor review. Training is obtained through any of the options previously cited: OJT; formal classroom in-house; formal classroom off-site, and symposia. In-house instructors can be company experts or external consultants. Off-site training can be obtained though professional commercial houses or at the local community college or university. Training records can be maintained in each employee's records jacket by the personnel department. From time to time a personnel supervisor or manager can make a facilitywide assessment of the state of training (another excellent application for the concept of state), as a corollary duty.

In brief, to meet ISO criteria a company needs to define a simple but formal training program. It is free to make all the decisions about it, including who needs training and how much and when. But the process must be a formal, documented system. All this is necessary but it is not sufficient for sustainability. You need to consider the curriculum to get to that level.

Training or Education

An earlier paragraph suggested that the purpose of training is more broad than to simply provide employees with the knowledge and skills necessary to do their job. Anderson et al. refer to the "learning organization," in which knowledge is widespread and its learning not limited to just management. They assert that employees should be taught statistical process control, problem solving, decision making, and communication, in addition to the skills needed for the work task. The authors say that Deming's concept of profound knowledge included such subjects as systems theory, variation, and psychology. They recognize that in the modern era employees are promoted to management levels and need to be prepared for it.

What we are talking about is, quite simply, a return to favor of education as opposed to training. Hurray! When I first went to work at IBM as an engineer, I had no engineering degree, but rather had simply a bachelor of arts in mathematics. This limitation was met with scorn by my peers, and I felt quite humbled and embarrassed about it for a long time. Then one day I realized that some of my peers could not read literature and a few could scarcely write at all. One fellow was obliged by university rules to submit a written request for his master's degree and could not compose the letter. Some of my associates were unfamiliar with many of the great names in history, including those of science. After a while I quit being embarrassed about the B.A. degree, realizing that it gave me a broader perspective, which is a driving force in my search for the systems concept.

Education helps to integrate knowledge. Therefore, a broad training curriculum can be justified for employees on more than the notion that it prepares them for management. It also prepares them for another force going on within industry these days—empowerment. Tuttle states that empowerment is an important part of total quality management and is the act of building power through cooperation, sharing, and teamwork. Suppose that a company wants to conduct a quality meeting of management and labor, with several levels of each group in attendance. Management has the top-down view, the knowledge of *why* things work. Labor has the bottom-up view, the knowledge of *how* things work. Somehow these two perspectives must be effectively integrated, and this integration is made easier if the employees have systems-level knowledge of their workstations: inputs, outputs, internal sources and customers, company mission and departmental role in that company mission.

A simple example will clarify this idea. Employees and management gather for a weekly progress meeting in a shipyard. Each knows the common schedule, the tasks to be done, and the resources needed for the tasks. Some of the tasks require common resources. Who gets them first? Who needs them the longest? Purchased parts delays occur. Some tasks are impacted. How can tasks be most efficiently reordered? Questions such as these are answered best by employees who are expert in what they do and familiar with their part in the total equation.

An Effective Training Program

Klöckner Pentaplast of America, Gordonsville, Virginia, manufactures rigid films for pharmaceutical packaging. It employs about 600 persons and has developed a training program that could serve as a benchmark for similar-size companies. Klöckner maintains a training department with a modest staff—three persons, including the director. The company employs a wide variety of skills, from machinery operation and clerical work to engineering and managing. The curriculum covers accounting, business courses, customer service, computer uses, quality control, and courses in the operation and maintenance of its machinery. They even offer courses in German and in labor law.

Training programs are offered both in-house and outside. Both the training department and the employees' supervisors work with employees in developing a personalized training program with two objectives: to ensure skill levels commensurate to the assigned task, and to encourage additional study for advancement and career development.

In-house courses are taught by Klöckner personnel or by consultants brought in from outside. Outside education is encouraged by educational assistance programs. In this way, the company effectively broadens its training capability by supplementing its own curriculum with those of the nearby University of Virginia and Piedmont Virginia Community College.

Personnel training records are kept in two places. Records of general training are retained by the company's training department; skill-level training records are kept by production managers. However, the two training record systems are integrated into a single computerized data base for central reference.

Summary

Sustainability in Clause 4.18 requires a formal, documented training program as structured in Exhibit 10-1 and 10-2. This program will define present and future training requirements for every employee whose work affects quality of product. Each employee will have a training record of past and projected training requirements, as well as a review process of training needs and opportunities. The training needs will be measured against job requirements. The program will include systems-level training.

References

ANSI/ISO/ASQC. *Q9001-1994. Quality Systems—Model for Quality Assurance in Design, Development, Production, Installation, and Servicing*. Milwaukee: American Society for Quality Control, 1994.

Anderson, J. C., K. Dooley, and M. Rungtusanatham. "Training for Effective Continuous Quality Improvement." *Quality Progress*, December 1994, pp. 57–61.

Bigliazzi, Marco, "Managing for Quality in Ancient Rome." In Marco Bigliazzi et al. "A History of Managing for Quality." *Quality Progress*, August 1995, pp. 125–129.

Breka, J., and L. Rubach. "Corporate Quality Training Facilities." *Quality Progress*, January 1995, pp. 27–30.

Cleary, B. A. "Relearning the Learning Process." *Quality Progress*, April 1996, pp. 79–85.

Department of Defense. *Mil-I-45208: Military Specification Inspection System Requirements*. Philadelphia: Department of Defense Printing Office, December 16, 1963.

———. *Mil-Q-9858A: Military Specification Quality Program Requirements*. Philadelphia: Department of Defense Printing Office, July 23, 1993.

Fairweather, J. S., and K. Paulson. "Teaching and Research in Engineering Education." *International Journal of Engineering Education* 8, no. 3 (1992), pp. 175–183.

Lamprecht, J. L. *Implementing the ISO 9000 Series*. New York: Marcel Dekker, 1993.

Malcolm Baldrige National Quality Award Foundation. *Malcolm Baldrige National Quality Award Criteria for 1996*. Gaithersburg: U.S. Department of Commerce, 1996.

Parr, W. C., and C. Hild. "Maintaining Focus Within Your Organization," *Quality Progress*, September 1995, pp. 103–106.

Tuttle, G. R. "Cascading Quality Through the Training Process." *Quality Progress*, April 1993, pp. 75–78.

Zaciewski, R. D. "Instructional Process Control." *Quality Progress*, January 1993, pp. 61–64.

Part Three

Quality System Requirements: Quality Assurance Purview

Chapter 11

Clause 4.2: Quality Manual

Brief: Clause 4.2 requires a quality manual that describes how the company meets the requirements of the Standard. The manual will include or refer to the company's quality procedures and related documentation.

A manual is considered a handbook of instructions or directions to be used as a reference. We might conclude from this that a quality manual would be a handbook of instructions related to quality. In fact, this is how the standard Q-10013 (1994) defines it, except not quite. There is an ambiguity in the terminology of quality documentation that needs to be clarified up front.

A quality system is described by a set of documentation: policies, plans, procedures, and instructions. The entire array can be considered the system quality manual, according to Q-10013, in the following words: "A quality manual should consist of, or refer to, the documented quality system procedures . . . which impact on quality within an organization." The key phase here is "or refer to," which has a major influence on the final form of a company quality manual.

Form of the Quality Manual

A company's quality program is manifested in company operations. ISO standards require that the program be defined and described in written documents, but a company is allowed a great deal of leeway in the interpretation of this requirement. The quality manual need not be a formal volume or set of volumes; it can be an assemblage of printed matter and software programs, although the total assemblage of documents must be defined and controlled.

In practice, however, companies often assemble a wide variety of documents and software as their total effort to meet the requirements of Clause 4.2, and present a small policy document that is called the "Quality Manual." The justification for this is the Standard's phrase "or refer to," which allows a company to present a policy document as a quality manual as long as it formally refers to the totality of quality system documentation. In fact, the guidelines for quality manuals, Q-10013, encourages this idea.

Accordingly, in this book, too, the quality manual is the Tier 1 policy book, the first in a set of volumes describing a quality system. The quality manual should be somewhat brief, forty to sixty pages, and written in such way as to require infrequent revision. Its brevity helps ensure that the manual remains a policy document and encourages its use by both company personnel and customers. Presumably, people will refer more often to a small, easily handled book than to a large and cumbersome one.

The total set of procedures and documentation describing the quality system is typically written in a three-tier system of controlled documents:

Tier 1: Quality manual
Tier 2: Departmental procedures
Tier 3: Work instructions and standard operating procedures (SOP)

The structure of Exhibit 11-1 is based on 1994 revisions to the ISO Standards. Earlier models used a four-tier arrangement, which is reflected in the manuals of thousands of companies. If your company is already certified, then yours may be one of them. In any case, the tiers of Exhibit 11-1 bear some explanation. The Tier 1 quality manuals contains policies and may also contain a few company-level procedures that do not fit anywhere else.

Exhibit 11-1. A tier system of documents.

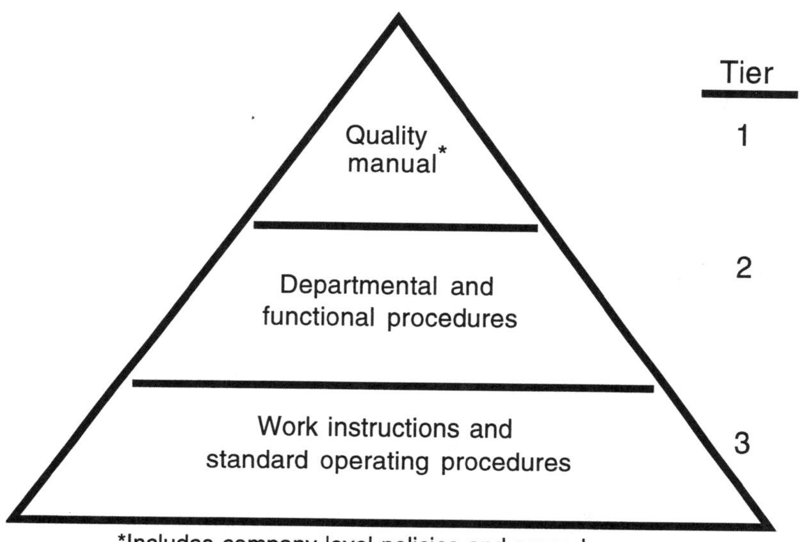

Most companies are organized according to some functional grouping. Usually, the highest level within a given facility is departmental. The functions within departmental purview should be described by procedures. A company may choose also to write procedures at some lower functional level. In any case, these are Tier 2 documents. The Tier 3 documents describe how a task is achieved. All three tiers will be discussed in more detail in ensuing paragraphs.

An Inherent Sustainability

The twenty clauses of ISO 9001 requirements are written with deliberate latitude so that each company can accommodate them to its own business as efficiently as possible. This provides flexibility to the criteria, but it also guarantees that some companies will have better-quality systems than others. Left to their own devices, some companies are simply more effective in what they do than others.

The criterion with least flexibility and with greatest assurance of capability is the one that refers to the quality manual. All registrars are quite strict about the form and substance of this document, regarding an applicant's quality manual as the baseline of its quality system. In other words, the system will be no better than the manual, so all registrars require a certain uniformity of effectiveness in the quality manual.

An effective quality manual exactly describes the company quality system and is easy to change. If a company alters some of its processes to effect stable and capable performance, the appropriate changes in the quality manual should be automatically triggered. Therefore, ISO-certified quality manuals tend to have the properties of stability and capability themselves. A quality manual is, after all, more than a document; it is also a process. So if you already hold an ISO 9000 quality system certificate, you may have a quality manual that contributes as effectively to stability and capability as it is going to.

The key to stable and capable quality documentation is the notion of triggers. Given that your company initiates a functional or organizational change in order to accommodate external or internal causes, the documentation system must have in place the triggering mechanisms that will change them also. These structures are discussed in Chapter 12.

The Quality Manual

Henceforth, the quality manual refers to a Tier 1 description of the quality system. By Tier 1, we mean policies and responsibilities related to each of the twenty clauses of ISO 9001. The quality manual should contain:

1. Company mission and quality policy
2. Quality manual revision and authorization page
3. Distribution list
4. Table of contents
5. Company organizational structure and brief history
6. Overview of the quality system
7. List of documents constituting the quality system, including an issue control matrix

8. Brief description of company policy with respect to each clause of paragraph 4, ISO 9001; Clause 4.1 will define the quality responsibility for each manager
9. Company-level procedures (documentation control, for example)

Item 1 is usually the personal work of the CEO and introduces the manual. Items 2 and 3 are used for control. Item 4 is self-explanatory. Items 5 and 6 are strictly voluntary, but they personalize the document. Moreover, organization charts will be useful to ISO auditors. A history is appropriate too, but companies are like people—it is hard to stop talking about yourself. Keep it brief. Item 7 is the master index for quality documentation. It is used for overall control, and its placement in the manual is absolutely necessary.

Item 9 bears clarification. Since company procedures are not policies, they don't belong in a Tier 1 document, strictly speaking. If there are only a few, they can be put into the quality manual as a matter of convenience. If there are many, their inclusion would fatten the manual, redefine its scope and mission, and lessen its prestige as a policy document. In this case it would be better to publish a Tier 2, "Company Procedures" volume, with limited distribution.

Item 8 is the meat of the quality manual. It specifies the company policies relative to each requirement of the Standard and who is responsible for what. The *who* is by title. Names should not be used in any control document, in order to minimize the frequency of revision. The *what*, of course, are the requirements of the clause. Thus, a properly written quality manual serves as a sort of three-dimensional matrix with one axis for requirements, one for policy, and one for accountability.

The reason persons are identified with each requirement is to make sure that the task is not overlooked, and that is a justification for assignment of accountability. As a lead auditor under the Mil-Q-9858, I was sometimes assured that "Ace Gyroscope will do . . ." when, in fact, things are done by people, not by corporations. They must know who they are.

Quality manuals use various formats in presentation. Two of them are shown in the following pages as Exhibits 11-2 and 11-3.

Exhibit 11-2. Sample A format for the quality manual.

COMPANY	QUALITY MANUAL	Date: Revision #:
PURCHASING	Section #: 4.6	Page 1 of
Prepared By:		Date:
Approved By:		Date:

4.6.1. Scope

This section describes the purchasing criteria of the Company in accordance with the requirements of Clause 4.6 of the Standard. Applicable procedures are found in *Departmental Procedures, Volume 3.*

4.6.2. Policies

General
Evaluation of Subcontractors
Purchasing Data
Verification of Purchased Product

4.6.3. Responsibilities

The Purchasing Officer is responsible for formulating purchasing objectives and conducting purchasing activities in accordance with the above described policies, in accordance with Paragraph 4.6 of the Standard.

The Management Review Board is responsible to ensure conformance of purchasing policies, objectives, and activities to the Standard, in accordance with Paragraph 4.1.3 of the Standard.

The Management Representative is responsible to conduct periodic quality audits of purchasing policies, objectives, and activities to the Standard, in accordance with Paragraph 4.17 of the Standard.

Exhibit 11-3. Sample B format for a quality manual.

THE COMPANY	Page
	Issue Date:
QUALITY MANUAL	Revision #:

9.0 PROCESS CONTROL

9.1 General

Assignment of Responsibility.

9.2 Planning

Brief description of policy & responsibility vis-à-vis planning.

9.3 Standards, Procedures, Documentation

Brief description of policy & responsibility vis-à-vis documentation.

9.4 Maintenance

Brief description of policy & responsibility vis-à-vis equipment.

9.5 Monitoring & Control

Brief description of policy & responsibility vis-à-vis control.

9.6 References

Procedures related to this requirement are available in Volume 4 of "Departmental Procedures."

Written By: Approved By:

The simplest one is organized exactly like the requirements themselves, with three sections: scope, policy, and responsibility. However, they should not be a rephrasing of the clauses, but must personalize (or "company-ize") the clause. The quality manual is a careful balance of general concepts and specific associations. The manual should not be generic. It should be sufficiently descriptive of the company's effort as to leave no doubt whose it is. On the other hand, there should be little or no procedural detail.

Procedures

Irrespective of the application or subject, all procedures should have the same format. There are many formats, and each company is free to choose one relevant to itself, but once chosen, the format should be used consistently. There are a number of good reasons for this. Iterative formats are easy to understand. Most people know their jobs, but the procedures are not written with experts in mind. Procedures are written for the occasion when a substitute comes on the job, or in case of complexity or infrequent use and the normal performer needs refreshment. Your newspaper or any periodical is a good example of the benefits of fixed format in ease of reading. You know where to find a specific subject and can go there quickly. So, too, uniform format procedures facilitate reference and encourage use. Another good reason for constant format is that several people may be engaged in writing one procedure or in writing the same part of many procedures. Without a uniform format, the result can be widespread inconsistency.

Perhaps some senior person or manager may be familiar enough to write a procedure for a process that someone else will do, but then it will be a mandate and resisted. Therefore, procedures should be developed and written by the person or persons who will conduct the procedure described. This is a form of "buying in." The procedure can be written in committee, but the persons who will execute the task must feel a responsibility to the document, and the best way to ensure that is to have them write it.

A procedure should be indexed for quick reference, identified by title, and include some statement about its purpose or scope. It should include supporting references or documentation, and any definitions that are necessary and unique to it.

Finally, it should describe the procedure and include assignment of responsibility. The process of writing procedures will benefit from the use of flowcharts. In this manner, procedure and flowchart form a check on each other.

Company Procedures

There are certain procedures that either are obviously company-wide or that do not easily fit into the purview of a specific department. Examples of company-wide procedures are the steering committee meetings, management reviews of the quality system, strategic planning meetings in which quality objectives are discussed, and perhaps disposition of nonconforming product. Examples of the procedures for which there is not an easy fit are training programs, calibration programs, and preventive maintenance system (PMS) programs. These activities certainly need formal description, and therefore they must be documented by procedures because they bear on quality of product or process.

Somebody must perform the procedures, which means that all procedures are assigned, even if force-fit. For example, if a company is too small to support a training department, it may assign training procedures to its personnel department. In this case, training procedures become departmental procedures by definition. Similarly, management review of records of the quality system may be assigned to the QA department.

On the other hand, steering committee procedures are likely to reside within the purview of executive management. Once procedure assignments have been made, the decision of whether to create a company procedure volume becomes clear. Whatever the appellation, company procedures will use the same format as departmental procedures.

Departmental Procedures

Procedure Description

ISO 9000 requires a Tier 1 quality manual that describes policies and responsibilities of management. It also requires a complete set of Tier 3 work instructions or standard operating procedures that describe how things are done. ISO 9000 does not require a set of Tier 2 departmental procedures at this time, but it is a good idea to have them anyway, for several reasons. First, removing procedures from the quality manual frees the manual to be only what it is supposed to be—a policy document. Second, departments do things and have certain responsibilities unique to themselves below the level of policy and above the level of work instructions. Third, and a corollary of the last idea, they provide an intermediate transition from Tier 1 to Tier 3. They allow a segmentation of descriptions by department. Tier 2 procedures:

1. Explain what the department does.
2. Provide the department organization chart and responsibilities.
3. Provide an index of the department's Tier 3 procedures.
4. Describe the department's input and output interfaces.

There need be only one controlled document for each department. If there are six departments, then there are six volumes of department procedures, each listed in the quality manual (see item 7 of the quality manual components). The advantage to this method is that each volume is stand-alone. A change in one affects no other, save the quality manual index, which will indicate the revision number of each company or department procedure. An example of a departmental procedure is shown in Exhibit 11-4.

Page Numbering

Departmental procedures will usually be rather large volumes containing many pages. Moreover, they will be living documents so that you should anticipate relatively frequent changes, additions, and deletions. Therefore, give a good deal of thought to how the pages will be numbered. Document changes require that the affected pages be reprinted, but the scope of the reprint problem is much larger than if a page is added or deleted.

Suppose that you have a controlled document of seventy-three pages, numbered consecutively, and you add a page of

Exhibit 11-4. Sample format for a departmental procedure.

SALES & SERVICE	DEPARTMENT PROCEDURES	Date: Revision #:
Written By:		Page 1 of
Authorized By:		Date:

1.0 Purpose

This document describes the structure and operating responsibilities of the Sales and Service department.

2.0 Scope

The scope of this procedure covers the responsibilities from initial customer contact until final customer sign-off on delivery and satisfactory installation of product.

3.0 Department Responsibilities

Initiate customer contact
Define customer requirements to other departments
Coordinate customer-company interface on specifications
Initiate job order
Maintain customer liaison during production
Arrange for installation of product
Ensure job closeout with customer sign-off

4.0 Individual Responsibilities

Department Manager
Sales Coordinator
Service Coordinator
Field Representative

5.0 Index of Work Instructions

information following page 2. Then seventy-one old pages must be reprinted because the old pages 3 to 73 will then have the wrong page numbers. Similarly, suppose that you delete page 2. Again, seventy-one pages will be numbered wrongly. This represents waste because, though the pages are now numbered wrong, the information on them is good. Obviously, consecutive page numbering is not a good idea.

There is an effective alternative strategy that is often used to solve the page numbering problem. Suppose that your seventy-three-page document consisted of, say, eight sections, each roughly nine pages in length. You might letter the sections and number the pages of each section accordingly. For example, the nine pages of Section B might be numbered B1 through B9. Then an additive change in section B will force a reprint of at most nine pages of the total document.

Companies sometimes number documents as "page 3 of 9," in order to indicate the size of the section so that readers may assure themselves that they have the whole section. Additions and deletions cause a lot of reprint trouble here because no matter where in the set the change takes place, or how few pages are affected, all nine pages must be reprinted. There is a more efficient strategy. Label the pages of Section B as B1+, B2+, . . . B8+, B9. You know, looking at page B2+, that there are more pages to Section B; the + means that more will follow. By the same reasoning, B9 is the last page. In this way, you need reprint only the pages following the changed page, just as you do the sectioned page numbering, yet you still have a way of identifying how many pages the section contains.

Work Instructions

A *work instruction*, sometimes called a standard operating procedure, is a document that describes, step by step, how a task is to be done. Because there is sometimes confusion on this matter, a work instruction should be distinguished from a *job description*, which is a document that describes what tasks a given employee performs. For example, Blanding (1991) provides a job description for a senior customer service representative, which in edited form looks something like this: "Functions as team leader. Primary contact for customer, responsible for taking orders and handling routine inquiries and complaints. Is expected to have extensive knowledge of account requirements. Often has specialized knowledge of company products" (p. 68). The job description describes *what* an employee does, but does not say how the task is done. The work instruction describes *how* the task is done.

Some companies use the term *work instruction* to describe craft activity, and use the term *standard operating procedures* to describe administrative activity. This distinction may be acceptable in a large company, where the twain never meet. In a smaller company, where workers might mingle with office personnel, the different appellations suggest a class distinction and can cause resentment. In this book every task description is called a work instruction.

Not every task requires a work instruction. You can determine whether or not a task requires a work instruction by asking two questions: (1) If the task is done incorrectly, will it affect the quality of the product? (2) Is how the task is done self-evident to a new employee? A yes to the first question means that a work instruction is required for the task. A yes to the second question means that a work instruction is probably not needed. For example, engineers do not need work instructions to design things. The task is self-evident based upon their qualifications.

Work instructions describe how to do the task. They are on-site reference documents and tell how to set up the machine or equipment with respect to a given job order. For example, a work instruction for a lathe does not describe how to do machining; it describes how to set the machine up. Similarly, running a test on a centrifugal chiller requires highly skilled electronic technicians. Despite their skill, the tests also require work instructions that describe test station set up for the particular kind of chiller under test: loop temperature ranges, pump pressure ranges, and so on. The purpose of the work instruction is to establish the conformance between the range of operation of the machine or equipment and the specifications on the job order.

Work instructions are often identified by an alphanumeric index, the lettered part indicating the cognizant department.

This idea is demonstrated in Exhibit 11-5. Thus, a marketing procedure might be indexed "Mkt.5," for example.

If work can be segregated by department, then each department will be responsible for control of its own work instructions. The departmental procedure volume will contain the work instruction index and issue control box. There is no need to have any work instructions in any parent document. You do not normally need a work instruction in the office of the department manager, with one exception shown in the following paragraph.

In the interest of avoiding extraneous copies of controlled documents, there should be at most two copies per instruction, with one copy at the work site and one copy in a training manual. The training manual is retained within the training department if there is one; otherwise it is kept in the appropriate department manager's office. This presumes that in the absence of a formal training department, the performing department is responsible for its own training program.

Many workstations have computer control and digital or video displays. It may, then, be useful to use software for the work instructions, particularly if there are many setup conditions at the station. If so, a hard copy of the instruction is redundant and not needed. Work instructions must be controlled and redundant copies add to the control problem.

Just as departmental procedures are written by persons at that level, work instructions should be developed and written by the person or persons who will do the task described. It is worth

Exhibit 11-5. Sample indices for assigning work instructions to departments.

Department	*Index*
Marketing	Mkt
Purchasing	Pch
Personnel	Prs
Production	Prd
Traffic	Trf
Service	Svc
Comptroller	Cmp

repeating that this is a form of buying in. If the persons cannot write, then the writing should be done jointly with their supervisor. The finished document (or software) should then be reviewed by this ad hoc committee of supervisor-performers so that all sign on. Two examples of a work instruction are shown in Exhibits 11-6 and 11-7.

Forms and Reports

As a rule of thumb, you can define a quality document as one that attests to a customer requirement. Therefore, a customer order is a quality document because it describes the characteristics of the desired product. A change order is a quality document because it describes the change to be made in a characteristic or specification in accordance with customer requirements. The trip report of a service representative is a quality document if it describes the status of the product delivered to, or under warranty to, the customer.

Forms and reports do not become quality documents, however, until they are completed. At this time some identification number is applied that associates the form to a particular customer and job order. Even a blank form should have several pieces of information on it, such as: title, identity number, and revision date. An example of this type of quality document is shown in Exhibit 11-8. This is a nonconformance report (NCR) form, identified in several ways. It is headed by a title and has further identification in the lower left corner. Nevertheless, it is not a quality record until it is completed.

Summary

Sustainability in Clause 4.2 requires a three-tier documentation system as structured in Exhibit 11-1. The system will describe quality responsibilities for all personnel, which are not in addition to their regular tasks but are integrated with them. The documentation will be current, easy to read, and available at all locations of work. The documentation will be written and signed

(text continues on page 183)

Exhibit 11-6. Sample A format for a work instruction.

PRODUCTION Work Instructions	PRD-3.5: Vertical Expander	Date: Revision #:
Written By:		Page 1 of
Authorized By:		Date:

1.0 Description: Construction of evaporator and condenser coils. Expands the copper tubes so that they fit tightly within the fins.

2.0 Materials In: Copper tubes, fins, header plates, hairpins, lubricating oil.

3.0 Materials Out: Evaporator and condenser coils.

4.0 References: Software Program Prd-3.5

5.0 Operations

A. Set up: The expander is set up according to the matrix provided in Program Prd-3.5, relative to the number of copper tubes and length of coil. The rods are lined up with a standard coil.

B. Coil Preparation: Required number of fins are lined up with the use of two rods. Header plates are put on both sides of the coil. Hairpins are lubricated and passed through the fins.

C. Expansion: The coil is placed on the machine and it is operated for expansion.

D. Inspection: The length of the coil is measured on each expanded coil. Tolerance for acceptance is ± 0.06 in. Corrective action: If the coil can be reworked, then expansion is iterated. If the fins are torn, then the coil is scrapped.

Exhibit 11-7. Sample B format for a work instruction.

PRODUCTION Work Instructions	PRD-3.5: Control Boxes	Date: Revision #:
Written By:		Page 1 of
Authorized By:		Date:

Title: Building control boxes

Purpose: Terminals, switches, relays, and related hardware are installed in a sheet metal housing, then wiring is accomplished to complete construction of a control box for heat pumps.

Documentation: The job order and associated drawings.

Procedure:

EL3.5.1. Hardware Installation: Mount all electrical components listed on the job order according to the drawings. There is no particular order of assembly.

EL3.5.2. Wiring: Wire the hardware of the control box according to the job order. When harnesses and wiring requirements exist together, the order is:

1. Install harnesses in the path provided.
2. Lash harnesses in the paths provided.
3. Install wiring according to the job order.

EL3.5.3. Inspection: The operator will make a visual inspection at the workstation to ensure the correct positioning of the hardware and wiring. A dynamic test of the control box will be made at Test Station 2.

Exhibit 11-8. Sample nonconformance report form.

Company Name

Nonconformance Report

Customer	Job Order Number	Job Order Owner
NCR Number	Date of NCR	Issuer of NCR

Description of Nonconformance

Signature of NCR Issuer

Signature of Owner

Part A: Fault Analysis

Signature/date

Part B: Corrective Action

Signature/date

Part C: Preventive Action

Signature/Date

Quality Assurance Dept. Evaluation

Signature/Date

Company Form NCR03, Rev.5, 16 October 1997

off by those who will use it. Each document will include the policies that support it. Each document will be amendable, with the procedures for amendment controlled but easy to use.

References

ANSI/ISO/ASQC. *Q9001-1994. Quality Systems—Model for Quality Assurance in Design, Development, Production, Installation, and Servicing*. Milwaukee: American Society for Quality Control, 1994.

ANSI/ISO/ASQC. *Q10013-1994. American National Standard: Guidelines for Quality Manuals*. Milwaukee: American Society for Quality Control, 1994.

Blanding, Warren. *Customer Service Operations*. New York: AMACOM, 1991, p. 68.

Hamilton, W. R. "How to Construct a Basic Quality Manual." *Quality Progress*, April 1995, pp. 71–74.

Chapter 12

Clause 4.5: Document and Data Control

Brief: Clause 4.5 requires control of the distribution of all documents and data related to quality, with associated procedures describing the control mechanisms.

Several times in this book I have asserted that the way to systemize a human-machine process is through documentation. A documentation system provides repeatability and improves stability. This may not be intuitive to all readers, but a more technical approach will show the reasoning.

Documentation as a Control Supervisor

The documentation system is like an event system control supervisor. Events are discrete—they either happen or they don't. Systems that are driven by events are called discrete event systems (DES). As in most systems, DES have states, and how the system should respond to a given event depends on the state that it is in.

A few examples will clarify this point. Let the state of an inventory system be described by the inventory. The event of a withdrawal will cause a different response to the system if the withdrawal removes the last item than it will if the withdrawal removes only one of two hundred items. Suppose the state of a pizza delivery system is described by delivery time and correct orders. Each delivery is an event and the response taken will depend on the delivery state.

Discrete event systems are controlled by a closed-loop process with an active controller called a *supervisor*. The job of the supervisor is to monitor the state of the system and the sequence of events, and to apply the proper correction for any given combination of state and events that is within its purview.

Business and industrial processes are driven by events. Sometimes the events are internal, initiated by the processes themselves; sometimes they are external, coming from the environment acting upon the processes. One of the jobs of management is to estimate all possible events that might occur and determine contingency plans. After all, preparing for the future is *la direction*. We have discussed strategic planning earlier, of which contingency planning is a subset. The point is that much of this planning eventually takes the form of documentation. For example, you may have a policy with regard to nonconformance. You will repair, regrade, scrap, or deliver by concession according to some scheme. This scheme is written down and so is fixed unless it is rewritten.

Thus documentation acts as a DES supervisor. What to do now and what to do next are written down, and if you follow your own plans you will respond correctly to any combination of system state and sequence of events that is within those plans. From time to time, unforeseen or uncontrollable events may occur that will render the existing supervisor ineffective. New ideas, plans, and data to accommodate the new reality will require an upgrade to the supervisor—that is, changes will be needed in the documentation. Therefore, the documentation system will require ready access to data banks and libraries, change processes, and all the components that will make it dynamic. Exhibit 12-1 outlines how the documentation control system serves as an effective supervisor, bringing to the overall system stability and the promise of capability.

The Control of Documentation

The model of control supervisor for the processes of a company appears appropriate and so demonstrates one of the assertions

Exhibit 12-1. Documentation process structured as a control system supervisor.

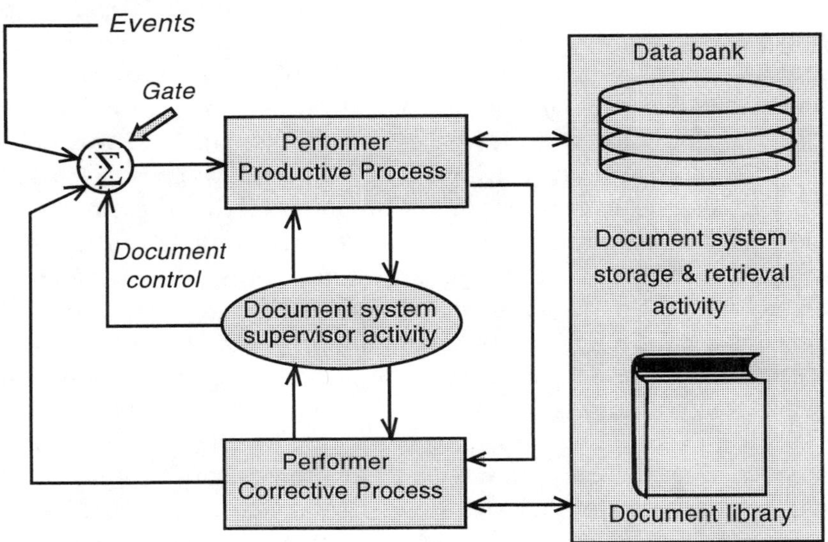

of this book: Documentation control enhances stability. This is an important idea because it means that properly structured, documentation control is a factor in sustaining a quality system.

Nevertheless, the conventional view of documentation control is a legitimate concern and an ISO 9000 requirement. In this view, documentation control refers to the control of all the quality documentation in the quality system. This idea is only a subset of the supervisor model. We will discuss the issue because it is the documented quality system that proves that you are doing what you say you're doing. The proper use of documentation is a cornerstone of an ISO 9000 quality system. But documentation is useful only if it is correct, so that there must be a method to ensure its relevancy. This is achieved through a process of document control, which governs the collection, storage, retrieval, and revision of documents and data. In many industries, such as pharmaceutical and aerospace, document control is necessary because of the distribution of powerful chemicals or of the sheer volume of change orders. Basically, document control consists of three processes: (1) an approval process; (2) an availability process; and (3) a revision process.

We are speaking here of quality documents—that is, those documents that attest to both the quality level of product and the process performance. These includes drawings, specifications, blueprints, procedures, and many types of records. The approval process concerns the authorization of a document for use in those activities affecting quality. The availability process has two particular concerns: Appropriate documents must be available where needed, and inappropriate documents must be promptly removed from use. The latter is often difficult to achieve because of the propensity of people to retain familiar documents—for example, procedures, which may have personal notes on them—and because of the availability of copying machines. Nevertheless, a superseded document at a workstation is cause for a nonconformity report in a quality audit. Finally, the update process concerns the authorized revision of documents as a result of corrective or preventive action analyses, research, or improvement processes.

Document and Data Approval and Issue

Documentation control is about the relationship of document control, quality records, and the processes of a company. Every process, productive or corrective, at every level of aggregation, is described by controlled procedures and documentation with regard to quality. Quality documents and subsequent revisions are to be reviewed and approved by authorized persons to establish their adequacy and currency.

Basically, the company must develop control procedures along the lines of identification, collection, indexing, and disposition. *Identification* refers to subject matter and revision level (date). *Collection* means that there must be an orderly distribution of documents. *Indexing* means that there must be a master list that delineates current documents. And *disposition* refers to the removal of obsolete documents. All documentation should be legible, dated, clean, readily identifiable, and maintained in an orderly manner. Data may be in hard copy form or stored in a computer.

Approval

An approval process begins by identifying the "owner" of a specific document. Usually, the owner is a specific department. An individual within the department can be assigned approval responsibility—by title, not by name. For example, the purchasing officer may be the responsible approval authority for all departmental procedures, standard operating procedures, and work instructions within the purchasing department, no matter who the person is that is holding this office. This authority can be delegated to supervisors or coordinators, so long as a procedure governs this delegation. Thus, an approval policy is implied. Approval policies would be defined in the quality manual under *4.5: Document Control.* Approval procedures would be described in a departmental procedure. An outline of an approval process is demonstrated in Exhibit 12-2. The figure shows that a procedure or work instruction is initiated by the user. This is in line with our "buy in" theory; nevertheless, the germination of the document might well have been determined in committee.

Exhibit 12-2. General process for documentation approval.

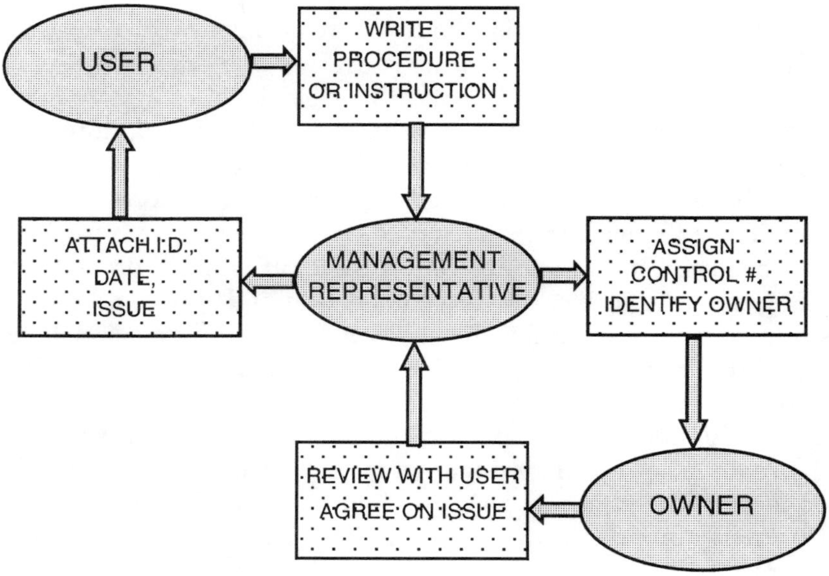

Document Control Steps

1. *Identification of copies.* Owner and users are to identify each copy of a document by a name and control number. If the quality assurance department or the management representative is to maintain document control, then that person can assign control numbers according to the numbering system developed by the owner department.

2. *Number of copies.* For each document, owner and users will determine the minimum number of copies required for effective use and where each copy is to be kept. Only controlled copies are to be used. Therefore, copies must be easily available to users.

3. *Date of copies.* Dating a document refers to its current date and revision number. Some companies also list last revision, but that seems extraneous. A current issue date, revision number, and approval signature suffice to ensure the validity of the document.

4. *Master list.* The master list of departmental procedures resides in the quality manual or in a company-level procedures index volume, itself identified in the quality manual. The master list of work instructions resides in the departmental procedures book or in a departmental index volume, itself identified in the departmental procedures book.

Plating

Exhibits 11-2 through 11-4 and 11-6 through 11-8 of the last chapter were examples of various documents. Some were taken from an arbitrary quality manual, others from various levels of procedures. Each contained a printed box at the top that is called a "plate," that is, a notation of some sort that makes it possible to identify and control the document. Control is possible because of the nature of the information that is on the plate.

Although there is no mandatory format for a plate, a quick referral back to the exhibits shows that while the plates vary somewhat, they all contain common information. This common information appears in the generic plate shown in Exhibit 12-3

Exhibit 12-3. Sample control note ("plate").

Checking Incoming Dyes and Chemicals
Against Specifications

Purchasing Dept. Issue #4

Date of Issue: ______________________ Page 1+

Authorized by: ______________________

and includes the title of the procedure, the locality of its purview (company- or department-wide), the issue number that reflects its currency, the number of pages to the procedure, and the authorization. It is the plate, then, that permits document and data control. Each document must be plated.

We wind up this discussion by clarifying two points. These exhibits in the last chapter contained two kinds of formats: one for the plate and one for the documentary information. Both are arbitrary. A company can choose any plating system it wishes, and can select any format it deems effective to present its information. Exhibit 12-4 presents yet another document format, with yet another control plate. In this case the exhibit represents an entry from a quality manual concerning *Clause 4.5: Documentation and Data Control*. Notice that this time the plate appears on the bottom of the page. In sum, you can use any format for a plate and put it wherever you wish. You can put the plate at the top of the page or at the bottom. You can plate every document or every section of every document. The plate format should be consistent. You can also use any format that you choose for the information.

Exhibit 12-4. Documentation control format for a quality manual.

4.5 Document and Data Control

Purpose

This document defines the policies and outlines a system of control of documents to ensure availability, currency, accuracy, validity, and authorization prior to use.

Scope

This process is applicable to all documents relating to quality of process and product. This includes, but is not limited to, specifications, drawings, standards, procedures, and instructions.

References

ISO 9001 (1994), Section 4.5
Quality Manual (Tier 1)
Department manuals, instructions, and procedures

Responsibilities

The Management Representative is responsible for maintaining the documentation control system, associated document indices, and coordination of the various departments for purposes of documentation control.

Each department head is responsible for maintaining an approval and change process for documents and data, in accordance with the following policies and outlines.

Approval and Issue Policies

Change Policies

Issuing Dept:	Date of Issue:
Written By:	Page:
Authorized By:	Revision:

Document and Data Changes

There are three major factors concerning the changing of a controlled document:

1. How changes are identified within the document
2. How and when current revisions are identified
3. The number of revisions before a document reissue

Documents fall into two categories: those that seldom change, usually forms such as test reports and purchase orders; and those that often change and so have revision levels, for example, drawings, procedures, specifications. For a document with revision levels, you:

1. Identify this level on the document
2. Review and approve changes to documents at the same level
3. Identify the nature of the change
4. Maintain a master list
5. Reissue the document after a practical number of revisions

Changes to documents should be reviewed and approved by the same functions that began them except when disallowed by specific directions. A master list or equivalent control procedure should be established to identify current revisions. They should be identifiable and dated. Current documents must be available where needed and obsolete documents removed.

The ISO 9004 guidelines provide examples of documents that require control: drawings, specifications, blueprints, inspection instructions, test procedures, work instructions, operation sheets, quality manual, operational procedures, and quality assurance procedures. There is a certain logic to this list, but each company can decide for itself which documents it wishes to control. Whatever the decision, there must be both a policy and a procedure to describe it.

Exhibit 12-5 sketches the documentation change process. It is much like the process used for initiating documents, as it should be. The major difference is that an individual user may

Exhibit 12-5. The documentation change process.

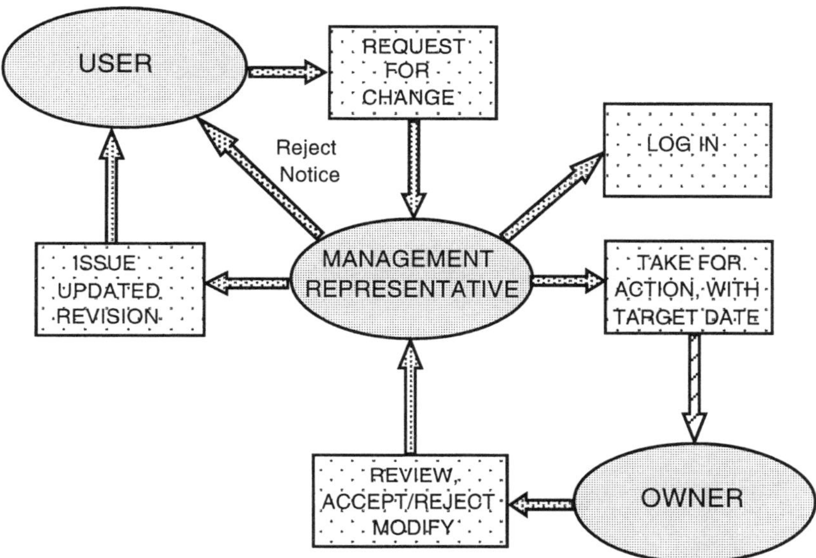

request a change; initial documents are often the result of the work of committees.

Uncontrolling Quality Documents

In principle, only controlled documents may be used in any process that affects the quality of a product. In some cases, there may be a demand for many copies of a document, say an SOP—too many to be controlled effectively. In other cases, the company may wish to circulate a controlled document among many people for review. The method to release item from control is to store one control copy of all such documents in a computer data base. Put them in a directory with a macro that will automatically print on top of any extracted document:

Review Copy, Uncontrolled (with printout date)

These uncontrolled copies can be distributed as necessary without concern to quantity or disposition. Recipients can easily verify the currency of their uncontrolled copy by referring it to the master index.

Summary

Sustainability in Clause 4.5 requires the use of documentation as a form of quality control, with a structure as shown in Exhibit 12.1. The complementary requirement is documentation control, consisting of approval, availability, and revision processes.

References

ANSI/ISO/ASQC. *Q9001-1994. Quality Systems—Model for Quality Assurance in Design, Development, Production, Installation, and Servicing*. Milwaukee: American Society for Quality Control, 1994.

ANSI/ISO/ASQC. *Q9004-1-1994. American National Standard: Quality Management and Quality System Elements and Guidelines.* Milwaukee: American Society for Quality Control, 1994.

Chapter 13

Clause 4.16: Control of Quality Records

Brief: Clause 4.16 requires documented procedures for the identification and disposition of quality records. Quality records are required to demonstrate conformance to the specifications and effectiveness of the quality system.

When we think of records we sometimes think of bureaucracy. Many people equate the two, which is regrettable because the two are not the same. Bureaucracy is the blind keeping of records with neither rhyme nor reason, but just in case. On the other hand, there are very good reasons to keep a few records.

1. *Evidence of quality*. It has been said that quality is in the eye of the beholder. What this really means is that the customer gets to decide what quality is. It does not mean that quality characteristics are visible. Sometimes they are and sometimes they are not. You might imagine that the quality of a piece of jewelry is in its beauty. If so, then quality is visible. But if the customer had specified a particular quality of jewel (no flaws) mounted in 18 carat gold with a special type of cement, then none of the quality characteristics is visible to the naked eye.

The only way to be sure of the quality of a product is to compare the specifications of the finished product with the customer requirements. This means referring to records. Therefore,

ISO standards absolutely require quality records because they are the final and authoritative evidence of quality.

2. *Corporate memory.* The notion of core competencies is in the *nouveau monde* of business conversation these days. Whether strategic planning, reengineering, or transformation, the experts tell us to identify and build upon what we know. Core competencies derive from the corporate memory, much of which is written down, fortunately. There are wildcat companies where people walk around with the company's business expertise locked up in their minds or in private vaults, but visionary companies do not operate that way. Knowledge is recorded and shared. The records may be drawings, test and inspection results, statistical histories, or special procedures. In short, the corporate memory of the company exists in its records. It is worthless if it is stored in some forgotten vault. It is knowledge if it can be readily retrieved.

3. *Legem requisit.* Many industries are required by law to keep certain records. This legal requirement, or *legem requisit*, applies, for example, to companies that produce or dispense drugs.[1] Pharmaceutical houses and hospitals must keep records of drug quantities, qualities, and locations. The federal government maintains a host of regulatory bodies: the Federal Communications Commission, Federal Aeronautics Administration, Securities and Exchange Commission, and Federal Housing Authority, to name a few, all impose requirements for records upon the industries within their purview. The type of records to be kept are usually specified by the regulatory agencies.

Even if you are not subject to legal requirements a priori, you may in future be challenged in court to demonstrate adherence to some criterion of quality. Failure to maintain what a court might consider prudent record keeping could put you at risk in its decisions.

Identifying Data to be Retained

How do you distinguish between documents and records? Brumm (1995) answers the question simply: A document exists

[1]Msgr. Raymond A. Barton, Holy Comforter Roman Catholic Church in Charlottesville, Virginia, provided the subtitle *legem requisit* ("required by the law").

before the fact; a record exists after the fact. A document is a written or graphical description of a policy, procedure, or instruction, and as pointed out in the last chapter, acts as a control supervisor of an activity. A record, on the other hand, contains data and information resulting from that activity.

ISO 9000 says that quality records must be filed, stored, and retained for a stated period. But just exactly what is a quality record? The concept is not defined explicitly, but you can identify some such records by careful perusal of the requirements clauses of the Standard. From time to time a clause of the Standard will contain the phrase "maintain records . . . (see 4.16)." This means that the particular item in question is to be stored as a quality record. If you go through ISO 9001 with a fine-tooth comb, you can identify fifteen such comments, summarized in Exhibit 13-1 for your convenience.

This list is necessary but may not be sufficient. For example, suppose that one of your operations consists of dyeing fabric. Then a record should be maintained of the list of colors available to a potential customer because color is a quality characteristic. Sometimes the record requirement is too vague. For example, Clause 4.18 requires that appropriate training records be kept. What does *appropriate* mean? This is why we saw earlier that among companies that were all ISO 9000 certified, some would have better quality systems than others.

Record-Keeping Policies

The quality manual should define policies in regard to quality records in its section devoted to this clause. These policies will specify the records, responsible storekeeper, and retention times. It should also state the purpose of the storage. Each company is free to determine some logical period of retention that is appropriate to its business, but this period must be stated. In many cases the period of retention is indicated by the purpose for storage—for example, to ensure that product quality was verified at the time of delivery. Consequently, in such a case, the warranty period suggests the retention time.

Identification and indexing are important to facilitate retrieval. In particular, test results can be used for statistical

Exhibit 13-1. ISO 9001 quality records.

	Requirement Title	*Required Quality Document*
4.1.3	Management Review	Records of management reviews
4.3.4	Contract Review	Records of contract reviews
4.4.6	Design Review	Records of design reviews
4.4.7	Design Verification	Measures taken for verification of design: calculations, tests, benchmarking, etc.
4.6.2	Subcontractor Evaluation	Quality records of acceptable subcontractors
4.7	Customer Supplied Product	Records of lost, damaged, or unsuitable product provided by the customer
4.8	Product ID & Traceability	Identification of product or batches required by specification to be traced
4.9	Qualified Processes	Records of special processes
4.10.3	Receiving Inspection	Purchased product released for urgent use
4.10.5	Inspection & Test	Inspection and test results
4.11	Measurement Equipment	Calibration records
4.13	Nonconforming Product	Records of repair and acceptance by concession
4.14	Corrective Action	Results of investigations
4.17	Internal Quality Audits	Audit results
4.18	Training	Training records

analysis, and so must be easily retrieved. Controlled documents are already identified, and the control number can become part of the storage identification process. The results of management, contract, and design reviews can be assigned some logical indicator similar to that of a controlled document, say an alphanumeric appellation.

Finally, storage must be secure and environmentally sound to protect the records from abuse and deterioration. Storage of documents is sometimes relegated to a place that is otherwise not used, and not used for good reason—a dark and dismal vault. This is the worst type of storage because it discourages retrieval, which means that it discourages analysis and improvability. The optimum storage of data is in software form, for ease of retrieval and accommodation of surroundings.

Brumm (1995) recommends that a company establish a records management program, which is a good idea, and that it be managed by a records department, which is less of a good idea. Records and documentation departments, as all institutions, build a raison d'être and identity of their own. They eventually become "them" rather than "us" to other departments. This means that other groups will tend not to release all records to them, nor always go to them for data and information. Sooner or later the company develops two data banks, the official one and the used one. ISO 9000 auditors regard this phenomenon as a nonconformance. The best people to maintain the records of a functional group is the group itself. They know what and how to prioritize their own information in terms of value and schedule.

Records Control

The process of identifying, utilizing, and storing data and information is dynamic and can be controlled as any other dynamic system. Exhibit 13-2 depicts this process graphically, in terms of the operations that are identified in the Standard as requiring maintenance of quality records. The basic feedback loop consists of some operation, say design, that is driven by the customer's requirements and compares these requirements to its own performance. At the same time, appropriate quality records are identified and stored in a records bank. This identification is made in terms of specifications and metrics and may not be definitive.

For example, the customer may specify mobile shelving systems to be mounted on a carpeted base. The units are built according to the job order, itself a very important quality record.

Exhibit 13-2. Generalized closed-loop system for quality records.

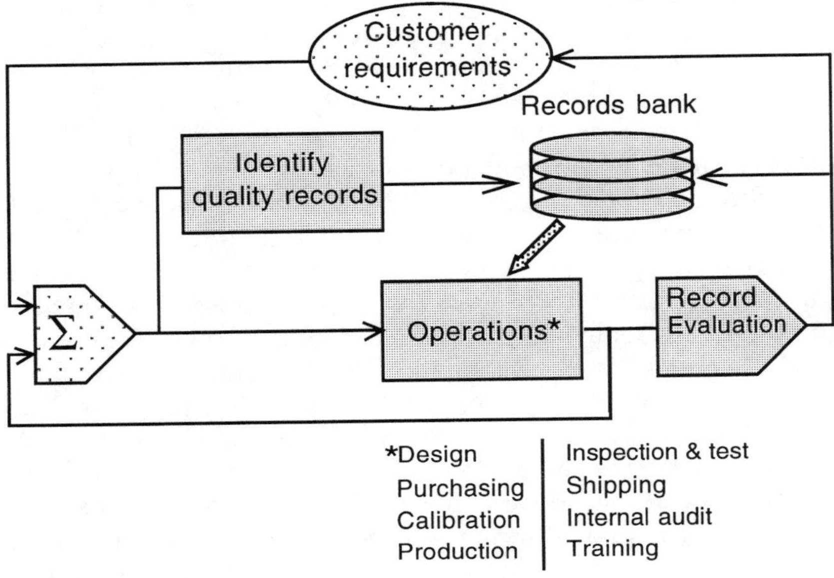

At some point in mid-process the assemblers find that the carpeting is insubstantial, or perhaps the customer changes his mind on its color.

So there is an ongoing evaluation of the operation's output relative to the records, which has two objectives. The first is to review the adequacy of the product relative to some governing record; the other is to verify the adequacy of the record itself.

Summary

Sustainability in Clause 4.16 requires control of quality records as indicated in Exhibit 13-2. Records policy should be to maintain as parsimonious a system as possible, commensurate with tracking quality data through the proposal-to-delivery cycle, with written expression of customer satisfaction and acceptance. Quality data will be retained with regard to reorders or for post-delivery verification and/or validation.

References

ANSI/ISO/ASQC. *Q9001-1994. Quality Systems—Model for Quality Assurance in Design, Development, Production, Installation, and Servicing*. Milwaukee: American Society for Quality Control, 1994.

Brumm, E. K. "Managing Records for ISO 9000 Compliance." *Quality Progress*, January 1995, pp. 73–77.

Chapter 14

Clause 4.17: Internal Quality Audits

Brief: Clause 4.17 requires a program of regular and periodic internal quality audits to determine the effectiveness of the quality system.

Management responsibility, within the meaning of ISO 9000, includes the maintenance of a quality system. There must be a way to ensure that the quality system is functioning and is effective; the best means to that assurance is through an auditing process. Larry Tate (1996), vice president for quality at Comdial Corporation of Charlottesville, Virginia, maintains that the power of the internal quality audit is the very best way for a company to sustain, and even improve, its quality system.

This view is widely held by quality experts. For example, Bishara and Wyrick (1994) describe the internal quality audit (IQA) at Eli Lilly, a pharmaceutical house, and point out that a properly conducted audit will improve quality, enhance the fitness of the product, and avoid delays in launching new products. Fiorentino and Perigord (1994) state that the impact of an IQA reaches far beyond a simple evaluation, and promotes openness with the customer, motivation, cohesiveness, and continuous learning.

ISO 9000, too, recognizes this potential, and in Clause 4.17 requires that an ISO company maintain an internal quality audit program. Properly set up, an IQA program monitors the quality system operation in real time, in a superimposed but noninterfering relationship in which the IQA team is, effectively, a customer. This arrangement is depicted in Exhibit 14-1, and should be compared to the structure of Exhibit 5-1. The exhibit from Chapter 5 showed a basic and sustainable business structure. Exhibit 14-1 is similar, but the IQA program acts as a system driver and the IQA team acts as the customer. The process is improvable because systematic problems can be identified through feedback and eliminated by management decision in a bootstrap cycle: self-evaluation ↔ self-improvement.

The Audit Team

There are several ways of establishing an IQA program. One method is to use external auditors on a contract basis. The company's management representative sets up the IQA program, including schedule, and provides record keeping and follow-up of action items established by the third-party audit team. This

Exhibit 14-1. IQA program in a bootstrap configuration as quality system monitor.

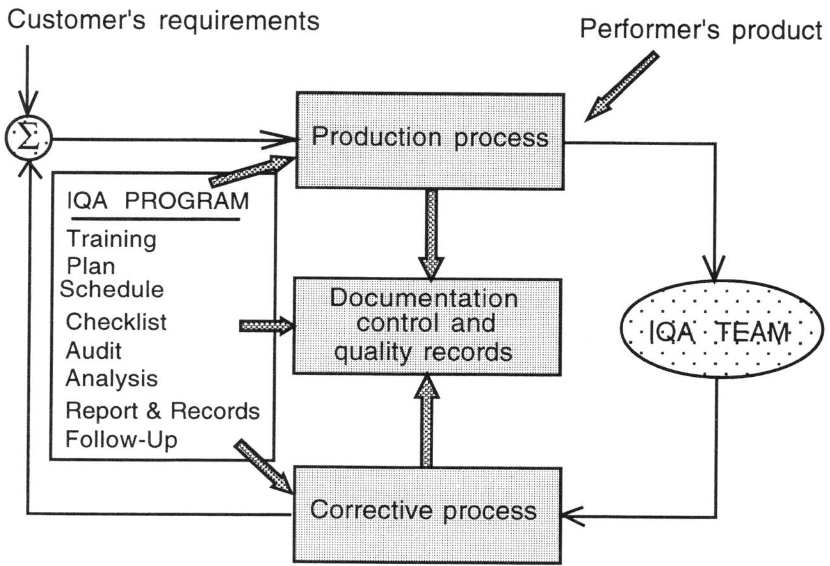

can be a cost-effective method, but ISO experts are in disagreement about whether this is permitted or not. The Standards require internal audits, but the composition of the team is not explicit. Audits are defined and described in ISO 10011.1 (1994), but it, too, is ambiguous.

In any case, most companies will establish an internal team, and this alternative is the one addressed in this chapter. This interpretation best reflects the spirit of Clause 4.17, which implies an in-house capability to improve oneself. As Fiorentino and Perigord point out, the true purpose of an internal audit is on-the-job training. The quality audit is not an investigative function but a formative one. Properly conducted, an IQA will improve the capability of both the company (by identifying systematic problems) and the IQA team itself (through positive experience). If the IQA team is composed of company employees, then the total audit experience is overall improvement—the bootstrap effect. Throughout this chapter, issues of internal auditing that apply only to in-house teams and issues that apply only to third-party teams are easily distinguishable.

Comdial Corporation uses an IQA team composed of employees from various functional units within the company who have been designated as auditors of opportunity. This means that auditing is a part-time and corollary duty. When an audit is scheduled of a particular function within the company, membership of the audit team is formed by drawing members from other functions. No person may serve on an audit team for an audit of his own function.

Audit team members are trained in audit skills, which stand apart from their technical skills or even their knowledge of the Standard itself. They have these things, of course, but they are trained in the art of auditing, too. Each team has a designated team leader who is trained as a lead auditor. The IQA manager is the vice president for quality, determines the schedule, and is responsible for the integrity of the audit program. In sum, Comdial has instituted an IQA program that is capable and improvable, is an integral part of its core competencies, and might well serve as a model of how the thing should be done.

Auditors

Auditors must be trained in the methods of auditing and must be independent. ISO 10011.1 (1994) is very clear about both of these issues. Training is not a big problem, as there are an abundance of companies in the business of providing such training. The training must be formal and include knowledge and understanding of the Standards; assessment techniques; and other relevant skills such as planning, organizing, and communicating. Competence should be demonstrated through written or oral examinations.

Auditors must be independent of the processes being audited—independence is required in order to achieve objectivity. This is assumed when external auditors are used and is one of the benefits of using them. When the IQA team is composed of employees, independence is obtained by selecting team members from departments other than those scheduled for the audit. The key to auditing is observation, or noticing what is happening rather than what should be happening.

Another important issue is judgment, or the ability to arrive at a decision about what one sees with respect to a standard, and maintain that decision in the face of peer (or superior) pressure. Independence enhances a person's ability to observe and to judge activities objectively. Auditors must have tact. Audits are absolutely not inspections and must not be perceived as such. Otherwise, the persons and processes being audited take a defensive "us versus them" position, hiding what must be seen, displaying what is irrelevant, and defeating the purpose of the audit.

The characteristic of tact is given a boost by independence because people tend to be more tactful when in an environment in which they are not experts. When they see something that appears contrary to a standard, they bring it up as a point of clarification, improving the chances of the audited person agreeing with the observation.

Auditors must possess the capacity for great attention to detail. This facility is the basis of every control system and so must be a property of monitoring also. Lacking expertise, people tend to see what is there rather than what should be there, if they see it at all. Processes tend to stray almost always because of some detail, and the error is often not easily observable until it is calamitous. Attention to detail can be tedious, particularly when the detail is documentation. The auditor must recognize that when a customer service representative is writing something down, that something may be a quality record; what and how she wrote it, and its recording and disposition are details that must be observed and evaluated against a standard.

Auditors should represent the spectrum of activities within a company. This notion goes beyond ensuring independence because it provides fresh, objective views of procedures and work instructions. Four auditors with different backgrounds will observe the same activity from four different perspectives, even when subject to the same rules of evidence. This breadth of evaluation enhances the possibility of larger-than-incremental improvement.

IQA Program

"And how his audit stands who knows save heaven?"
—William Shakespeare, *Hamlet*, III, iii

As Shakespeare's words suggest, there are audits, and then there are audits. We began this chapter with strong notions of how effective auditing can be as an instrument of quality improvement, but this effectiveness comes neither free nor easily. Internal quality auditing can be a force for sustainability when implemented in a solid program within the structure shown in Exhibit 14-1.

Training

Earlier I talked about training requirements in general terms: knowledge of the standards, knowledge of auditing techniques, capability in personal skills. Specifically, the auditor should be trained in how to set up a schedule, develop and use a checklist, effectively and efficiently conduct the audit, report on nonconformances, write a report, and verify follow-up activities.

Efficient auditing requires a sampling method; because of time constraints, not every item of a quality system can be observed. The audit plan must accommodate this reality. Effective auditing requires acceptable techniques in examining, questioning, and evaluating. Therefore, training should include exercises in:

1. Comparing a quality system to a Standard
2. Defining the scope of an audit
3. Conducting an opening meeting
4. Performing an audit
5. Writing up nonconformances
6. Conducting a closing meeting
7. Writing a report

Audit training can be obtained through either formal courses or OJT. Both are valuable experiences. The first level of audit training should be accomplished formally. The management representative, at least, should obtain internal audit training from one of the major companies providing this service. In general, this training takes place off-site, necessitating travel and per diem costs as well as per capita costs. Lead auditors should also obtain this type of off-site, formal instruction if possible. Regular members of the IQA team can be trained similarly, or if training costs are prohibitive, a training team can be brought in. Not only does bringing in a team save travel and per diem expenses, but training consultants may be willing to negotiate a flat rate for the class, no matter how many students.

Formal training provides the basis for gathering audit expertise, but the polish comes with OJT. A number of benefits are obtained through actually conducting the audit. Both the auditors and the auditees learn to see the operations of the company through the customer's perspective. The auditors get this perspective by acting in a customer's role. The auditees, most of whom will never see a customer if they work in a manufacturing plant, get the sense of the customer perspective through the auditor-as-customer-agent.

The auditor also learns through the auditing experience that auditing is, as Rice (1994) puts it, for problem solving, not for fault finding. This perception is important to improvement. If the auditor is seen as an inspector, then the audited function may well try to hide symptoms and thus obscure systematic problems. They may even deny the observations of the auditor, with resulting escalation of blame, denial, and obstruction up the chain of command. Audit team leaders have the responsibility to monitor the cooperation level of their audits from a training point of view, ensuring that auditors develop tact and objectivity.

Management

The management representative should be the IQA program manager. As such, she is responsible for defining IQA policies, procedures, plans, and execution of the program. Management representation may be a corollary duty of one of the managers within the company. (If so, this should be specified in the quality manual.) Clearly, IQA management becomes a subset of a subset of responsibilities. In any case, she is the leader of the IQA team, although she is not necessarily required to take part in the auditing itself. That depends on the competence and size of her team and her own availability.

The IQA program has two very important roles. First, it is the driving force behind certification, using its capabilities and responsibilities to bird-dog the company to a completely functioning quality system. Second, once certification is achieved, the IQA program monitors the quality system forever for compliance to the Standard. According to the quality manual, the management representative provides the leadership and direction in this dual effort. Considering the scope and depth of activities, it is likely that the quality system implementation phase will require the MR's full-time participation. Once the quality system is in place and operational, and the company has achieved certification, management representation may revert to corollary duties, depending upon the size of the company.

Schedule

The Standard requires regularly scheduled audits, but does not specify frequency. The general rule of thumb is to audit the quality system at least once per year. Although the Standard itself is noncommittal on this issue, registrars are not. They will almost always insist on a complete internal audit cycle being accomplished before they come in for their annual audit. Thus, an IQA frequency of at least once a year has become the industry standard.

Annual quality audits can be accomplished in several ways. One method is to do it the hard way—once per year audit everything. An alternative is to divide the company operations to be audited into groups of two, four, or twelve, then perform partial quality system audits semiannually, quarterly, or monthly. At the end of one year, the entire quality system will have been audited at least once, thus meeting the requirement.

Scope and Basis

The scope of an audit depends on both the activities to be audited and the reason for the audit. In the first case, we may choose to audit only certain departments because of an annual cycling system. Beyond that, we may specify the sampling rate or purview—only so many procedures, instructions, and interviews, for example. The reason for an audit is called its *basis*. We have discussed scheduled audits, but there may be some other rationale: customer complaints, results of statistical analyses, or increase in nonconformances in a given area. These kinds of problems amount to system-level special causes and may require an audit effort to track them down.

Checklist

A checklist is composed of several columns. The first might be a specific requirement of the Standard. The second column might be a space for a simple yes or no, relative to compliance. The third column might be available for auditor comments. The checklist, of course, is made up in accordance with the scope and basis of the audit.

Planning

The management representative is responsible for an audit plan, which will include schedule, scope, basis, and checklists. Beyond that, it includes strategy: which departments will be examined, and where and why. Previous audit results, special cause reports, and auditor training are factors in deciding how to execute the audit. Finally, the planning phase allows the MR to select and meet with the audit team. The objectives are laid out and brainstorming can take place in order to define, develop, and finalize the plan.

Report

The audit report may be written by the audit team leader, but it is the responsibility of the MR. A copy of the report becomes a quality record, but a copy should also be provided to the responsible managers of the audited activities. The report should be dated, and list those who conducted the audit. A fundamental purpose of the report is to discuss nonconformances, so it should identify items to be taken for corrective action and suggest a schedule for doing so.

The report should be in a standard form, especially that part devoted to reporting nonconformances. One possible format might be: audit number, responsible department, responsible auditor, nonconformance, issue date, response due date.

Follow-Up

The minimum goal of an internal quality audit is to verify conformance of a quality system to its standard. It follows that in the event of a nonconformance, corrective action is required and its accomplishment verified. Corrective action is always in addition to the planned and scheduled regular activities of the productive unit found in nonconformance. This means that the responsible manager, often a peer of the management representative, may take his time responding. One way of encouraging compliance to the audit report is to make things clear about the matter in a quality manual policy. For example, Clause 4.17 of the quality manual might say: "It will be the policy of this company that corrective action items will be assigned a response date by which time the identified problems must be resolved. Problems remaining uncorrected beyond this date will be brought to the attention of executive management for resolution." This is a hammer, but it is a hammer up front. Presumably, all management partake in the creation of the quality manual, work together on policies, and agree to abide by them. A policy that requires a formal resolution of action items enhances respect for the audit process.

Companies that are interested in sustainability have another purpose for conducting audits that goes beyond verifying conformance to the Standard. Sakofsky and Vitale (1994) express it this way: The purpose of an internal quality audit is to improve the value of the audited activity. Value-added activities are important and easily measured in manufacturing. They are equally important in service, but perhaps a little more difficult to measure.

Russell and Regel (1996) have written extensively on this notion and identify a concept that they call the "audit function improvement process." This is a formal mechanism by which those who conduct an audit are brought into the corrective process. Auditors, auditees, and other stakeholders work together in teams to ensure a constructive resolution to systematic problems identified in the audit. The authors recommend it as superior to a postresolution review of corrective actions by the QA department because it reduces misunderstandings.

Consider a calibration program, for example. It should provide a mapping of equipment to be calibrated and calibration equipment. Suppose that an auditor finds that the calibration software program lists the specifications of a unit to be calibrated, but does not list the specifications of the device used for the calibration and so records the discrepancy. It is possible to misunderstand exactly the discrepancy here. Is it one of accuracy, precision, or both? The auditor did not quite clarify the nonconformance, yet the calibration program can be improved with a follow-up discussion of the matter with the affected persons.

Summary

Sustainability in Clause 4.17 requires above all a philosophy—the IQA, representing the customer, is the company's trump card in self-evaluation and improvement. This notion encourages an investment in the IQA in terms of personnel training and program influence. Auditors will be trained in both ISO 9000 requirements and auditing techniques, in addition to their own expertise and skills. The management representative will provide scope and direction to the IQA.

References

ANSI/ISO/ASQC. *Q10011–1994. Guidelines for Auditing Quality Systems.* Milwaukee: American Society for Quality Control, 1994.

Bishara, R. H. , and M. L. Wyrick. "A Systematic Approach to Quality Assurance Auditing." *Quality Progress,* December 1994, pp. 67–70.

Fiorentino, R., and M. Perigord. "Going from an Investigative to a Formative Auditor." *Quality Progress,* October 1994, pp. 61–65.

Rice, C. M. "How to Conduct an Internal Quality Audit and Still Have Friends." *Quality Progress,* June 1994, pp. 39–41.

Russell, J. P., and T. Regel. "After the Quality Audit: Closing the Loop on the Audit Process." *Quality Progress,* June 1996, pp. 65–67.

Sakofsky, S., and D. D. Vitale. "Value-Added Audit Training." *Quality Progress,* May 1994, pp. 45–47.

Tate, Larry. Interview with author, August 22, 1996, Charlottesville, Va.

Part Four

Quality System Requirements: Engineering Purview

Chapter 15

Clause 4.4: Design Control

Brief: Clause 4.4 requires a system to control, verify, and validate the designs of products and processes to ensure adherence to specifications.

The essence of design is creativity. No standard in the world can mandate or bestow creativity. You either have it or you don't, but creativity is brought to market through a design process that, properly organized, is sustainable. A sustainable design process is one in which creativity won't get lost or inadvertently abridged.

Every company designs something, if only in personalizing some function—say, customer service. In a very real sense, design and planning overlap, so that any planning function designs, and any designing function plans. Nevertheless, Clause 4.4 does not apply to every company that seeks ISO certification; indeed, the requirement distinguishes ISO 9001 from the other standards within the 9000 series. So how do you know if Clause 4.4 pertains to you or not? The question is answered in the summary quote from ISO 9001 that begins this paragraph: ". . . the design of the product. . . ." If you design your products, then Clause 4.4 applies to you and ISO 9001 is the relevant standard for certification. If not, then Clause 4.4 does not apply to you and you can march to some other standard, say ISO 9002 or ISO 9003.

Although this requirement applies only to those companies that design product, its application covers the entire spectrum of design activity. For example, the ISO 9004 guidelines point out that design of product entails materials and processes also. Companies that design products may also design the processes used to make the products. Clause 4.4 is applicable to both kinds of designs and is thus quite extensive in its overview of the design process.

The Design Scheme

Specifically, design control is concerned with the operations of design and development planning, design input and output, verification, and design changes. Consider Exhibit 15-1. The basis of any design is the set of requirements defined by the customer. The design process will transform these requirements into specifications and will include the development of the initial design into various prototypes or configurations. The various stages of development may well call for in-process testing;

Exhibit 15-1. Capable design control configuration.

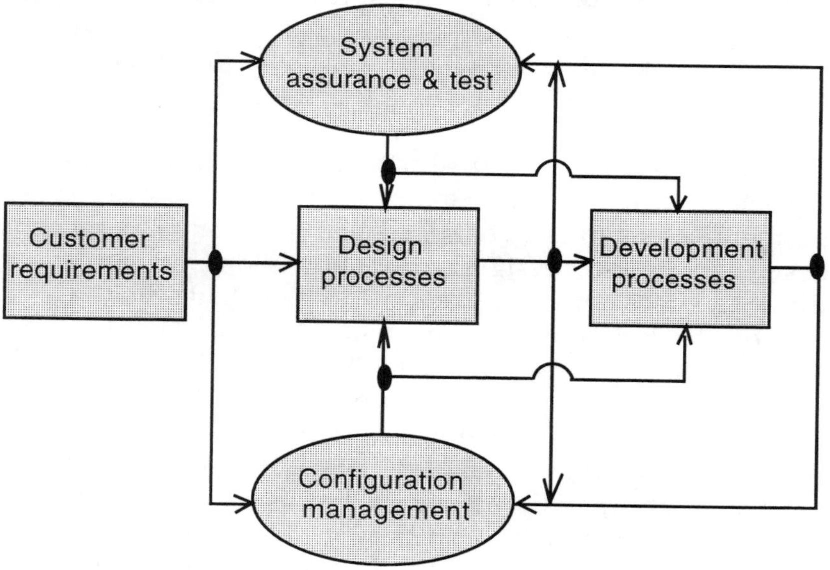

System assurance & test

Customer requirements

Design processes

Development processes

Configuration management

William A. Stimson, *The Robust Organization* (Burr Ridge, Ill.: Irwin, 1996). Reprinted with permission.

this is particularly true in the design of software programs or complex hardware systems. Exhibit 15-1 depicts the feed forward of requirements to test program formulation, as well as feedback following some initial progress.

Similarly, there is feed forward to configuration control. Configuration management is an important part of the process. In the early stages of design in particular, when requirements may be fuzzy, configuration changes can be undisciplined. Without a paper trail it may be difficult to review why design changes were made. This loss of information can limit design reviews and reevaluation of alternatives.

Development, test, and configuration require constant iteration in this closed-loop cycle because it is in the iteration that improvement is possible. Time is not a factor in the structure of Exhibit 15-1. There is always a feedback loop in permanent structure so long as a given product is on the market. Design, development, and redesign are life-cycle functions.

The Control Problem

The company will have plans and procedures that identify the responsibility for each design and development activity. These plans and procedures should include the assignment of qualified personnel to each phase of the design problem, irrespective of his assignment on the organization charts. There will be provision of adequate resources for design, analysis, and test phases. In addition, technical and organizational interfaces should be identified, with necessary information exchange documented.

Design and Development Planning

In contract review you are concerned with translating customer requirements into specifications. This is more than just coming up with numbers, of course; it also means determining materials, drawings, skills, and all the resources required to achieve this translation. The ISO requirement is that this process be formalized. A company is free to choose its design process, and there are many models to choose from. Most design processes have certain similar characteristics whether the product is hardware or software. These universal properties are what make the design process effective and are shown in the dynamic sketch of Exhibit 15-2. The overall process provides the closed-loop mechanisms that are required for robustness.

The design dynamic begins with a translation of customer requirements into the design specifications. A preliminary set of drawings represents the initial design, and this process is iterated in a model development loop until an optimal design is arrived at in terms of the final customer requirements. I say "final" because it is quite possible that initial requirements may change also, either because of unforeseen costs, unavailability of material, the discovery of a better way to do something, or simply because the customer has changed her mind about one or several product characteristics.

Clause 4.4 requires that the subprocesses of Exhibit 15-2 be formalized, not necessarily in organizational structure as in documented operations. The design, development, and planning responsibilities and interfaces must be identified, as well as customer input. The paper trail from customer through acceptance testing must be recoverable for those documents that pertain to product quality.

Exhibit 15-2. Dynamic closed-loop design process.

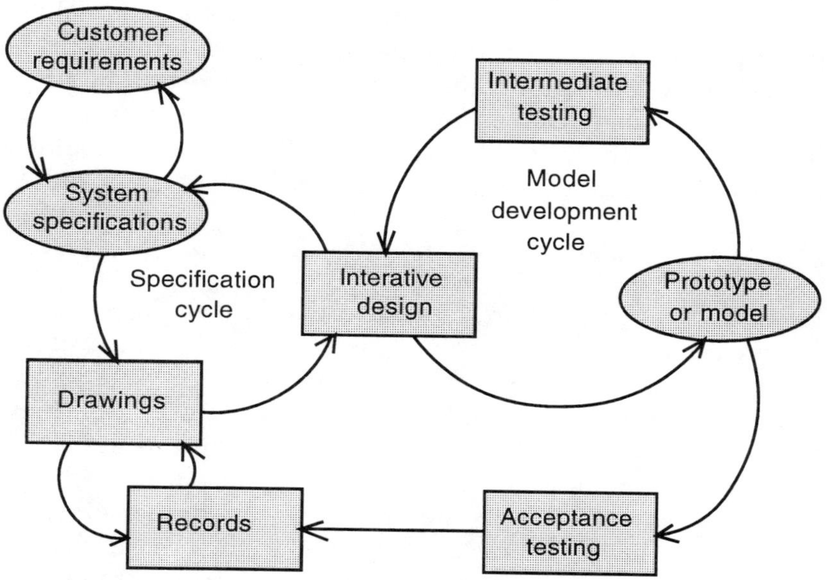

What does it mean to establish a paper trail? Is this simply more bureaucracy? The answer is an emphatic no. It is not necessary to retain brainstorming or intermediate notions about a product's design; documenting fuzzy ideas would inhibit the creative process. But as the design is developed, its connection to the customer requirements must be traceable. This is because traceability permits later reappraisal of earlier options, and because if there is a clear or nuanced departure from the customer requirements, that departure must be identified.

For example, suppose the customer is a manufacturer of medicinal ointments and you are a producer of metal and plastic squeeze tubes. The customer orders a large number of metal tubes of a certain size, but it turns out that there is a possibility of interaction between tube and ointment, so it is necessary to add an internal protective coating to the design of the tube. This sort of design change should effect several loops in the process of Exhibit 15-2: the specifications cycle, the development cycle, and the specs-to-customer loop.

System *specifications* should be interpreted as a very general term. It is more than the translation of customer requirements into quantitative or measurable data. Specifications include the necessary supporting information: drawings, software, policies, procedures, technical manuals, environmental constraints, safety issues, regulations, and all other information necessary to effect the design of a product.

Intermediate testing goes on throughout the development phase, as each model should be tested for verification and validation of the model. Verification answers the question Are we doing things right? with respect to specifications. Put another way, Is the model responsive to the specs? Validation answers the question Are we doing the right things? with respect to customer requirements. Again put another way, Is the model what the customer wants? As shown earlier in Exhibit 15-1, test requirements are fed forward for development into a test program that responds correctly to these questions.

Product and Process Redesign

ISO 9000 standards do not evaluate redesign processes, but it is reasonable to expect a positive correlation between long-term stability of the quality system and the ability to adapt to changes in customer requirements. Let's consider first the notion of product redesign. Why would you want to redesign a product already on the market? You probably would not if it were doing well. At some point sales drop off sufficiently that it becomes clear that product redesign may be an option whose time has come.

A robust company will not wait for that voice from the sky. It evaluates its existing products on an ongoing basis in terms of customer appeal and satisfaction. One way of doing this, according to Rupp and Russell (1994), is to identify a customer, select an appropriate measure of customer satisfaction, then determine if there is a difference in performance between the customer's needs and what the product provides. Then a problem-solving approach is taken to improve the product in this characteristic. This approach includes root-cause analysis.

The authors point out that sometimes the root cause of the problem with the product is in the process used to make the product. For example, a particle counter that is doing fairly well in the marketplace might do even better if its accuracy or precision could be improved. The count is achieved by means of a laser beam and jewel target. Root-cause analysis might show that too much noise is generated in the vicinity of the target and a totally new design is required to reduce this noise. The lesson that Rupp and Russell offer is that a redesign process should always be dual channeled, with one channel in product analysis and one channel in product-process interface.

Organizational and Technical Interfaces

As with everything that you do, there is a minimum way and a most effective way to implement the requirements of this clause. The minimum way is simply to provide an organization chart to the ISO auditors, accompanied by a procedural description that is in accord with it. The effective way is to establish horizontal as well as vertical interfaces in the design process. In this sense, *vertical interfaces* refers to the communication between line organizations relative to a particular job order. *Horizontal interfaces* refers to the exchange of ideas, data, and information between appropriate groups while the design process is within a particular phase of Exhibit 15-2.

For example, early design meetings should include marketing, customer service, production, and purchasing personnel, if not the customer herself. Purchasing people are there as a reality check for materials costs and availability. Production people are there to ensure conformance of requirements to capability. Procedures are required to demonstrate this integration and exchange of information.

An appropriate phrase comes to mind here: falling between the cracks. Things almost always fall between the cracks in horizontal interface. There is another descriptive cliché: rice bowl structure. This phenomenon of human organization results from a tendency to "we" versus "they" in human affairs. Perhaps it is a hand-me-down from tribalism. Whatever the reason, rice bowl structures seem to be a natural phenomenon and must be fought. Organizational interfaces are almost always vertical, and the lead-subordinate relationship is effective in establishing communications, albeit filtered. Technical interfaces are lateral and almost always left to random communication. The company that wants to be dynamic must take overt steps to ensure technical interface in design as well as in all other processes. This is all the more necessary in the modern era, when so many products have unrelated technical characteristics. Consider the following example of a product manufactured by the INOVA Corporation of Charlottesville, Virginia.

INOVA manufactures data display systems used in telephone call centers and in large-scale transit authorities. Design considerations include mechanical, electrical, electronic, and software features. Each design is distinct in its discipline but cannot stand alone. Mechanical engineers must consider the spatial requirements of the electrical and electronic components. Electronic design must consider the electromagnetic fields generated by the electrical circuits. Software design must consider the physical displays that will be driven by their contribution. INOVA has succeeded remarkably well in the integration of the disciplines into effective products. The bases of this integration are shared experience, mutual respect of the disciplines, and iterative meetings of key design personnel throughout the development cycle. These meetings are effected through two kinds of teams: a formal design review team and an engineering design team representing the different design functions.

Design Input

We have touched on design inputs earlier in discussing the formal procedures required to ensure timely availability of supporting information (drawings, software, policies, procedures, technical manuals, environmental constraints, safety issues, statutes, regulations) to effect the design of a product. This clause is closely related to the previous one because it often happens that design input data are identified but simply do not arrive from an allied function. As an example, consider the following illustration.

Plagued with specification problems in a series of expensive ship repairs, the U.S. Navy finally assigned two ships of the same class to the same shipyard for consecutive overhauls. Moreover, the two ships were built by the same builder within the same epoch. The rationale for the Navy strategy was to ensure that, whatever the problems with specifications and drawings on the first ship, they should all be identified and resolved for the second ship. In fact, it did not happen. The drawings of the first ship did not agree with the actual configuration of the ship. Fine. They were brought into alignment and returned to the builder for update for both ships. However, the drawings still disagreed with the configuration of the second ship. This complex morass can occur only when people who need to talk to each other aren't talking. Beyond obtaining the necessary inputs, adequacy, ambiguities, and conflicts must be resolved, and a procedure is required that will bring together a mechanism for this purpose.

Design Output

The design output must be documented, verified, and validated with respect to the design input requirements in each phase of the development cycle. Crucial characteristics of the design must also be identified at this point, such as safety, storage, weight, and other features required by law or critical to operation. Final design is often preceded by iterations of fuzzy preliminaries. What the designers do with their intermediate designs is up to them, but the final designs must be documented. They must also be reviewed for conformance, verification, and validation prior to release. This confirmation usually takes the form of well-designed acceptance criteria. In other words, the design of test and acceptance criteria is as important as the product design itself.

Design Review

The design process model of Exhibit 15-1 automatically meets the criteria of this clause. Review meetings should be formal, documented, and include all the players concerned with the design. The outcome of these design reviews is considered a quality document and falls under the requirements of Clause 4.16, as do the outcomes of contract reviews. We have already discussed the example of INOVA's effective use of the design review process. INOVA maintains tight control of its design review iterations. Integrity of design is maintained for both the physical and the documented quality systems.

The scope of the design has a great deal to do with the magnitude of the review. A large software program, for example, may take over a year to write, and the design process would include many reviews and walk-throughs. ISO requirements are not concerned with this scope other than that it be formal and suitable to the product.

Design Verification

Both verification and validation are part of the design control and need to be delineated. For the moment, let us consider verification only, which will continue through each phase of the design process, through system testing and delivery.

There are commonly recognized procedures:

1. Hold design reviews.
2. Conduct feasibility tests and demonstrations.
3. Determine alternative calculations.
4. Compare the new design with a similar proven design, if available.

Some of these procedures have already been discussed but are repeated here because of the interaction of these clauses.

Procedure 4 is a type of benchmarking and is always done. If the performance of your prototype is in the ballpark of a related product, this lends credibility to the design approach. These methods are not mandated unless they are appropriate to your business, but if carried out must be recorded. ISO policy is that if you do something, it must be recorded.

Design Validation

A rule of thumb for the design of a relatively simple product is that validation takes place twice, once at agreement on contract and once at acceptance testing—that is, before delivery. This rule is completely inadequate for the design of many products and complex systems. Both a contract review and a design review are appropriate for each development cycle. So also is design validation. It is just too easy to lose sight of the goal in a process as introverted and tunnel-viewed as design. John Gibson (1990) often referred to the need of software people to just "jot down a few lines of code to get things started." This temptation almost guarantees a divergence from the design as it is and the design as it should be.

You do not have to look far to find extensive examples of how not to conduct validation procedures—just look at the personal computer industry. You can buy an off-the-shelf for immediate capability or you can buy for later expansion. If you buy for immediate capability, there is a good chance that the system will not do what you had expected.

Take the first case. You buy a Windows platform with word processor and spreadsheet programs, but every time you attempt to use the spreadsheet graphics the computer crashes. There is not enough read-only memory (ROM). Yet the computer system passed all acceptance tests before delivery, tests designed to verify individual programs. But the total system does not work in unity, which was what you wanted in the first place.

Take the second case. You buy a Windows platform with Internet capability, and this time you get enough ROM. You are not going to get burned on that one again. You pass on the fax-modem for the moment, stating that you already have a modem and you intend to update to fax later. Your system arrives and has no receptacle for your modem! The PC went through its verification test with flying colors, but it cannot do what you intended for it even though you had expressed a desire for this potential to the vendor. System verification is usually established, in some sense, in most industries. But are you getting what you want? That is validation.

ISO 9000 standards do not ensure the adequacy of product validation. They ensure only that some validation procedure exists. ISO standards allow a company to define its processes and procedures as it chooses, so long as the documented and actual quality systems are the same. If you want sustainability, you need to go a step beyond ISO 9000.

Design Changes

There must be a procedure to effect changes to a design. This is a universal step in the design process and makes sense with or without ISO considerations. The procedure should include documentation, review, and an approval process before a change can be implemented. It seems redundant to say that design changes are intimately connected to validation procedures, yet businesses sometimes fail even here.

A very good example involves a case that we can all identify with. You contract for new roofing tiles of a national, respected brand, guaranteed for thirty years. On installation day the crew finds no tiles of that brand in the shop, and brings out another brand, less well known but also guaranteed for thirty years. About a week after the job is completed you receive the roofing tile guarantee from the roofer for Brand X tiles. Has the product been verified? Yes, it meets the numbers criteria. Has the product been validated? Not at all.

The roofing tiles example is a good one for two reasons. First, many of us can identify with the experience. Second, it indicates just what validation is. The roofer does not have to give you your first choice. He can appeal to you for a change in the specifications, and if you approve, validation has been achieved. We will approach this subject again under the name of "agreement of expectations" when we discuss contract review.

Summary

Sustainability in Clause 4.4 requires an iterative, controlled design process similar to that of Exhibit 15-2. There are three key cycles: requirements↔specifications; specifications↔prototypes; prototypes↔acceptable design. The methodology for each cycle has three parts: verification, validation, and participation by external and internal customers. The internal customers represent cross-functional expertise in process, product, marketing, purchasing, and customer service.

References

ANSI/ISO/ASQC. *Q9001–1994. Quality Systems—Model for Quality Assurance in Design, Development, Production, Installation, and Servicing*. Milwaukee: American Society for Quality Control, 1994.

ANSI/ISO/ASQC. *Q9004–1–1994. American National Standard: Quality Management and Quality System Elements and Guidelines.* Milwaukee: American Society for Quality Control, 1994.

Gibson, J. E. *How to Do Systems Analysis*. Workbook. Charlottesville: School of Engineering, University of Virginia, 1990.

Rupp, R. O., and J. R. Russell. "The Golden Rules of Process Redesign," *Quality Progress*. December 1994, pp. 85–90.

Chapter 16

Clause 4.11: Control of Inspection, Measuring, and Test Equipment

Brief: Clause 4.11 requires the control, calibration, and maintenance of equipment, hardware and software, that is used for inspection, measuring, and testing of product conformance to specifications.

We usually think of *measurement* and *mensuration* as synonyms. In a semantic sense they are, but it is worthwhile to distinguish a difference, to separate the concept from the measurement itself. Mensuration is the process of measuring something and of obtaining a result. For example, it is the activity of measuring the speed of light, the percentage of dissatisfied customers, or the weight of a bolt of cloth. It is the pure act of making a measurement.

In the physical world, we often need physical things to do the measurement. Sometimes the measuring devices are fragile or complex and require care. Sometimes the measuring device and unit being measured interact and therefore change the measurement. Other times the measurement requires proper procedures. Always, the measuring device must be capable of performing the measurement. Clause 4.11 is not about mensuration. It is about the equipment used in the measuring, about its capability to make the required measurements, and about its care.

The Mechanics of Measurement

Suppose you have decided that there is some aspect of your business that requires measurement. Determining to do so, you find yourself somewhat unsure of what to do next and the question arises: Just what is a measurement? The topic is quite complex, but for these purposes a practical definition from Lamprecht (1993) will suffice:

> *Measurement: The quantitative determination of a physical magnitude by comparison with a fixed magnitude adopted as the standard, or by means of a calibrated instrument. The result of measurement is thus a numerical value expressing the ratio between the magnitude under examination and a standard magnitude regarded as a unit.* (p. 59)

From this definition you see that measurements require a parameter to be measured; a metric to measure it by; a standard to compare it to; and a device of sufficient accuracy, precision, range, and sensitivity to effect the measurement. These issues are equally pertinent for either hardware or software units to be measured, or devices to make the measurement.

Control Procedure

Explicitly, documented procedures are required for control, calibration, and maintenance of inspection, measuring, and test equipment, including software. For example, a measurement made with a device that is beyond its calibration period is a nonconformance. Implicitly, however, Clause 4.11 is concerned with the integrity of a measurement and relies on proper procedures to ensure that integrity.

We have been discussing measurement as a process. Now let's address the subject as a procedure. Every measurement that is made requires a procedure that defines the parameter; the metric; the measuring device; and the required range, accuracy, precision, and sensitivity. The parameter to be measured is a quality characteristic if possible, or a variable indicative of a quality characteristic. The company is responsible for meaningful measurement. Since many of its processes have variational characteristics, statistical measurements will be required also, but will be discussed in Chapter 17.

Instrumentation

When it comes to measuring a physical characteristic, the validity of the measurement depends as well upon the instruments that are used. The instrumentation used must have the appropriate parametric range, accuracy, precision, sensitivity, and calibration required by the associated procedure. By *parametric range* is meant that the instrument can cover, over its linear capability, the domain or range of the measured variable.

Accuracy is the ability of the measurement to determine the true value of the characteristic being measured. Accuracy is expensive, so you need to determine and meet the requirements, but you do not need to exceed them. Suppose that you want to measure a voltage level known to be five volts. Progressively accurate measuring devices would report 5.0, 5.01, 5.001, and so on. The required accuracy depends on the specifications. If the specs called for an accuracy to within 1/100 of a volt, then a voltmeter accurate to 1/1000 of a volt would exceed requirements and would probably cost more.

Precision refers to the variability of the measurement, and therefore differs from accuracy. A voltmeter that repeats the same reading for the same measurement time after time is more precise than one whose reading varies. Since the characteristic being measured also has variability, it is possible to confuse the two. The precision of the measuring instrument must be established by first measuring a known, fixed quantity.

Sensitivity of the instrument refers to its ability to detect small differences in the measured unit. We are often concerned with the change in a value and, in control systems, want to detect that change as quickly as possible. A measurement is sensitive to the degree that it can detect small changes.

You can use poll taking to distinguish among accuracy, precision, and sensitivity. Suppose that a polling group wants to forecast the nation's political leanings prior to an election. The accuracy of their poll will decide its mean value, say 52 percent of those polled intend to vote for a certain candidate. A poll is often accompanied by a caveat saying "accurate to within three percentage points." This means that the 52 percent poll result is within three points of the true value of the population at large. The precision of a group of polls is defined by the variation in their results. The sensitivity of the polls is defined by their ability to detect trends or shifts in voter mood.

Color analyzers offer another example to explain the difference among accuracy, precision, and sensitivity. A spectrophotometer is one such device that determines color by measuring individual wavelengths and then computing values for light and hue. Its accuracy is the degree to which it can read a specific wavelength, say 5000 angstroms (Å). If it reads 5000Å for all wavelengths between 4900Å and 5100Å, then it is accurate to within 2 percent. Its sensitivity is the degree to which it can detect a shift from the wavelength. If it can detect a shift from 5500Å to 5550Å, then it is sensitive to shifts of 1 percent. Its precision is the repeatability with which it will report a measurement of 5000Å, as such, time after time.

The dynamic operation of any equipment is established by the manufacturer in making adjustments of variables, gains, and power within the unit. These adjustments establish the accuracy, scale factors, and linearity of the equipment. With time, minute wear and tear occurs in the equipment, which must be readjusted to restore it to its required operational capability. This is called *calibration*. You usually do not wait for equipment to be obviously wrong, but schedule calibration periodically. Many states require periodic calibration of devices used to measure some commodity such as gasoline pumps and grocery market and butcher shop scales.

Calibration and Metrology Equipment

Test equipment to be used in measuring, inspection, or testing must be maintained in calibration in order to provide valid data. The very nature of calibration implies the need of associated calibration procedures and records. On the other hand, concentrating on calibration can miss the big picture; it is only a subset of metrology. For example, some industries do not manufacture a product measurable by a machine; subjective judgments are required. Even here, it is useful to maintain records of ordinal reference. In this case, the subjective standard used becomes the calibrated standard. There is no substitute for thought.

For example, identical colors will appear different on different kinds of cloth or on different kinds of roofing shingles. Industries that deal with this sort of product rely more heavily on samples of cloth, carpet, or shingles than they do on the measured colors themselves. Their standards, or calibrated colors, if you will, are their product samples.

There are commonly recognized criteria in determining the what, when, and how of measurement. First, you identify the measurements to be made and the accuracy needed to make them. Then you select appropriate equipment. A calibration program must be defined for the measuring equipment. This program will include procedures and schedules, the former to account for the complexity of the measurement or equipment, the latter because accuracy tends to drift with time, so that calibration is a transit state.

Specifications and Standards

In measurement, specifications provide the detailed technical requirements that ensure verification and validation. As a general rule, the more specific the technical description or requirement, the more costly is the measurement. There are, of course, exceptions. In measurements that utilize models, specification error refers to the correctness of the theoretical model. Specifications are often defined in terms of upper and lower limits, in recognition that infinite precision is not possible. A good deal of thought is needed in determining these limits, along with recognition that they may have to be changed. For example, you may specify that a cylinder should be three inches in diameter, ± 0.001 inch, only to discover that your production system cannot consistently meet these specs. Very often, a certain amount of Kentucky windage (intuition) goes into specifications. If the production system is not capable, there are only two choices: widen the specs or buy a new production system.

Standards provide uniformity in the conduct of the measurement. They allow the same measurement to be made of the same parameter irrespective of place, time, or conditions. In some cases, a standard is a procedure. In others, it is a physical property such as a 1 ohm resistor or the wavelength of a radioactive element. We sometimes speak of standards of behavior. Since measurement is defined in terms of comparison to a standard, there can be no measurement without one. Quality performance requires standards throughout the organization.

Calibration Programs

We have seen that measuring devices undergo changes in their dynamic characteristics as time goes by. These characteristics must be brought back to proper operating range on a regular basis, which means that there needs to be a program to ensure this restoration. There are many software packages available that help do this, but they are bookkeeping programs—necessary but not sufficient. Even with software help, you still need to set up a dynamic calibration program.

Consider Exhibit 16-1. You have an inspection, test, or measurement instrument that needs to be calibrated—call it the unit under test (UUT). It may itself measure certain properties of your product. For example, if you produce wide-band amplifiers, then your instrument may be a bandwidth analyzer. It needs to be calibrated from time to time, and in this scenario it is the UUT. If you dye materials, then your measuring instrument may be an oven that is controlled by a thermostat. The thermostat needs to be calibrated from time to time, and within the concept of a calibration program, it is the UUT.

Either the original equipment manufacturer of the UUT or your engineering group will determine the periodicity of calibration, which varies from unit to unit depending on the fragility of the unit and on the wear and tear imposed by testing. This set of periodicities will be the basis of a calibration schedule.

I arbitrarily use the term *measuring device* (MD) for the instrument that will do the calibrating. Calibration costs money.

Exhibit 16-1. Schematic of a calibration program.

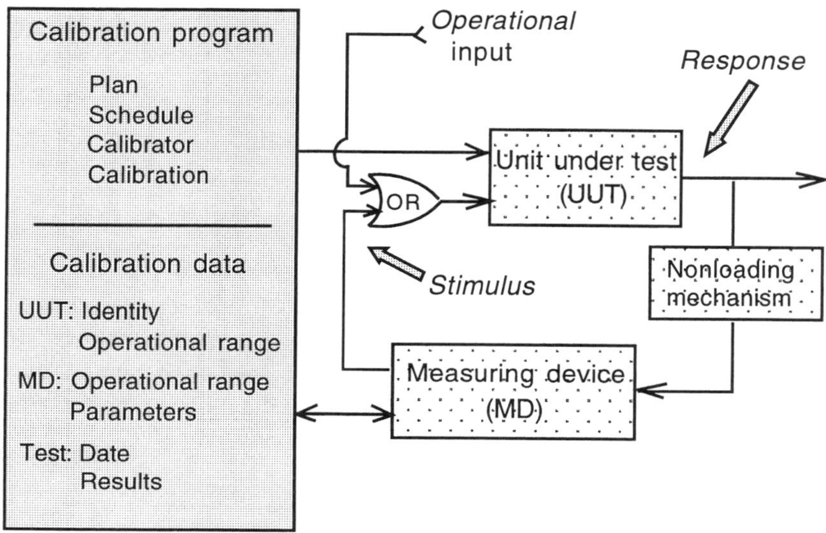

If the measuring device is expensive relative to the period of calibration, it may be cost-feasible to use external calibrators. You can ship the UUT off-site, or if the MD is portable, bring in a calibrator. ISO standards do not require that all your calibration capability be in-house; this is solely a cost consideration. Measuring devices can be as complex as an electromagnetic spectrum analyzer and as simple as a 6-inch rule. All must be calibrated. Technicians can be seen, in many shops, walking around with their own personal tape measures hooked on their belt. If one of them measures a quality characteristic with a personal, uncalibrated tape measure and is spotted by an ISO auditor, a nonconformance results.

Engineering will determine whether a UUT is best calibrated with an operational input or by injecting a stimulus from the MD. This option is indicated by an OR-gate in the exhibit. Similarly, it is engineering judgment whether the UUT output is loaded down by the MD—that is, whether the response is affected by the measuring. If so, then some kind of isolating or nonloading device is required. Auditors do not make these judgments and will respect the company process as long as there is a written procedure that describes it.

As a final comment, it should be obvious that the MD must have an operating range greater than the UUT, and if the measured property is dynamic or variable, the MD must have greater accuracy, precision, and sensitivity.

Summary

Sustainability in Clause 4.11 requires the company to determine the measurements to be made, including parametric issues, identify the equipment necessary to achieve the measurements, establish a calibration and maintenance program for the equipment, maintain records of maintenance and calibration, and maintain records of final measurement results as quality records.

References

ANSI/ISO/ASQC. *Q9001–1994. Quality Systems—Model for Quality Assurance in Design, Development, Production, Installation, and Servicing*. Milwaukee: American Society for Quality Control, 1994.

Lamprecht, J. L. *Implementing the ISO 9000 Series*. New York: Marcel Dekker, 1993.

Litsikas, Mary. "Practical Use of Color Measurement Devices Grows." *Quality*, March 1996, pp. 26–33.

Chapter 17

Clause 4.20: Statistical Techniques

Brief: Clause 4.20 requires that the company identify statistical techniques needed to verify adherence to product specifications and system capability.

Clause 4.20 is about measurement. Unfortunately, its title may scare off those to whom it is best addressed. Many executive-level managers, including a few quality assurance managers, may gloss over Clause 4.20 on the grounds that it is for the "technical weenies." But the importance of measurement is so great, and its conduct so often neglected, that we shall take advantage of the occasion to explore the idea of measurement itself. In order to fully appreciate this clause, you should think about why measurement is important to you.

Why We Measure Things

I often say that when you can measure what you are speaking about and express it in numbers, you know something about it; but when you cannot measure it, when you cannot express it in numbers, your knowledge is of a meagre and unsatisfactory kind: it may be the beginning of knowledge,

> *but you have scarcely, in your thoughts, advanced to the stage of science, whatever the matter may be.*
>
> *—William Thomson, Lord Kelvin, 1891*

Managers need to measure performance for two very important reasons: (1) to evaluate process performance relative to goals; (2) to be able to control the process. You cannot improve a process if you don't know how good it is or if you cannot control it. Yet we hear executive management bandy the word *improvement* about as though it were simply a matter of willing it so. The word appears in every mission statement. Well, Lord Kelvin throws cold water on the notion of willing an improved product or process. Indeed, he goes further than that, saying that without measurement, we simply don't know what we're talking about.

Okay, Lord Kelvin, you've shamed us into it. *Mea culpa, mea culpa, mea maxima culpa*. We resolutely determine to start measuring as the first step in the goal to dynamic improvement and sustainability. But what do we measure? According to Grant and Leavenworth (1988), "Measured quality of a manufactured product is always subject to a certain amount of variation as a result of chance. Some stable system of chance causes is inherent in any particular scheme of production and inspection. Variation within this stable pattern is inevitable. The reasons for variation outside this stable pattern may be discovered and corrected." (p. 1)

Although the mathematical sciences are not known for it, from time to time you come across real poetry—some idea beautifully, completely, and concisely expressed. I submit that the summary of Grant and Leavenworth is the most complete, concise, and beautifully expressed description of statistical process control that one can find. I have marveled at this short paragraph many times, but can't find a word that can be omitted and cannot think of a word that can be added.

Variation

When you think about the words of Grant and Leavenworth, you realize what it is about your processes that you must measure. In Chapter 4 we identified variation as the enemy of quality. Then it is variation that you will measure, everywhere that it exists and affects quality of product. This is a potentially large task because variation exists in all processes throughout a company, not just on the production floor, and it is difficult to imagine some process that does not affect quality directly or indirectly.

Nevertheless you need to bound the enterprise. The limit of measurement is not determined by function but by state or quality variables. If a function, say comptroller, provides an output defined by one variable, then you need measure only one variable. If a function, say production, provides a product with three quality variables, then you need measure only three variables, not 15 or 180. We discussed this issue in Chapter 4 and will sum it up this way: Measurement of quality should be widespread and parsimonious.

There will always be variation in a production process owing to random causes; you cannot clone output. Nevertheless, it is possible to arrive at some bounded variation, some stable pattern induced by chance causes. The chance causes of Shewhart's (1931) time are called common causes today. Variation within this stable pattern is inevitable. Deming (1986) and others have implored management not to overreact to *stable variation*. Overreaction can be shown to increase variation rather than reduce it. There may also be variation owing to external forces acting upon the system. This is called *assignable variation* and the causes are assignable causes. They are also known as special causes.

Deming (1986) and Juran (1992) in particular have gone to great lengths to show that variation, common and special causes, and overreaction are problems that concern general management. Deming describes these statistical concepts relative to employee evaluations, for example. This is why Clause 4.20 should not be relegated to the "technical weenies" but rather provide appropriate food for thought throughout company operations.

Identification of Need

The company needs to read the requirements of Clause 4.20 carefully because there is some ambiguity. Previous versions of this clause were undemanding, but the 1994 revision has been toughened up—at least one can interpret it that way. Some registrars will tend to a laissez-faire interpretation and leave it to a company whether it wants to use statistical techniques or not. Others may go to the other extreme and insist that process capability be statistically demonstrated. So what's the best alternative?

In this book we are not concerned with politics. We are concerned with what is right. Clause 4.20 (1994) says "The supplier shall identify the need for statistical techniques required for . . . verifying process capability. . . ." To an engineer this is hardly ambiguous. Process capability has a strict engineering meaning; it is the ratio of product specification to process variation. Most companies adhere closely to specifications. They accompany a job through the production line and provide the standard of performance. This is all to the good. But it only measures *goodness*. Statistical techniques permit the measurement of variation, and hence of stability and capability. Pursuing Lord Kelvin's challenge, you want to know whether your processes are stable and capable, and the cost of finding out is much less than the cost of not knowing. And as you will see, the pursuit is applicable to any process within the company.

Procedures

There are a wide variety of statistical techniques that provide qualitative insight into process capability—time series, run charts, Pareto diagrams, Ishikawa (fishbone) charts, to name a few. They can tell if something is wrong, and often what it is. Moreover, they are intuitive and do not require a strong statistical background. There are also powerful techniques that do require an understanding of statistics, such as control charting, regression analysis, and experimental design. These techniques have been made easier through the development of user-friendly software and are worth considering for general application.

If any of the above methods are adopted, a procedure should be drawn up that describes the events for which they will be used. (You do not need to describe how they are done.) Beyond this, you want to establish stability and capability of your key processes at least, and once at that level, to then move on to improvability.

Stability Analysis

As mentioned in Chapter 4, a process is stable if its variability is bounded. Stability is measured by determining if the mean and variance of samples of product are constant and within control limits established from evidence of the process itself. Stability of process can be established by Shewhart control charting in the following sequence:

1. Identify the quality characteristics to be measured.
2. Select the metrics.
3. Determine the distribution of each characteristic.
4. Select the appropriate control limits.
5. Using recent past data, compute process mean and control limits.
6. Begin charting.

Items 1 and 2 are presumably within the expertise of every functional manager, since they require knowledge only of what the function is supposed to do. Items 3 and 4 are more difficult because some rudimentary understanding of statistics is needed. A first estimate of parameter distribution can be made by using histograms or by referring to common assumptions about certain kinds of characteristics. The silhouette of a histogram indicates whether or not the distribution is even-tailed or skewed. If it is symmetric, you might begin with an assumption of normality. Probability distributions are simply models, an attempt by wise men to describe the real world, which is under no obligation to conform. Nevertheless, many natural and industrial processes are quite robust, and a normal model may well be suitable, at least while the process is in control.

Many assumptions about distributions derive from years of study of industrial processes. For example, where the characteristic is the number of surface imperfections that is observed on a plated surface of a given area, the distribution can be modeled as Poisson and a C-chart may be appropriate (Grant and Leavenworth). You could use the same model to determine the stability of a publications process, where you might be concerned with the number of spelling or typographical errors per page. A 100 percent inspection is usually not cost-feasible in this kind of evaluation, so a metric of errors per page is preferable to a metric of the number of total errors in the document. In any case, once the distribution and control limits of a process are found, then items 5 and 6 are straightforward.

Process Capability

A process is capable if its variability is within specifications. Capability is measured as the ratio of specification limits to control limits. To determine the ratio of specification to variation, they must be put in the same units. The units may be in the selected metric or they may be in terms of σ, the process standard deviation.

Some quality experts use the term *productive process* in the sense of manufacturing, where production has come to refer to the assembly or production line that terminates in a product for market. They refer to other kinds of processes as *nonproductive*. I dislike this terminology and consider it degrading. In a sense, every process is productive. You put something in and you get something out. This is more than a semantic problem—its result has placed a devastating constraint on the application of statistical techniques, and especially the use of these techniques to determine process capability.

So for our purposes we shall create some new terminology, something borrowed from the armed services. The Army refers to its infantry, armor, and artillery as fighting forces. Other units are not called nonfighting forces, which would be both degrading and sometimes untrue. Rather, they are called support forces. We shall adopt a similar nomenclature. All processes within a business enterprise are constructive processes. Those whose output is a product destined for direct sale in the marketplace are productive processes, in recognition of tradition; there is no sense in shoveling sand against the tide. Those whose output *contributes* to productive processes are support processes.

A process capability can be determined for any constructive process. Just as do productive processes, support processes suffer variation in their output. Support processes do not normally have specification limits, but they have the equivalent—targets or goals. If these goals have a range about them, then they are effectively specifications. Therefore, a capability index can be defined for support processes that will provide a measure of effectiveness for self-evaluation.

Improvability

A process is improvable if incremental variation is measured and can be reduced. Improvability is measured by a penalty function. Penalty functions are systematic reactions, administrative, hardware, or software that force a response back into compliance. The amount of force depends on the amount of error. It may follow a square law, as does the well-known Taguchi Loss Function, or it may be proportional to the error, as discussed in Chapter 4.

Penalty functions are often called cost functions to avoid the negative connotation of the word *penalty*, even though they are always a penalty. They always exist. If the company does not impose them, the marketplace will. For example, the cost of failing to detect an assembly-line error early on increases as value is added to the product and can be enormous to correct if the fault is not detected before delivery. Imagine the cost of rectifying a faulty condenser in an industrial air conditioner made in Florida and detected in Oregon!

In sum, sustainability is ensured through the achievement of stability, capability, and improvability of constructive processes. These properties are achieved through statistical techniques. Procedures for sustainability are required to ensure systematic and cohesive (to company-wide goals) measurement and operation, but the statistical techniques themselves need not be described. The procedures do need to include the quality characteristics and metrics that are to be measured.

Measuring Support Processes

Exhibit 17-1 provides a brief summary of support functions for which statistical techniques apply. The list is hardly comprehensive and is offered solely to stimulate the imagination of management in any company function. The intent is to aid the management of support processes. For example, some of these activities are used in service companies and therefore are, by

Exhibit 17-1. Some metrics for support applications.

Support Function	*Metrics*
Accounting	Accounts receivable and payable; agreement to general ledger
Comptroller	Productivity measures; cost reductions
Computer programming	Defect density; percent of single function modules
Contracts	Change orders
Data processing	Service volume; turnaround time
Finance	Return on investment; net present worth
Handling and storage	Damage incidence; retrieval rates
Information systems	Annual post hoc cost/benefits ratio
Inventory	Turnover rate; holding and shortage costs
Marketing	Market share; average time to market; return on investment
Planning	Forecasting variation
Publications	Defect density; timeliness of distribution; cost of rework
Purchasing	Price reductions; source selections; inventory control
Receiving and shipping	On-time schedules; condition; count; correct product
Safety	Accident rate; training rates
Sales	Contacts/bookings ratio; quotes/bookings ratio; new dealerships
Service	Percent orders entered versus received; percent delivery on time
Traffic	Transportation costs per product
Training	Average and variance of annual training

definition, productive processes. In that case, the marketplace has probably forced an MOE of some sort.

One suggestion is that a support function as benchmark to an equivalent productive function. For example, some service companies provide data processing (DP) as their stock in trade. If this is their main line of business, they will, through marketplace evolution, find a practical and effective way to measure the quality of this service to ensure success in business. A DP department in a manufacturing plant can benchmark to this kind of service company, adapting its measures of effectiveness as a means of self-evaluation.

The metrics of Exhibit 17-1 are specific in some cases, very general in others. Some of the support functions will require considerably more variables than suggested by the examples. Consider a management information system. It may be evaluated by a cost/benefits ratio, but both costs and benefits have a number of components and not all of them are quantitative. The challenge is to quantify a benefit—say, ease of obtaining timely information. Even if this effort is successful, then the manager must decide if a single number, the ratio, is as informative of quality as the dozen or so costs and benefits independently considered, or if something is lost in the translation. For example, if a sizable change in cost is not reflected in a comparable change in the ratio, then the index is insensitive and some other MOE must be defined. Similarly, if the information system can absorb a significant user increase without having to be updated, the cost/benefit ratio should be able to reflect this. The key is to remember that a dynamic system is properly described with a minimum of state variables.

Metric Considerations

Some of the entries in Exhibit 17-1 are deliberately brief. Blanding (1991) lists several dozen metrics that measure service. Neufelder (1993) provides over forty metrics in software development in categories of error, product, and process. You can beat yourself to death with this thing, or you can come up with a minimum number of state or quality variables that describe your system.

Some metrics are vaguely put and must be thought out. In the accounting example, a state variable must be defined that will relate, say, accounts receivable to the general ledger. It could be the number of dollars in error or the number of accounts in error, whichever is the most useful. Although the goal of each support function should be an MOE of capability, the initial work can be installed rather quickly. Using a technique described by Zierden (no date), each manager in the company determines her customer, works out a set of requirements with him, then endeavors to meet them every time.

In many companies the comptroller is responsible for optimizing time and materials relative to output—in short, the productivity of the company. This responsibility can be measured in whichever way is most meaningful: cash flow, resource expense reductions, or even stability of costs. The ability of the comptroller to specify costs precisely allows the company to set a sale price per product for a target profit.

Intuitively you might suppose that sales is the most easily measured support function. However, the warning about measuring something because it is easy to measure is appropriate here. The first metric that comes to mind is dollars, indisputably easy to understand. But dollars can fool you, too. If sales volume in dollars is up and profit owing to high costs or competition is down, what have you gained? Nor does sales establish production costs or pricing; that function is responsible only for things within its authority. Two effective MOE might be the ratios of contacts to bookings and quotes to bookings. The first measures big-picture effectiveness—the ability to cast the net, as it were. The second measures the ability to close, given a promising lead. *Quote* can also mean estimate—that is, the customer has come to you for a proposal.

Measuring Productive Processes

Manufacturers usually track their productive processes quite well because a direct line can be traced from these systems to profitability. Nevertheless, in the interest of completeness I will review some of the commonly used metrics of productive processes. Exhibit 17-2 lists a few metrics that measure the various characteristics of productive processes.

Stability and availability are interrelated because if assignable causes stop production, then you begin to measure system down time. Nevertheless, both measurements are needed. Stability is a fundamental property of a process and needs to be verified. Availability is often defined as the ratio of system up time to system (up + down) time, but this is a biased measurement because the down time may include time when no work is scheduled—a holiday, for example. We should prefer the ratio of up time to production time, where the latter is the scheduled work period.

Exhibit 17-2. Some metrics for productive applications.

Process Characteristic	*Metrics*
Stability	Constant mean and variance
Capability	Specification/variation ratio
Improvability	Cost function index
Productivity	Product price/cost ratio
Availability	Machine up time/production time ratio; reliability
Efficiency	Scrap and rework ratios; first pass yields; setup times; percent of incoming product inspected; on-time delivery
Cycle times	Inventory turns; work-in-process inventory turns; order-to-shipment lead times
Customer factor	Customer reject rate; warranty costs
Innovations	Adoption of employee ideas; new products

Thinking About Methods

There are many statistical techniques that are useful in the conduct of business. One of them, control charting, has been described in some detail in Chapter 4. Some of them, such as run charts and cause-and-effect diagrams, are fairly well known. Another of them, experimental design, is actually a family of techniques. The purpose of this book is not to provide a comprehensive list of statistical techniques, nor to describe any of them in sufficient detail as to use it. The purpose of the book is to familiarize line management on some of the methods to the point where curiosity leads to inquiry.

Cause and Effect Methods

These methods are designed literally to help establish a relation between a problem and contributory effects. Two of the very popular are fishbone charts and Pareto charts. An example of a fishbone chart is shown in Exhibit 17-3, where it is obvious how it received this name. The chart is more correctly named an Ishikawa diagram after its designer, Kaoru Ishikawa, according to Ryan (1989). This particular example might be from a producer with shipping delays.

Exhibit 17-3. Example of a fishbone chart for cause and effect analysis.

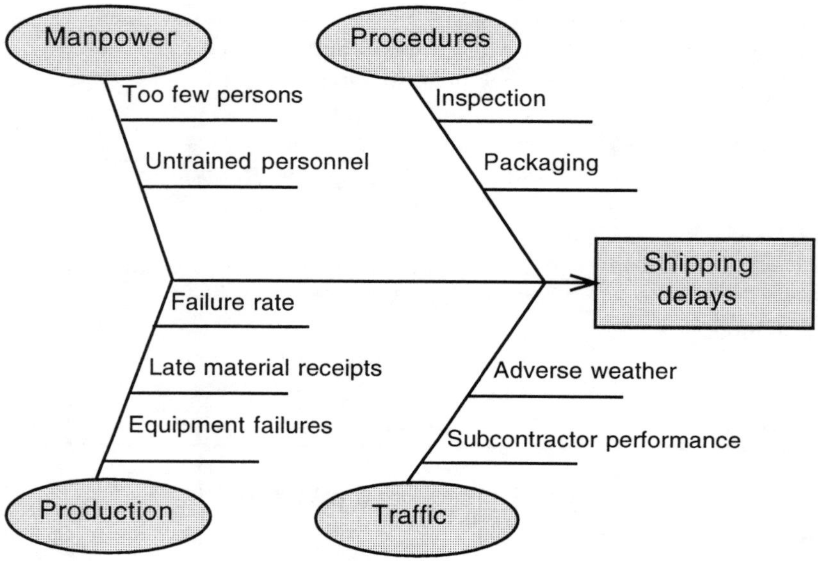

The major possible causes are indicated with radial lines, or bones, from a main trunk. Then subcauses appropriate to the main causes branch off each bone. The Ishikawa diagram is particularly effective in brainstorming, with concerned support functions gathered together for the analysis. How did someone determine that a problem existed in the first place? One method might be control charting of a key shipping parameter, say delivery time. Control charts detect instability, but do not identify causes. Ishikawa diagrams work together with control charts to complete the problem-solution process.

Vilfredo Pareto was an Italian economist earlier in this century who developed several important statistical ideas which we shall take the time to distinguish. Both ideas are commonly used and you do not want to confuse them. The first is known as the *Pareto optimal frontier* and describes a boundary relating two unlike and independent variables. The other notion is known as the *Pareto diagram*. It is the Pareto diagram that you are interested in here because it offers a quantitative relationship of cause to effect as shown in Exhibit 17-4. The strategy of this diagram that is used today, and was developed by J. M. Juran for industrial use, is to separate the vital few causes of a problem from the trivial many.

Exhibit 17-4. Pareto diagram of causes effecting customer complaints.

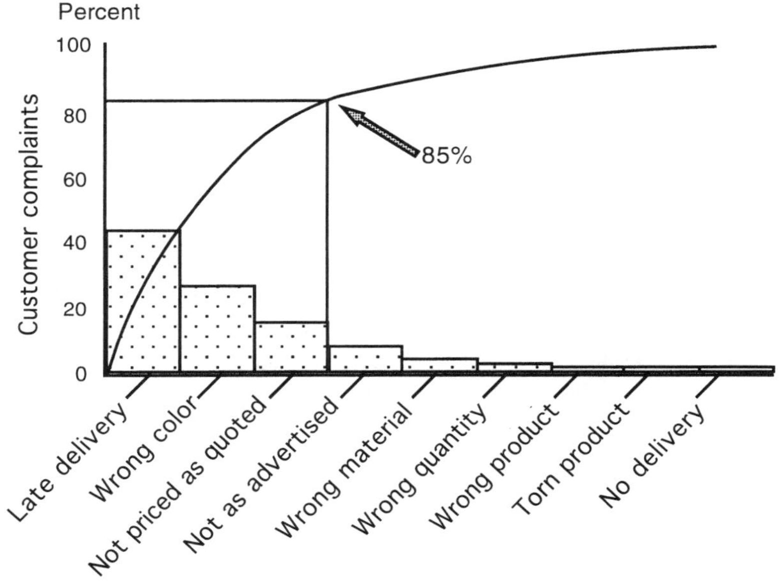

In Exhibit 17–4, the effect is the number of customer complaints, and the causes are distributed throughout the various constructive processes of a manufacturer of garments. There are two graphs in the figure. The bar graph presents a bar that assigns to each cause a percentage of the effect to which it contributes. The second graph is a curvilinear plot of the cumulative percentage. Clearly, the first three problems cause 85 percent of the customer complaints. You conclude that the wisest strategy is to attack the problems of late deliveries and sending out the wrong colors and price quotes.

As with Ishikawa diagrams, Pareto charts help determine the source and magnitude of problems. How were the problems detected in the first place? Again, the best detector of assignable causes is control charting. Cause and effect tools are identifiers of problems, not detectors. Of course, a single customer complaint is self-identified; you don't need analytical tools to tell you of a dissatisfied customer. But you do need analysis to tell you if the complaint represents a common cause or an assignable cause, because the two kinds of causes are approached differently. Common causes are inherent to the system and can be reduced only by changing the system. This is nearly always a management problem.

Design of Experiments

The modern idea in quality is to design a system that operates as well as it can in a given environment, and that maintains this efficiency even when disturbed by external factors. The system may be in the design, development, or operational phase of its life cycle. It is never too late to redesign, but obviously it is best to do it right in the first place. One way to effect an environmentally resistant system is through a family of techniques called design of experiments (DOE), or sometimes experimental design.

Blake et al. (1994) argue that experimental design improves a company's position in the global marketplace by designing robust processes, reducing time to market and life cycle cost, and increasing reliability. The authors identify a strong need for this family of statistical techniques, and evidently this need is real because the use of DOE seems to be increasing, as manifested by an increasing number of software programs that support the techniques.

The basic principle behind DOE, a powerful one, is that internal and external factors acting upon a system often have an interactive effect that cannot be detected by the traditional engineering strategy of varying one parameter at a time in order to design an improved response. DOE techniques identify interactive factors and vary them simultaneously in a parsimonious sequence of experiments, whence derives the name of the methods. Some of the techniques that fall within the genre of experimental design are analysis of variance, factorial arrays, Tuguchi techniques, and response surfaces. And this is the problem. All the methods require a significant background in statistics. The software programs aid in computation, of course, but the strategy of experiment must be determined, and the analysis performed, by persons with expertise in both the system and in statistical inference.

Nevertheless, the use of DOE should be encouraged, as the following example might make clear. Suppose that you manufacture clear plastic film. Your factory is located in Alabama and your machines were designed and built in Germany. The operational values of parameters of the machines were established by the original equipment manufacturers. However, your environment is greatly different from that of Germany, and of course as the years go by, the machines age.

You notice that white spots are occurring on the film and your control charts indicate that the problem is systematic. Through an Ishikawa analysis you determine that the factors causing the white spots are dryer temperature, line speed, and film tension. A DOE technique can establish the interaction of these parameters, if any, and what their optimal settings should be for a given environment. The actual conduct of the experiments may be achieved by you or by the OEM, depending on contracts and warranties, but the methods will solve the problem.

This example also teaches a second lesson. Some companies that use DOE methods have abandoned control charting. Experimental methods do not replace detection methods, although they may reduce their use. No system reliability is constant; age will introduce variation, and that variation must be detected if it is to be limited.

Summary

Sustainability in Clause 4.20 requires the company to recognize that the enemy of quality is variation, which exists in all operations. Productive *and* support processes should demonstrate stability. Variation within a stable pattern is inevitable, but variation beyond this can be "discovered and corrected." Reducing variation improves capability, which is the only meaningful way to bring about improvement. The key to improvement is to understand a process, its states, and its quality characteristics, and from these to derive metrics that permit process control.

References

ANSI/ISO/ASQC. *Q9001–1994. Quality Systems—Model for Quality Assurance in Design, Development, Production, Installation, and Servicing*. Milwaukee: American Society for Quality Control, 1994.

Blake, S., R. G. Launsby, and D. L. Weese. "Experimental Design Meets the Realities of the 1990s." *Quality Progress*, October 1994, pp. 99–101.

Blanding, Warren. *Customer Service Operations*. New York: AMACOM, 1991.

Crider, Janet. Discussion of accounting practices and quality indices. Telephone and facsimile communication, November 2, 1996.

Deming, W. E. *Out of the Crisis*. Cambridge: Center for Advanced Engineering Study, Massachusetts Institute of Technology, 1986.

Grant, E. L., and R. S. Leavenworth. *Statistical Quality Control*. New York: McGraw-Hill, 1988.

Juran, J. M. *Juran on Quality by Design*. New York: Free Press, 1992.

Lamprecht, J. L. *Implementing the ISO 9000 Series*. New York: Dekker, 1993.

Neufelder, A. M. *Ensuring Software Reliability*. New York: Dekker, 1993.

Ryan, T. P. *Statistical Methods for Quality Improvement*. New York: Wiley, 1989.

Shewhart, W. A. *Economic Control of Quality of Manufactured Product*. Princeton, N.J.: Van Nostrand, 1931.

Thomson, William (Lord Kelvin). *Popular Lectures and Addresses*, vol. 1, 2d ed. London: Macmillan, 1891.

Zierden, W. E. "Pursuing Excellence Through Quality." Productivity Brief No. 42, ISSN 0741–6448. *American Productivity Center* [no date].

Part Five

Quality System Requirements: Operations Purview

Chapter 18

Clause 4.7: Control of Customer-Supplied Product

Brief: Clause 4.7 requires a process of control of any product that is provided by the customer for use in the company supply systems.

Clause 4.7 is at the same time brief and unique among ISO requirements. It pertains to that singular case where a customer will provide the company a part or parts to be used in the manufacture of a product to be delivered to the customer. At first blush this might seem a rare occasion, but it is in fact a common enough occurrence in some industries and has two responsibilities to it: stewardship and quality control.

Stewardship

The U.S. government, as customer, will sometimes supply the product in certain of its contracts to industry. On occasion the provision can be sufficiently large as to carry with it a significant burden of stewardship. For example, a private shipbuilder or repairer typically receives millions of dollars' worth of government-furnished equipment (GFE) and government-furnished material (GFM) to be installed on a ship to be delivered to the

U.S. Navy by some specified date. In some cases the GFM or GFE will be held in inventory beyond the contract date, and even for long-term storage. The reasons for this are several. The cost estimations of Navy ship repair are usually quite rough. The ship to be repaired is almost always in deployment until just before the repair period. The bidders do not get to see the ship prior to bid; the contract winner does get a ship visit prior to start of work and gets to negotiate a cost update.

In some cases, long-lead GFM will be in excess of that needed and the shipyard will be required to store this material over the long haul, with the Navy paying storage costs. In other cases, work may be rescreened from the ship's force to the contractor, or conversely, so that not all the GFM or GFE purchased for the job order will be used. Again, the Navy may require the shipyard to store the material. Although paid for the service, the performer is required to supply responsible stewardship.

Government agencies sometimes purchase systems piecemeal, obtaining subsystems at a cost advantage, then hiring a contractor to put the system together. The U. S. Army's Redstone Arsenal let a contract to Hewlett-Packard's Automatic Measurement Division for a computer-controlled calibration system. The computers and software for the system were provided by HP, but the video displays were provided by the Army.

Customer-supplied products are less frequent in the private sector, and when they occur the dimensions are bounded by the tighter inventory philosophy that the commercial sector employs. For example, custom home builders often receive such products when a customer provides certain tiles, lumber, or built-ins of choice. A just-in-time inventory technique is often used, minimizing the stewardship problem to the period of performance. Another example is the provision by a music company of tapes to be converted to compact discs, or of discs to be replicated, by a CD manufacturer. Presumably, but not always, the provisions are appropriate to the job order and the final product is purchased by the customer and delivered upon completion of the task.

Stewardship means that the performer is responsible to safeguard the customer-supplied product as inventory until such time as it is put into production. At that time the material falls into the mainstream of the company's quality control processes. Safeguarding means that the material must not only be protected from theft but also from the weather or from damage on the floor or in the yard. Clause 4.7 is concerned with written and actual procedures on the details of how this stewardship is achieved.

Quality Control

Obviously, the quality of customer-supplied products will impact the quality of the final products, and this, too, is a concern of the Standard. The company is responsible for recording and reporting to the customer the event of lost or damaged products or delivered products unfit for use. This report is a quality record, in accordance with Clause 4.16, because the customer will deliver its product to the performer in good faith and assume that its responsibility has been fulfilled. If the product is somehow unfit, then this is potential grounds for dispute and customer grievance.

Just as the company must maintain quality overview of its subcontractors, so also it must maintain quality overview of its customer-suppliers. However, a rating or evaluation system is not required. In fact, Clause 4.7 provides a disclaimer: "Verification by the supplier does not absolve the customer of the responsibility to provide acceptable product." This disclaimer is worded in the terminology of the ISO program. The "Supplier" is the performing company, that is, the manufacturer of the product or provider of the service. It is not the customer who is providing (supplying) the product.

The Dynamics of a Sustainable Process

We have discussed two major considerations in regard to customer-supplied products: stewardship and quality control. The processes used to effect these concerns must be formal and sustainable. That is, they will work all the time, for long periods of time. A schematic of how to arrive at this level of performance is shown in Exhibit 18-1.

Exhibit 18-1. Sustaining process for product supplied by the customer.

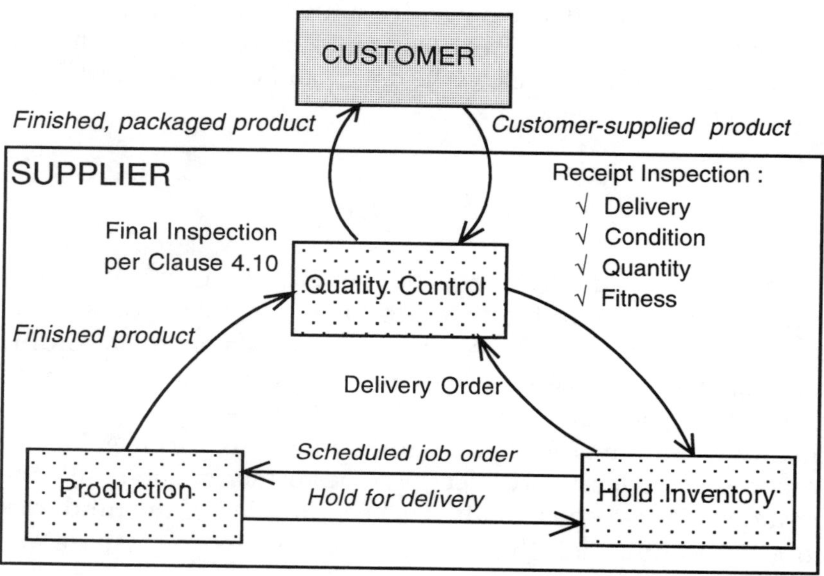

Customer-supplied products are received in the same manner as others—they go through a receipt inspection. Delivery date is noted, and the condition, quantity, and fitness of the material is recorded and compared to contractual requirements. Generally the material will then go to inventory until it is required on the production line. Nevertheless, the material should be marked "from purchased parts and other inventory" by labels and location. It does not belong to the manufacturer; it belongs to the customer. The holding area need not be unique—other material can be in the general storage area—but the customer-supplied product should be sufficiently isolated as to be readily distinguished. And of course, it must be safe from damage or misuse.

The material is integrated into the final product according to the job order, but this final product may not be called for immediately. If not, it again returns for hold, and again it has a unique status. At some point, presumably, the final product will be called for delivery and will undergo transition in accordance with the standard quality control procedures of Clause 4.10.

The bottom line in a sustaining system of customer-supplied products is determined by a quite simple criterion: Can an internal or external auditor readily identify customer-supplied products at any time, anywhere, and verify their security and integrity?

To simplify a discussion of contractual issues, we shall adopt an abbreviation: customer-supplied products will be called CSP. The customer provides CSP to a manufacturer or provider of service that is to be used in making a final product. The CSP will either be physically integrated into the final product or will not. It may be a tape of data or music that is to be converted electronically to compact disc. In this case, the CSP maintains its identity and is never a physical part of the final product.

The customer intends to buy this final product, by definition. He is the customer. There are three concerns that should be resolved in the contract up front. The first is the issue of stewardship. An end date of responsibility should be included. Whether or not the customer accepts delivery of the final product in accordance with the contract, the product contains material belonging to him unless spelled out otherwise in the contract. This places the performer in an untenable position if the customer delays or refuses delivery.

The second issue is related to the first and calls for an agreement on how long the CSP status should be retained. If it is information, the CSP never belongs to the performer. This is easily resolved by simply returning the data source to the customer, whether or not the final product is purchased. If it is a physical device that becomes part of a final product, then perhaps the two parties can agree that at some point the CSP belongs to the customer only in the same sense as the final product—upon delivery. The performer, of course, is obliged to deliver according to the contract.

The third issue is quality control. The performer has some help on this one because the Standard disclaimer can be worded within the contract in such way that the customer understands that the quality of the final product may not exceed the quality of the CSP. In the end, the terms of the contract will determine whether the final product falls under the purview of this clause or under Clause 4.15, which concerns regular handover issues.

Summary

Sustainability in Clause 4.7 requires the company to accept two responsibilities relative to customer-supplied product: stewardship and quality control. These tasks can be unified by a structure similar to that of Exhibit 18-1. Both stewardship and quality control have unusual aspects with respect to customer-supplied product. These aspects should be defined and clarified explicitly in the contract.

References

ANSI/ISO/ASQC. *Q9001–1994. Quality Systems—Model for Quality Assurance in Design, Development, Production, Installation, and Servicing*. Milwaukee: American Society for Quality Control, 1994.

Chapter 19

Clause 4.8: Product Identification and Traceability

Brief: Clause 4.8 requires, where demanded by specifications or suitability, a system to identify and trace purchased product during all stages of production. Traceability will include identification of product within batch or lot.

Clause 4.8, too, is a brief and unique clause, pertaining as it does to identification and traceability of purchased parts. These are not the same issues, so there are two requirements in this clause. Nevertheless, they are both related to the character that the purchased part contributes to the final product.

To begin, what does "where appropriate" mean? One obvious answer is that it is appropriate if spelled out in the contract. Beyond that, the general notion is that if a purchased part used in a manufactured product contributes a unique quality characteristic to that product, then it should be identified throughout the production process, from receipt of part to delivery of product. Traceability is closely related because in order to trace something, its identity must first be known. As Arnold (1994) points out, traceability has two parts, extending rearward to a point before receipt and forward to a point after delivery.

The Standard and Standard Business Practices

Rube Goldberg cartoons always had the same theme: a wondrous array of unrelated and indescribable parts that somehow all fit together, so that when a singular event triggered the system, a desired response resulted. For example, a smoker might drop a match that missed the ashtray, but that would ignite a piece of string placed nearby for the purpose, which would burn and release a book suspended from a ceiling, which would fall on a dog's tail, who would howl and leap, knocking over a bucket of water, which would douse the burning match. Rube Goldberg scenarios did not require logic, only imagination.

Manufacturing is done with a little more control. The parts that go into making a product or system are always spelled out with some sort of identification: so many pounds of a certain kind of steel, a certain color and brand of paint, and so on. The identification necessary to get the correct part is found in the company's material requirements planning system or similar logistical program. After all, how do you order parts if not by some nomenclature? Let's assume that this is the reasonable thing to do and not imagine that unassigned parts or random selection is involved in the process.

The ISO Standard Mystique

ISO standards assume nothing. Processes must be spelled out. Parts should be identified from receipt through delivery in drawings and specifications, for several reasons. The first is to verify that the appropriate part is available and being used throughout the production process. The second is to be able to identify quality failures by part or lot. Suppose, for example, that a lot of tuner circuits was found to have been poorly designed, yet installed on a set of 300 television sets, of 10,000 manufactured in a given period. Without being able to identify the lot, it might be necessary to recall all 10,000 sets rather than the suspected 300. The most common way to identify a part is through a part number listed on the job order, which then accompanies the part through the production process.

There is a tendency to believe one of two alternatives about ISO Standard requirements: (1) They impose an unnecessary paperwork burden; (2) they provide a magic bullet to quality. In fact, ISO standards provide neither. They are a convention, an agreement by signatories, that standard business practices themselves ensure quality. Therefore, those that seek ISO certification will find it an easy goal if they use accepted business principles and will find it difficult if they don't. The secret to ISO 9000 sustainability is the same as ordinary business sustainability.

Business Inventory Practices

Consider a large manufacturer of product containing, say, 100 parts that receives, on average, about 100 requests daily from customers to change delivery dates. That combination represents 10,000 parts schedule changes daily. This dynamic cannot be sustained on track except by a mature inventory-to-production process such as a material requirements planning (MRP) system. The core of the MRP system is a software program that at the very least identifies every part for every product, by scheduled need and production floor location.

Purchasing will handle the arrival of these parts, factoring in lead time and other considerations, but their timely distribution will be a combined effort of purchasing, production, and material parts management. The MRP can explode to arbitrary detail the parts requirements for a given product on a given day in a material status report. The parts are delivered to the production floor in some well-defined way, perhaps in a Kanban distribution. Each part will be identified in the job order by part number and quantity. Experienced workers will recognize the parts, but a good system will not depend on this experience. Procedures will call for comparison of job order data to the physical objects themselves.

It is difficult to imagine a large business operating in any other way. Small businesses may be able to use a much simpler MRP system, perhaps even a manual one, but the mapping of part to task via job order is always accompanied by a written part identity. The basis of an MRP system is provided by two kinds of files. The first, a bill-of-materials file, is a master list of all the parts for all subassemblies and products built by the manufacturer. The bill of materials file establishes the breadth of inventory. The second, an inventory file, provides information and status of all parts, subassemblies, and products on hand, and on order, with associated quantities and lead times.

An inventory system based on parts identity and schedule permits the evaluation of several dynamics in both logistics and production. You can index inventory turnover, the first step in improvement; you can determine the cost of inventory of different kinds: storage and in-process. You can track raw materials input to machine centers, finished parts input to assembly areas, and final product held for delivery. You can determine, and perhaps improve, lead times and queue times. The usual refrain is pertinent here. Measurement enables control; control enables improvement. The essential component of inventory and production dynamics is continuous parts identification, and can be integrated into a closed loop of inventory support as shown in Exhibit 19-1. This structure, suggested by Sheridan (1989), can lead to optimal parts control and, incidentally, to ISO certification.

Exhibit 19-1. Controlled inventory-production loop with parts identification.

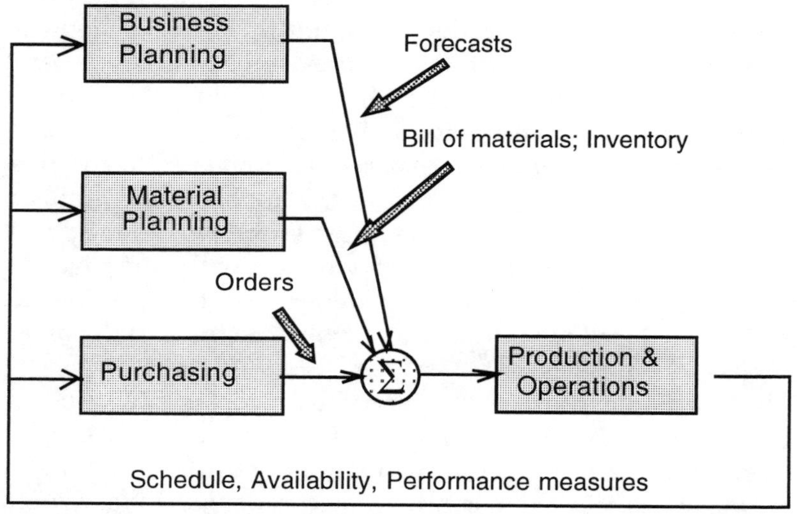

Note: Parts identification and quantity are listed in forecasts, orders, bills of material, and inventory.

Adapted with permission of *Industry Week*.

Traceability

The ability to trace a part from its supplier through to the consumer is clearly understandable in the case where the "part" is the active ingredient in a powerful drug. Traceability is often determined for us by government regulation or industry protocol. Even when there is no regulation or protocol requirement, a manufacturer might still want traceability if she envisions having to go back to the supplier, or forward to the customer, *after* delivery of a product. This can come about as a result of customer complaints or of court actions concerning a product, whose failure is identified as caused by a particular part.

We saw an example earlier in this chapter of a manufacturer of television sets who found it advantageous to maintain traceability because when it became necessary to track down bad tuners, the magnitude of the problem was reduced by a factor of 33. The traceability problem can be of enormous proportions in the automotive industry, where recalls may number in the tens of thousands. Even relatively small manufacturers can limit liability costs, though, if they can trace parts. For example, a manufacturer of mobile shelving systems may rely on several sources for drive motors. If one of the brands develops a systematic fault in the field, then the ability to identify which of several hundred products contain the drive motor can significantly reduce travel as well as replacement costs.

In the rules of ISO, traceability is a quality record factor. This means that a retention period must be assigned to the records of those products subject to this factor. Usually the law or industry custom will suggest a reasonable retention period of traceability. ISO auditors will not challenge this issue, but will look for a retention policy of some sort in the quality manual.

Summary

Sustainability in Clause 4.8 requires the company to regard the inventory and the production processes as a unit relative to parts identification. This integration is achieved by a structure similar to that of Exhibit 19-1. Policies will identify those parts whose identification must be traceable from receipt through delivery, and the company will define procedures to implement this accounting.

References

ANSI/ISO/ASQC. *Q9001-1994. Quality Systems—Model for Quality Assurance in Design, Development, Production, Installation, and Servicing*. Milwaukee: American Society for Quality Control, 1994.

Arnold, K. L. *The Manager's Guide to ISO 9000*. New York: Free Press, 1994.

Sheridan, J. N. "MRP II Still a Sound Strategy?" *Industry Week*, July 3, 1989, pp. 39–45.

Chapter 20

Clause 4.9: Process Control

Brief: Clause 4.9 requires the planning and implementation of production, installation, and service processes affecting quality. Furthermore, it requires that these processes be operated under controlled conditions.

This book is about process control, broadly interpreted. It is about how to organize a constructive process so that it can sustain its effectiveness in a changing environment—robustness, if you will. This is not a traditional view. Conventionally, the term *process control* is narrowly interpreted. It refers to the organization of productive processes. Clause 4.9 is about this conventional view. Its domain is the control of basic processes used to generate products. Up to now we have focused primarily on support processes because most of the requirements of ISO 9001 apply to them. Sooner or later we had to arrive at the control of production processes themselves, and Clause 4.9 is that time.

Productive Process Control

In a manufacturing environment a productive process is the human-machine system used to make the product. The product may be hardware or software, digital data or printed word. For example, in a software industry such as engineering or computer programming, the productive process is again the human-machine system used to make the product. The "product" may be the design of a bridge or a computer spreadsheet program; the creative process must be under control.

Process control is fundamental to manufacturing, but in modern industrial systems can be quite difficult to maintain. The structure of a controllable and capable process is shown in Exhibit 20-1. Notice that the customer is in the loop at all times, providing initial requirements for planning and production, and approval or rejection of deviations to specifications or schedule. There is also a mechanism for changing schedule, objectives, or specifications. This capability is in addition to being able to change the process itself. The ability to change some factor in the process or its environment in order to maintain dynamic equilibrium or to achieve improvement is what process control is all about.

In Chapter 2, we discussed the basic elements of control and identified them as responsibility, authority, and accountability. To review, control is achieved through responsibility by precisely defining and assigning the task and metric of the performance function. Control is achieved through authority by the provision of resources

Exhibit 20-1. Process control implemented in a capable structure.

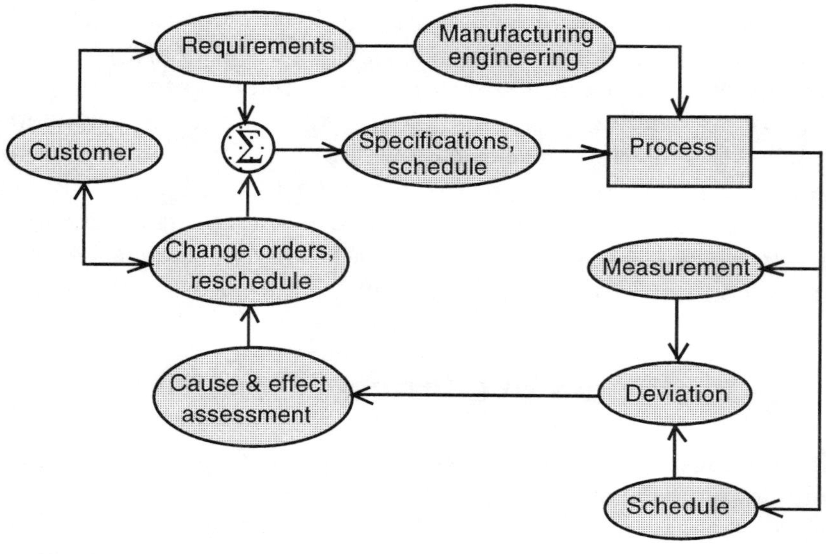

William A. Stimson, *The Robust Organization* (Burr Ridge, Ill.: Irwin, 1996). Reprinted with permission.

required to achieve the task. Control is achieved through accountability by imposing a penalty function for off-target performance.

The Standard requires that the processes used to make the product be identified, the production be planned, and the processes be operated under controlled conditions. Being able to identify the processes that make the product seems to be a trivial requirement. In general, it is—but not always. Some operations are rather complex, and important processes that affect quality of product do not touch it. For example, we may send a sheet of metal through an automatic punch press. Clearly, the punch press is one of the processes that must be controlled. But the process that generates the tape used to control the press is also part of the system. So is the equipment used to calibrate the machine positioning system.

We assume that all production is planned, but that is not always true, and even when it is true it may not be done well. Inadequate planning is manifested in the production process in many ways, but the two most common are bottlenecks and fire drill mode. Bottlenecks are often caused by inadequate strategic planning, which has not been able to align supply and demand. Fire drills are often caused by inadequate tactical planning, which is unprepared for perturbations in the day-to-day routine. There are other reasons for bottlenecks and fire drills, of course, but these events will catch the eye of an ISO auditor as honey attracts bears.

On the other hand, use of flowcharts, process layout diagrams, Gantt charts, PERT (program evaluation and review technique) diagrams, and materials requirements planning (MRP) programs indicates that the planning function is understood and utilized. Here again, the use of planning techniques separates serious companies from the bicycle shops, and allows the ISO registrar to quickly identify which is which.

Flowcharts and Such

We sometimes believe that we have an understanding about the general flow of a process until we try to draw it. Then we find inconsistencies, illogic, and just plain disconnects. At first we are tempted to blame our lack of drawing skills and to wish that we still had draftsmen around. But of course a draftsman merely formalizes whatever doodling we may offer; so if we offer garbage, then the final product will be well-drawn garbage. In the end, we admit that we really hadn't thought it out and now it is time to do so.

The discipline required to draw a process is well worth the effort because it will reveal the logic of the thing. We need some symbols to start with. Exhibit 20-2 shows some conventional symbols used in process flowcharting, functional layout drawing, and decision making. You can create your own if you choose, as long as there is consistency throughout the quality manual and supporting procedures.

Exhibit 20-3 shows how these symbols can be used to create a flowchart. This particular chart is a general one of a typical manufacturing plant with design capability—that is, an ISO 9001 candidate. The flowchart must reflect the organization as it really is. In this way you can compare what you have to what you thought you had. For example, the flowchart shows a feedback loop from contract review. If you cannot identify the persons and functions in your organization that complete that loop, then you have a control problem. And you may be sure that an ISO auditor is going to check this out.

Exhibit 20-4 shows a functional layout of a sheet metal process. Functional layouts appear to have a similarity to flowcharts in that they use some of the same symbols, but they have a

Exhibit 20-2. Some conventional symbols used in process flowcharting.

SYMBOL	MEANING
Rectangle	Operation; Task
Ellipse	Inventory; Storage
Circle	Test; Inspection
Triangle	Holding; Delay
Diamond	Decision
Arrow	Direction of flow

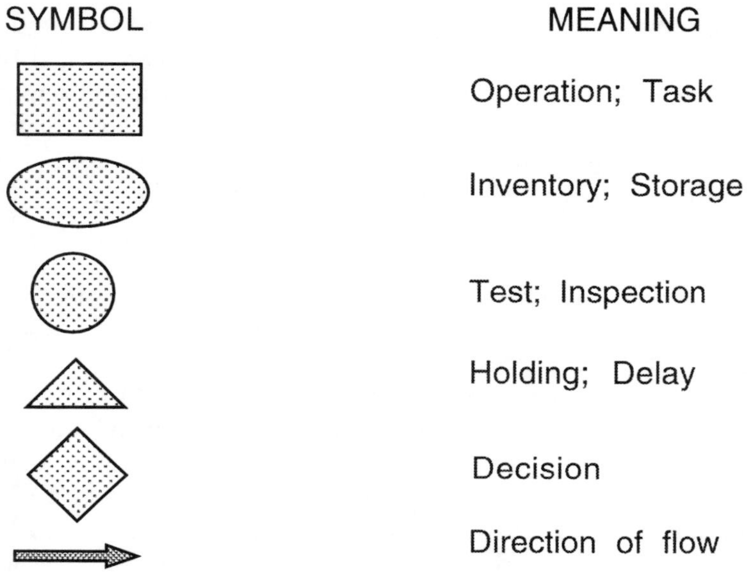

Exhibit 20-3. Flowchart of a generalized manufacturing operation.

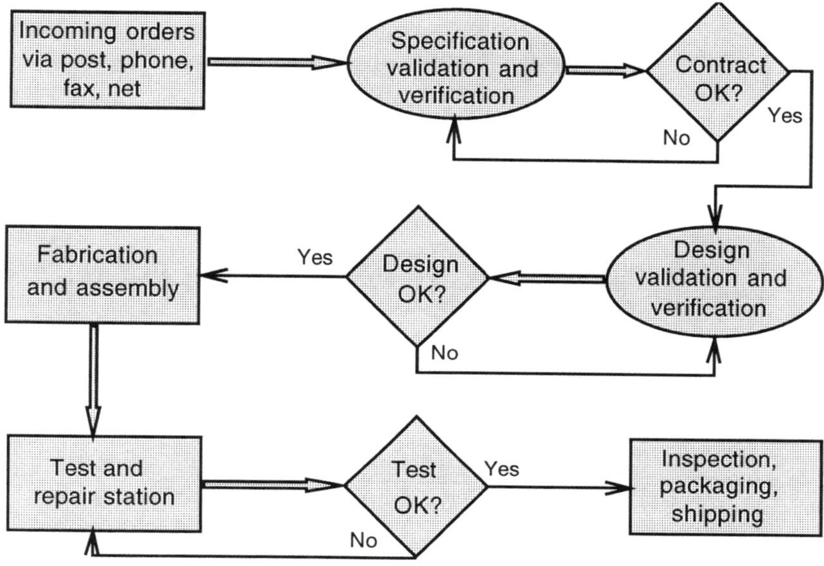

Exhibit 20-4. Drawing of the functional layout of a sheet metal process.

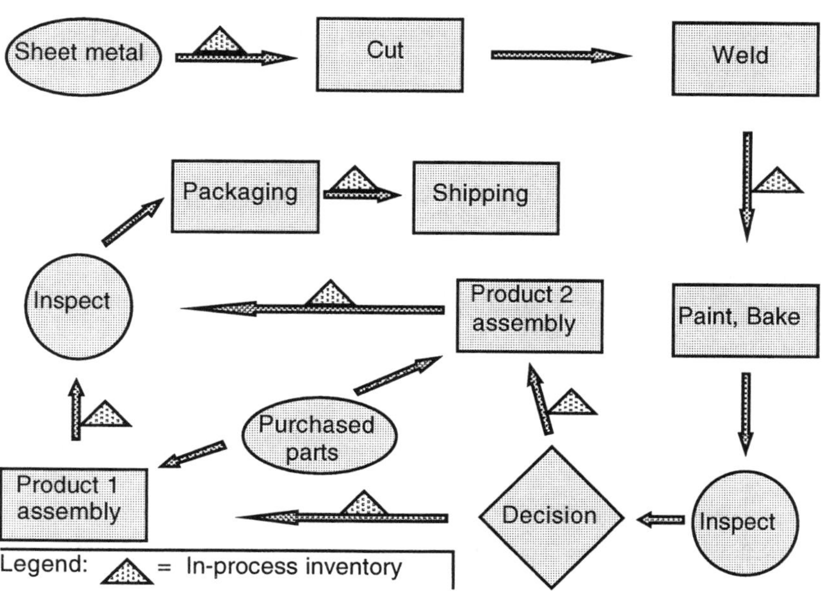

different purpose. The purpose of the flowchart is to reveal the logic of a process. The purpose of the functional layout is to reveal whether the physical plant agrees with the logic of the flowchart.

Flowcharts and functional layouts are useful in support of quality documents. They make it easy to see that you have what you think you have and that you are doing what you ought to be doing. They also help your IQA auditors (the good guys) to understand what it is that you should be doing, and they help ISO auditors. You might think at first blush that you do not really want to help the ISO auditors (the bad guys), but you really do. The more quickly an auditor can understand a process and verify that it is in agreement with documentation, the less digging around she will do. And that's good.

Controlled Conditions

Procedures

The first condition of control in the ISO hierarchy is that documented procedures define the production, installation, and servicing processes if their absence adversely affects quality. Such procedures should be part of the departmental log, and are easy to generate from flowcharts. Work instructions describe the next lower level of aggregation. The advantage to flowcharts as the basis of this documentation is that they describe the logical sequence of production and identify critical points in the process, factors to be measured, and the method of control. They suggest policy by revealing potential operational problems. In addition to flowcharts, departmental procedures, and work instructions, other documentation of process control are inspection reports, test results, standards and specifications, and the job order.

Equipment

Production processes require equipment to accomplish the task at hand. Clause 4.9 requires that this equipment be suitable to the task of production, installation, or service. Again, this requirement tends to separate the serious contenders from the hacks. Wiring people need wire strippers, not knives. Heavy items require forklifts, not strong backs. Precision welding requires welders, not burners, and so on. In general, most companies provide the appropriate tools for a job, so that this requirement is not a difficult one to achieve, and yet the wrong use of tools or the use of a wrong tool is more common than you might think. Such events naturally attract the eye of the ISO auditor. There is a strong interaction between proper equipment and proper training, and process control is where it all comes together.

The proper use of proper equipment includes the requirement for a suitable working environment, which usually means a safe, well-lighted area in which to work. Safety refers to the use of equipment, the area immediately surrounding the operational range of the equipment, and the discharge of waste, particularly toxic waste. Safety, then, is an important element in process control because so many injuries occur owing to misuse.

There is a certain amount of rote on the subject of safety in work areas or in areas of heavy equipment. Companies are often very strict in their enforcement of hard hats and safety glasses; I suppose that state and federal rules have had much to do with this. They are usually quite strict in toxic waste cleanup. But where you might see a great deal of laxity is in the area of nontoxic liquid waste, grease spills, refuse, and just plain trash. A visionary company will lead the industry in reducing accidents owing to things that shouldn't be there in the first place.

Process References

Process control includes the provision and use of standards and codes; quality plans or procedures; and technical, operational, and maintenance manuals. The first control condition, *procedures* refers to the generation of these documents. *References* means that they must be provided, available, and used.

This criterion is not as easily met as it ought to be. Many companies will have been in operation for a considerable period and documents associated with a particular process, function, or equipment sometimes get lost, become outdated, or are so dirty and ragged as to be unreadable. I know that most operations or production bosses already put in long days, but some regular, if infrequent, verification must be done to ensure that appropriate references are on-site.

Monitoring Parameters

Clause 4.9 requires that suitable process parameters and product characteristics be monitored and controlled. This requirement squares perfectly with the notion of system state that was discussed in Chapter 4. We understand that the state of a process describes what it is doing. In the language of ISO standards, a parameter is a variable whose value describes some characteristic or property of a system. For example, speed, thickness, position, rotation, and smoothness are all parameters. Some of the parameters describe the state of the process, and you can assume that your state variables are the "suitable process parameters" required by the clause. Other parameters describe the quality of the product or process—that is, whether it meets specifications. These parameters are called quality characteristics in Chapter 4, and we shall assume that our quality characteristics are the "suitable product characteristics" required by the clause.

Every process has characteristics or attributes that can be considered as variables. Some of them describe the state of the process. Some of them describe the quality of the product. Some of them can be seen, some not. Some are controllable, some not. You must consider these issues in deciding what parameters to monitor. In keeping with engineering, monitoring variables are those that can be seen; state variables are those that describe what the process is doing. The easiest quality to monitor is that in which the two sets are the same, but in general, they are not.

Let's look at a few examples. The first example, that of a punch press, was discussed briefly in Chapter 4, but let's take a closer look at its parameters this time, relative to Clause 4.9.

A Punch Press Process

Assume that you have a punch press with stops and a turret of punches. You place a sheet of metal against the stops of the machine and, when you are ready, start punching holes into the sheet at desired locations. Setup instructions tell you where to put the stops and what size punches to use. For simplicity, let's assume that many holes will be punched, but they will all be the same diameter. You can regard the setup instructions as *initial conditions* of the process, and can define the state of the punch press in some useful way. Since what the press is doing relies more on positioning of things than their motion, you can define its state with the following state variables:

X_1 = position of the sheet against the stops
X_2 = position of the stops with respect to the turret
X_3 = size of the punch

Next, you want to know how well the punch press is doing its job relative to the quality of the product. At this point, quality of product has to do with whether the holes are of the right diameter and in the right place. Therefore, the quality characteristics are:

Q_1 = size of the holes
Q_2 = position of the holes

You can easily establish the relationship of quality to process state in this example. In fact, the relationship is exact in one case: $Q_1 = X_3$. The size of the hole, a quality variable, will be determined by the size of the punch, a state variable. The relationship of Q_2 is more complicated, as it is a function of both X_1 and X_2. Thus, some understanding is required of how process state relates to quality because you cannot necessarily control the process by looking at the quality. You control a process by looking at its state, and you control quality by knowing the relationship of state variables to quality characteristics.

A Painting Process

Assume that you paint sheet metal by first preparing the metal in a "bonderizer" process, then mixing the paint for the right color, adding a catalyst of some sort, then painting and drying the metal panels. After thinking about it, you define the following state variables:

X_1 = bonderizer temperature
X_2 = thickness of phosphate coating
X_3 = paint mixture
X_4 = nozzle aperture setting
X_5 = oven temperature

You then define the quality of the paint job by its appearance and durability. The appearance is described by two characteristics: color and texture. Durability is exactly that: how long the paint will adhere and maintain its colors. Thus, quality characteristics are:

Q_1 = color
Q_2 = texture
Q_3 = durability

Q_1 is directly related to X_3. Q_2 is a function of X_3 and X_4. Q_3 is a function of all state variables, and moreover, cannot be ascertained by inspection.

Clearly, the relationship of state to quality can be complex. Every industry has its own decisions to make in deciding what parameters to measure to ensure quality. In choosing to monitor a parameter, pick one that makes sense. If a parameter can serve as both state variable and quality characteristic, it is the first choice. Second choice goes to the parameters that have an isomorphic relationship between state and quality. This means that for each value of state there is a single value of quality, and conversely.

Above all, don't measure something just because it is easy to measure. Choose parameters that can really measure the effectiveness of your control system. O'Guin (1995) provides some interesting examples of metrics used in process control of the aerospace and defense industries. A few of direct interest here are purchase order change rate, drawing change rate, repair and rework hours per 1000 direct labor hours, average dock-to-stock time, and ratio of shop order released on time to those scheduled.

Approval

There are two aspects to an effective approval process; the first is that there is one. The second is that it works. This may sound facetious, but it is not. Let's consider them one at a time. First, every process must be subject to an approval control. Isn't this a motherhood statement? Isn't there usually an approval process? Yes, usually, but not always. I remember attending a briefing on the impending sea trials of a surface ship whose overhaul was nearing completion. Upon asking two people as to which of them was going to write the sea trials agenda, each pointed his finger at the other. The way that you ensure an approval governance is by always assigning authority, responsibility, and accountability to each process.

The second concern is whether the approval process works in a timely way. Getting approval for engineering change requests (ECRs) is a good example of the subject. In many plants, an ECR is initiated by a technician recognizing a problem, perhaps in the production process. It must be logged, checked by document control for revision commentary and proper form, passed through a periodic quality review process, finally approved, then the path retraced back to the person wanting the change. Although this narration sounds bureaucratic, all of the steps are necessary for valid document control. The problem is the time it takes. Many companies are solving this problem with automated workflow management systems such as that described by Taninecz (1995). These computerized systems provide terminals at various stations on the floor so that personnel can gain quick access to document control processes such as an ECR. At least the transit time is greatly reduced and the document control problem eased. The approval delay time is thus reduced to its necessary and sufficient components: quality and engineering review.

Criteria for Workmanship

A correctly designed and completed job order represents the standard of performance. It contains the specifications required to do the job. Samples may be provided to aid in the specification. For example, a dye shop may attach a sample of the desired color to the job order as it proceeds to the dye mixing area. In addition, there might be standards and qualifications required—for example, welding or soldering certification, typing speed, hygiene requirements, fire watches at welding sites.

Maintenance

This control condition can be met with a maintenance program aimed at grooming the equipment. Regular and routine preventive maintenance and alignment of equipment adds to its reliability. The program would include maintenance schedules and describe the nature and extent of the periodic cleaning, lubricating, alignment, and other grooming concerns.

Who does the maintenance of productive equipment? Quite often this task is done by a maintenance force of personnel trained specifically to align and groom the equipment, rather than just to operate it. However, there are notable exceptions and Turbide (1995) describes one of them at the Yamato plant in Japan, makers of motorcycle control cables. Employees are trained and scheduled to maintain their own equipment, with the idea that this encourages ownership, pride in craftsmanship, and responsibility. The company keeps a maintenance force for training and backup purposes. Will this notion work as a general strategy? It must depend on the individual company, its workforce, and the complexity of its equipment. Routine maintenance improves reliability, but it is also true that machines begin to give signs of problems and an experienced cadre of maintenance persons would be better at predicting failure before it occurs.

Maintenance periods, of course, will be integrated with operations because they usually represent down time. In keeping with the notion of measuring things, a good maintenance program improves reliability and an optimum integration with operations improves availability. Reliability and availability are important indices of effectiveness in process control.

Shift Work

All of the issues we have discussed about process control are the concerns of management. On the day shift, at least, they will get the managerial attention and leadership that they require. But Penkata (1995) points out that managers do not really manage late-shift operations. This job is left to the floor supervisors. Multishift operations do not usually enjoy an equal distribution of information, training, and resources.

Some industries that conduct multishift operations make no pretense of treating each shift the same. Hospitals are a good example. The various shifts in a hospital have somewhat different objectives, as in late-night periods the nature of treatment swings from active to passive activities. Even in manufacturing, a company may not commit management to late shifts, but instead assign certain tasks to these periods that are oriented to tactical rather than strategic importance. Maintenance of equipment is often scheduled for late-night shifts. Nevertheless, if production takes place on a late shift, then there should be a proportional output relative to the day shift.

Apart from the fact that an IQA team or ISO audit team will audit late-shift operations, it is good business practice to ensure an even distribution of leadership and resources on all shifts. Even a cursory MOE will show if the shift efficiencies are similar. This comparison will establish the quality of the overall process control system.

Summary

Sustainability in Clause 4.9 requires a process control system that is structured similarly to that shown in Exhibit 20–1. The two important features of this structure are flexibility and customer overview. Flexibility means that the process can adapt quickly to changes in objectives, process, or product. The "customer" refers to both internal customers and external customers. Clearly, the final paying customer should have overview, but in process control the internal customer sets the pace and the baseline quality. The relationship between process state and product quality characteristics are identified and monitored for stability, capability, and improvability.

References

ANSI/ISO/ASQC. *Q9001-1994. Quality Systems—Model for Quality Assurance in Design, Development, Production, Installation, and Servicing*. Milwaukee: American Society for Quality Control, 1994.

O'Guin, Michael. "Aerospace and Defense Contractors Learn How to Make Their Businesses Soar." *Quality Progress*, June 1995, pp. 35–42.

Penkata, Don. "It's 10 pm: Do You Know Where Your Quality Program Is?" *Quality Progress*, February 1995, pp. 91–93.

Taninecz, George. "A Flow to the Floor First?" *Industry Week*, July 3, 1995, p. 53.

Turbide, D. A. "Japan's New Advantage: Total Productive Maintenance." *Quality Progress*, March 1995, pp. 121–123.

Chapter 21

Clause 4.10: Inspection and Testing

Brief: Clause 4.10 requires that inspection and testing activities be conducted in order to verify adherence to specifications. Appropriate records will be maintained of the results of these activities.

Quality of product is usually verified through a system of inspection and testing (I&T). An I&T system is often quite complex in its entirety. To begin with, it includes the test equipment necessary to the task. Following the inspection or test, either the quality characteristics are acceptable or they are not, so that a subsystem of dealing with the nonconformances is included in the overall I&T system. If there are nonconforming parts, their status must be declared in some way, and corrective procedures will be needed. These different components of the total I&T operation are governed by different clauses of the ISO 9001 requirements: Clauses 4.10 through 4.14. Respectively, Clause 4.10 deals with the I&T process itself; Clause 4.11 deals with the control of measuring equipment used to accomplish the inspections or the testing; Clause 4.12 concerns the status of product having been inspected or tested; Clause 4.13 concerns control of nonconforming product, and Clause 4.14 concerns corrective and preventive actions.

All of this is by way of saying that Clauses 4.10 through 4.14 are very closely related. Each represents a subprocess, if you will, of a total I&T operation. ISO standards treat each of the subprocesses separately, but an effective I&T system will integrate them all, perhaps along the lines shown in Exhibit 21-1. For example, owing to an urgent need on the production line for a purchased part, receipt inspection may be waived. If so, the waiver must be recorded and the part traceable. Although the concern here is with Clause 4.10, it does not stand by itself. As I go through the details of this clause, bear in mind that the objective is sustainability and that the system we are really talking about is the complex one in the exhibit. A sustainable inspection and test process is an integration of checks and balances.

Acceptance Sampling

Vince Lombardi, the legendary coach of the Greenbay Packers professional football team, used to say that football was simply a game of blocking and tackling. That seems a marvel of understatement when you think of the complexity of the modern game, but although stark, it is nevertheless true. In a similar

Exhibit 21-1. Schematic of the overall inspection and test process.

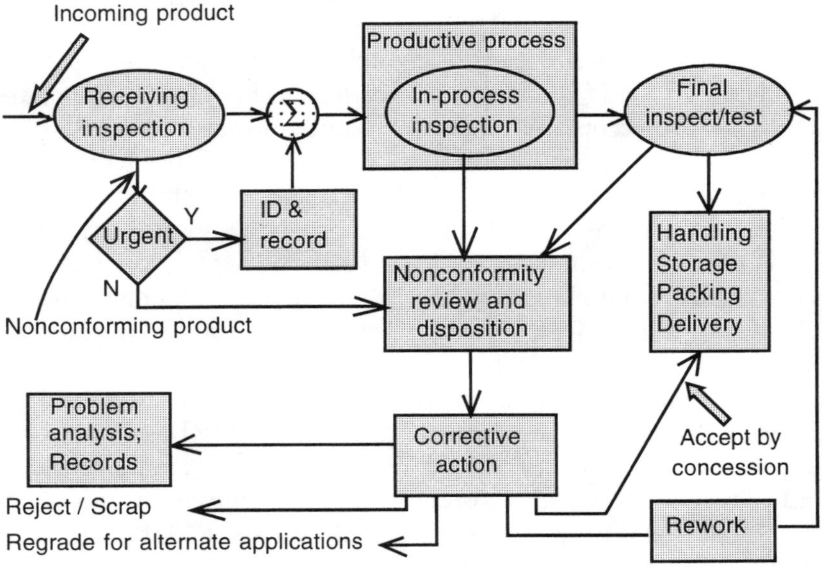

William A. Stimson, *The Robust Organization* (Burr Ridge, Ill.: Irwin, 1996). Reprinted with permission.

vein, manufacturing is simply a process that makes one thing from something else.

The quality of the product depends on the quality of the production process *and* the quality of parts from which the product is made. Error is possible in both places. It is possible to receive parts of inferior quality. Having selected only good parts, it is then possible to manufacture inferior quality. A manufacturer must reduce the occurrence of both.

The Logic of Sampling

One way to do that is to maintain an inspection system that will verify the quality of every single incoming part and every single outgoing product. This is called 100 percent inspection. The general view of 100 percent inspection in industry is that it is too expensive. The general view among quality experts is that it is too ineffective. Inspectors are humans and they are subject to fatigue, boredom, inattention, and variation in judgment.

Another way to reduce the occurrence of poor quality is by using a statistical technique called acceptance sampling. Acceptance sampling is performed on incoming parts, and it is performed on outgoing product. The method is quite simple in principle. You have a group of items, be they product or parts, that is called a lot. Rather than inspect the entire collection, you inspect a sample from the lot, and according to some rule you then decide whether to accept or reject the lot. The basis of this decision lies in the assumption that the distribution of nonconformances in the sample is the same as the distribution of nonconformances in the lot. Therefore, knowing the number of units in the lot, number of units in the sample, and number of nonconformances in the sample, you can estimate the number of nonconformances in the lot.

It is important to realize that the estimate need not be zero. Few manufacturers would be willing to reject an entire lot because it may or may not contain a few nonconforming items. Therefore, the manufacturer specifies an acceptance number: the number of nonconforming items that will be acceptable in a sample. The acceptance number is a fundamental element in the company's quality control policy. It is the basis of decisions about whether the lot should be accepted, rejected, or screened. Screening means that the entire lot will be inspected.

This decision implies risk. It is possible that a sample will exceed the acceptance number even though the lot has a lower proportion of nonconformances. Thus the lot is rejected and the manufacturer incurs unnecessary cost. The risk of rejecting a good lot is called *producer's risk*. It is also possible that the sample will contain fewer nonconformances than the acceptance number even though the lot has a higher proportion of them. The risk of delivering a bad lot is called *consumer's risk* because the consumer will buy from this lot.

The Illogic of Sampling

Acceptance sampling is as common as apple pie in American industry. It is also extremely controversial. Statisticians have shown that if a process is not stable, then the distribution of nonconformances is unknown. Conversely, if a process is in statistical control, then the distribution of nonconformances in the sample is independent of the distribution in the remainder of the lot, so that inference about a lot based upon a sample is invalid.

Beyond the mathematical issues, Deming (1986) condemns the idea of acceptance sampling because it guarantees the delivery of bad product. Ryan (1989) recommends putting in quality improvement methods and getting rid of acceptance sampling altogether. On the other hand, Grant and Leavenworth (1988) devote a significant part of their book to acceptance sampling methods, for obvious reasons—they are used widely and extensively.

I can bring in dozens of arguments for and against acceptance sampling and fill up a bibliography, but Sower et al. (1993) summarize the problem very well. According to the authors, there are two key issues: (1) Does the customer require acceptance sampling? (2) Is the process in statistical control? The U.S. government provides a good example of the first issue. It often requires acceptance sampling to be used by its contractors, and it is used at both ends of the production process, receiving parts and final product output. The government is a massive buyer and its will establishes policy. Other customers may prefer a policy of acceptance sampling too, particularly if they themselves are manufacturers depending upon high quality of incoming parts. The basic strategy in acceptance sampling of incoming parts is, if the rule calls for rejection, to return the entire lot to the subcontractor. This definitely gets their attention.

The second issue is a little more difficult to appreciate because we are committed to the idea of sustainability. Our processes will be stable, capable, and improvable, amen. Therefore, the notion that acceptance sampling may be a valid method of quality control for unstable processes is irrelevant, we think.

It is time for pragmatism. The paper by Sower et al. presents several realistic scenarios in which an ISO-certified, sustainable operation might use acceptance sampling, and you should consider them:

1. If a subcontractor has not achieved statistical control, then acceptance sampling methods can be used to verify the quality of incoming parts until such time as the subcontractor is able to demonstrate stability.
2. If a process shifts out of statistical control, then acceptance sampling can be used as a temporary means of verifying quality of final product. There are a number of reasons why a process in control may shift for some appreciable period, among them a change in operators or in equipment.
3. Acceptance sampling will definitely be used to verify quality if the customer requires it.

Receipt Inspection and Testing

Inspection and testing activities are conducted at general stages of a production process: receiving, in-process, and final. We are concerned here with the first activity in this sequence—receiving. Incoming material may not be used in production processes until its conformance to specifications has been verified. This is usually achieved through inspection. We have just discussed acceptance sampling, and in Chapter 8 we discussed various quality control procedures that might be conducted at the subcontractor facility. In other words, you might require the subcontractor to verify the quality of its own product because that is what you pay him for. At this point you can assume that some appropriate statistical technique will be adopted, on- or off-site, by the subcontractor or performer, to verify the quality of incoming parts. This process of receipt inspection will, of course, be described in an associated procedure.

If the subcontractor is providing quality control of the incoming product, then there must be recorded evidence in the form of inspection results or statistical data from the final inspection conducted at the subcontractor facility. These data need to accompany the parts, and if they are separated—say, the parts go to storage and the confirming data to the QA office—then there needs to be a procedure that describes this policy.

Quarantine

Incoming parts must arrive somewhere; usually there is a particular area within the plant that is designated for incoming inventory hold. The problem is that this location may not be clearly isolated. What seems clear to the person logging in the material may not be clear to someone who did not see it arrive. It is important to ensure that the material not be integrated into production prior to its being inspected and approved for use. Therefore, some means of tagging or marking will serve to indicate whether the material has been inspected or not, and of having passed inspection or not.

Not only should incoming material be tagged as such, but quarantine areas should be established to keep it in. Quarantine is needed for that material not yet inspected, and rejection areas identified for unacceptable product. Auditors sometimes find quarantined material kept in stock areas, adjacent to material that is customarily thought of as ready for use. The delineation of quarantine areas, by however simple a method, eliminates this ambiguity.

Waiving Receipt Inspection

In some cases of urgency, the purchased product may be needed immediately and the receipt inspection therefore waived. This practice is permissible in the ISO organization, providing that the part is identified and recorded as having been waived of inspection, and there exists a procedure describing the conditions of waiver and the policy behind it. The reason for identifying and recording this event is to be able to recall the final product and replace the culpable part in the event that a later nonconformance is discovered.

In-Process Inspection and Testing

In-process inspections should be performed by the persons who did the value-added activity that is being inspected, because each person is responsible for her own quality control. Testing is more complicated, and dedicated test personnel might be required, particularly at the final stage, where the product is likely to have system characteristics. As with receipt inspections, you must maintain procedures and records for in-process inspections and testing. Product must be held until these I&T activities have been completed, except under waiver rules previously discussed.

Exhibit 21-2 depicts a typical inspection and test arrangement for a production process organized as a workstation

Exhibit 21-2. Inspection and testing integrated into a workstation sequence.

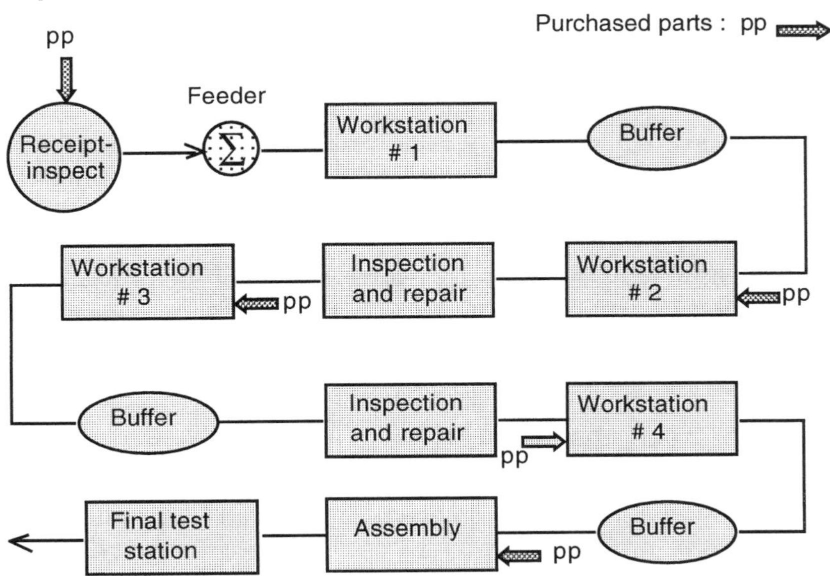

sequence. A workstation is a place and time in which an activity occurs. Examples of relevant activities are work, inspection, measurement, and decision. The activities are grouped into functional subsystems, each displayed as a block in the exhibit. The location of inspection and repair stations and test points is only partly dictated by the technical process itself. If there is statistical dependence between the workstations, then the effects of serial dependence decrease the process reliability, so that this, too, should be a consideration in the location of inspection points.

Although Exhibit 21-2 depicts an assembly line, it must be viewed in a completely general sense. The flow of activity shown in the exhibit can be hardware production, of course, but it can also be the flow of services or even of software production. A software development process would be quite similar. In this case, the inspections would include reviews and walk-through. Tests would include the structure of the computer program modules as well as their functional or operational use. As with hardware, software inspections are sensitive to workstation location. We defined a workstation as a place and time activity, so that location can refer to a translation of either time or place. This flexibility of view is appropriate to software development. Kennett (1994) presents several metrics for software inspection that relate to when in the life cycle particular errors are found, where in the process they were created, and where they were detected.

Exhibit 21-2 could also represent a service industry in which a sequence of services is provided. The workstations would then be servers, and people rather than hardware would be in queue. Hospitals, department stores, and airports are examples of multiservice activities that might be similarly modeled. Exhibit 21-2 is simplified for clarity. Each inspection and test station should be organized to function as shown earlier, in Exhibit 21-1.

Final Inspection and Testing

There is almost always a requirement for final verification and validation of product. In modern quality theory, each person is responsible for the quality of his own work, and as the product proceeds from station to station, the quality control is continuous, assuming a process with integrity. Then do you always need a final test activity? Perhaps not always, but more often than you might think. The final product often takes on characteristics of its own that are arrived at synergistically. The sum total of quality is simply greater than its parts. This is clearly true in the building of complex structures such as electronic systems, but it can be true even of relatively simple products.

The Stamp of Approval

Liberty Fabrics of Gordonsville, Virginia, offers a good example of this notion. Liberty manufactures Raschel lace and elastic fabrics; the Gordonsville plant is its dyeing and finishing facility. Various intermediate processes within the plant maintain quality control procedures in the modern sense; each worker is self-responsible. Nevertheless, the finished product proceeds to Quality Assurance for final tests. The reason is that a piece of fabric has characteristics of stretch and recover, curl, color fastness, and shrinkage that cannot be evaluated during the activities of fabrication, dyeing, and finishing. Liberty's final test, conducted by objective QA personnel, provides the stamp of approval for the quality that the customer will see.

Final I&T requires the same general pattern of activity as does receipt and in-process I&T. This will be (1) the policy described in the quality manual, (2) a departmental procedure describing the rules of I&T, (3) work instructions describing the detail of the I&T process, and (4) a means of barring uninspected or nonconforming product from continuation in the productive process. In the case of final inspection, this means that a process of tagging or isolation is needed to prevent the product from being delivered to the customer until it has passed the final I&T.

Objectivity

It is fairly easy to determine whether to conduct a final acceptance test of a product before delivering it to the customer. It is not so easy to determine who should do it. Final I&T is often conducted by quality assurance specialists independent of the production process. Although this way of doing business is common, it is not mandatory. ISO 9000 standards do not require a division of responsibility between production and final test, only that a policy and procedure governing the strategy be defined. Companies are free to use a strategy of individual quality control all the way through to delivery, and many of them do.

There are two schools of thought on the matter of final test authority. The first notion is division of responsibility. Production fabricates the product, and Quality Assurance conducts acceptance testing. The justification behind this division is to gain objectivity. Presumably, those who did not make the product have no sense of ownership and can look at the job impartially. The second notion is continuity of responsibility. Production is responsible all the way through, from receipt inspection to delivery. The justification behind this strategy is accountability. People who have pride in what they do want to be held accountable for their work.

Most people believe that they are reasonably objective in their judgments. If you take away a responsibility from someone because you want to give it to someone you think more objective, you have offended that person. Where is the course of wisdom? The Bible (Matthew 6:24) tells us that no one can serve two masters. We usually take *master* literally, but it can apply equally well to motivation. Objectivity is often decided by motivations. The job of a test director is to conduct a test. The job of a production boss is to meet a production schedule. When you assign final test responsibility to production, you have given the production boss two masters.

If the final product has quality characteristics whose goodness has not or cannot be determined during the production process, then a final test is required for sustainability. The decisions about that quality should be made objectively.

Inspection and Test Records

The company must be able to provide evidence of the integrity of its inspection and test program. A test program has integrity if it is comprehensive, continuous, and complete. A comprehensive I&T program ensures that all of the specifications have been included in the program. A continuous I&T program ensures that inspections and test overlap the specifications so that no characteristic, static or dynamic, is omitted. A complete I&T program concludes all of the scheduled inspections and test, including the data, evaluations, and reports.

Records contribute to process control because they represent corporate memory of the dynamics of quality and reliability. Often, the raw data end up in a vault. This may be a necessary evil, but before the data go into the vault, quality, reliability, and maintainability analysis should be performed, not only to determine present status but also to indicate trends, and equipment and process life cycles. You need to bear in mind why you make measurements in the first place. Analytical results should be graphic and automated, available at a moment's notice.

Records of inspection and testing should be maintained for other reasons also. I mentioned inspection of incoming product. Suppose that a company has a policy of acceptance sampling but in some cases finds it necessary to waive inspection, perhaps for urgent production purposes. If incoming product is released on a waiver, it must be identified and recorded in order to permit immediate recall in the event of nonconformance. This is certainly true of chemical and pharmaceutical processes, but is a good idea in any industry.

Finally, I&T status of product should be identified with tags or labels, records, or test software. Records demonstrate that only a product that has passed the required inspections and tests is used in installation or is delivered to the customer. In every process, there should be quality procedures that define and describe the company inspection and test requirements. Procedures "on station" ensure operator consistency, a necessary element in control and robustness.

Summary

Sustainability in Clause 4.10 requires a cohesive, integrated system of inspection and testing, as indicated in Exhibit 21-1. Every process has policies, procedures, and documentation, including quality status, and employs methodologies that are comprehensive, continuous, and complete.

References

Deming, W. E. *Out of the Crisis*. Cambridge: Center for Advanced Engineering Study, Massachusetts Institute of Technology, 1986.

Grant, E. L., and R. S. Leavenworth. *Statistical Quality Control*. New York: McGraw-Hill, 1988.

Kennett, R. S. "Assessing Software Development and Inspection Processes." *Quality Progress*, October 1994, pp. 109–112.

Ryan, T. P. *Statistical Methods for Quality Improvement*. New York: Wiley, 1989.

Sower, V. E., J. Motwani, and M. J. Savoie. "Are Acceptance Sampling and SPC Complementary or Incompatible?" *Quality Progress*, September 1993, pp. 85–89.

Chapter 22

Clause 4.12: Inspection and Test Status

Brief: Clause 4.12 requires that the status of a product be identified relative to its conformance to inspection and test criteria. The identification process, defined in appropriate procedures, will be maintained throughout the production and postproduction processes to ensure that only an acceptable product is delivered.

Clause 4.12 is among the brief ones and its intent is easily understood. There should be no ambiguity about the quality of a product delivered to the customer. You build processes that will establish and maintain the quality of manufactured product. This basis is necessary but not sufficient. Material goes through an evolutionary process on its way to becoming product. During this development its quality is in transition. To preclude the accidental or mistaken delivery of a nonconforming product, there must be procedures that declare its status throughout the production process. The status is usually determined by inspection, so that there are three categories:

1. Uninspected
2. Inspected and rejected
3. Inspected and accepted

It seems at first blush that Clause 4.12 is easy to do. In the general case it is. But in the case where the product may contain complex or fragile parts, then it is easier said than done. If the product is a system composed of subsystems, each with its own modes of operation, such as a television set, then its status is very likely to be dynamic and safeguard procedures are especially important. In the last chapter we discussed how to isolate incoming parts according to their inspection status, and these common-sense procedures, while valid throughout the production process, have more details to consider. Where the status may get blurred is in repair areas. The reason for this is physical displacement of the units from the production line. Exhibit 22-1 gives some indication of the displacement problem.

The Dynamics of I&T Status

To simplify things, a unit is simply a product in some stage of its development. Assume a workstation scenario similar to the one shown in Exhibit 21-2 of the last chapter. Let there be a number of value-added activities with inspection stations here and there in the sequence. Exhibit 22-1 is a sort of blowup of a workstation sequence, showing the *n*th workstation, followed

Exhibit 22-1. The disposition of inspection status in the production cycle.

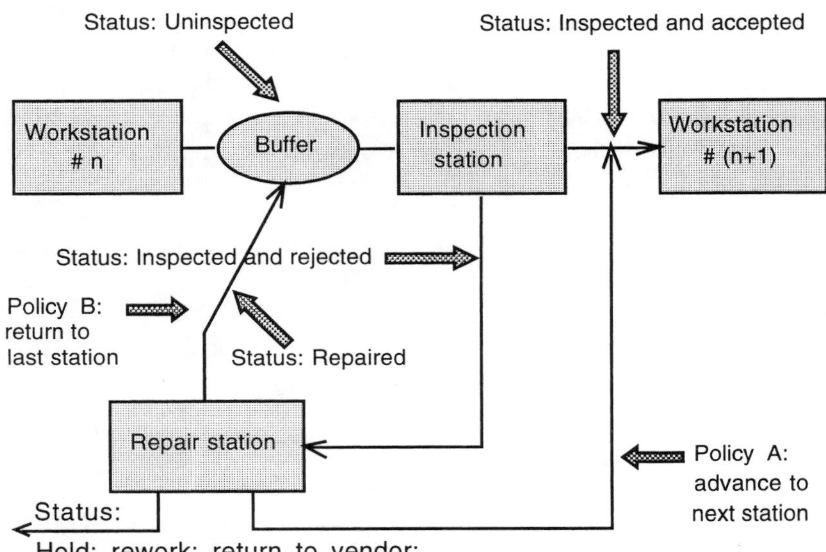

by a buffer and an inspection station, followed by the (n +1)th workstation. The status of the units in the buffer is clear and need not be declared because they are in a well-defined sequence. (This example differs significantly from the example discussed in receipt inspection, where incoming parts may be lying around awaiting inspection and their status not clear at all unless declared.)

As long as a unit stays on-line its status is known simply by its position in the sequence. A unit passing inspection goes on to workstation number (n+1) with a different status, which is again clear. Now suppose that a unit fails inspection. Then it is taken off-line and sent to repair. Because it is off-line, its position no longer indicates its status, so the status must be declared. The declaration can be in the form of a tag or label firmly attached.

A unit in the repair area is either in repair, awaiting repair, or in hold waiting for a part. During this time its status continues to be "inspected and rejected," and it should retain the label saying so. After it is repaired, the unit will move back to the production line according to one of two policies. The policies are formed based on what is done to the unit while in repair.

Some repair stations have the capability to perform the exact test, or a similar one, that was performed at the inspection station. Having been repaired and having passed a similar test, the unit may advance to the next workstation in accordance with Policy A. In this case, the unit receives an "inspected and accepted" status and rejoins the production line as shown in the exhibit.

Some repair stations have no test capability, or have a test different in kind from that conducted at the inspection station. For example, the inspection station may conduct an operational or "light off" test on a unit coming from the nth workstation, whereas the repair station may be set up to conduct a continuity check only of the repaired unit. In this case, the unit may be returned to the buffer in accordance with Policy B. Hence the repaired unit receives the status of "uninspected" and rejoins the production line as shown in the exhibit.

Policy

ISO 9000 standards never dictate policy, although they require the company to establish its own. The policies of the previous example are equally acceptable to ISO certification, so long as they are defined in the quality manual. But our intention is to go beyond ISO 9000. Within the context of sustainability, Policies A and B are not at all equally acceptable. Policy A recognizes the following sequence as logical: detect nonconformance in a unit; repair nonconformance; advance unit to the next stage. But there is a logical non sequitur in this train—the assumption that the repair job has put the unit in condition for the next stage. Depending on the nature of the unit, there are two possible alternatives that render this argument invalid: The repair job did not really remove the nonconformance; or there are two nonconformances in the unit, with one masking the other. The second alternative is not uncommon in electronic units, for example.

Policy A can be made logical if the repair station has the capability to conduct the exact test or inspection of the unit as does the inspection station. The repair station can then test the state and condition of the unit, verify that the identified nonconformance is eliminated and that no second is masked, and approve the unit for advancement. If the repair station does not have this capability, then the unit is properly returned to the buffer for reinspection.

Declaration

It is reasonable and economical to accept the position (location) of a unit on the production line as prima facie evidence of its condition. From feeder station to final assembly, the unit is in development. Prior to an inspection station, it has the status of "uninspected" by that station. Following an inspection station the unit has a status of "inspected and rejected" or of "inspected and accepted." The status is assumed and no declaration is necessary.

However, if the unit is taken off-line at any time in its development cycle, its status must be declared. The categories can be identified by either some sort of printed record or area placement. Printed records can be color-coded tags or labels, or a check-off sheet. In any case, the printed indicator must be attached to the product in such a manner that it is not easily separated. Some companies use areas on the factory floor as quarantine or reject areas. However, fixed areas can be wasteful if not fully utilized, and undefined areas can lead to confusion.

The best arrangement is a combination of printed attachment and area placement. The area can be marked off by rope to fit the required space. Just a few products in the uninspected or rejected categories mean that only a small space of the production area is needed, making the unused space available for other purposes. A large number of products in these categories would require more space for a finite period of time, meaning that production heads would factor in this extra lost space in their process flow plans. The rope, supplemented by a sign saying "Rejects" or "Quarantine" identify the area where a product is not to be used in the production process. Then each product within the isolation area is likewise tagged or labeled, providing a redundant and fail-safe system of I&T status.

Summary

Sustainability in Clause 4.12 requires a vigorous distinction of inspection and test status, in both declaration and disposition. There must be no ambiguity in regard to a part having undergone an inspection or test. Its status must be securely identified and its movement controlled according to policies that direct its disposition. Exhibit 22-1 shows an appropriate discipline. The policies of reinsertion of repaired product into the production line must reflect test integrity.

References

ANSI/ISO/ASQC. *Q9001-1994. Quality Systems—Model for Quality Assurance in Design, Development, Production, Installation, and Servicing*. Milwaukee: American Society for Quality Control, 1994.

Stimson, W. A. "Principles of Systems Testing." *Naval Engineers Journal*, November 1988, pp. 48–58.

Chapter 23

Clause 4.13: Control of Nonconforming Product

Brief: Clause 4.13 requires a system that will control product that fails to meet specifications, preclude unintended use, and define product disposition.

Clause 4.13 of the Standard is closely related to Clause *4.10: Inspection and Testing*. In fact, all the clauses from 4.10 through 4.14 are related in the sense that they have to do with testing work that has been completed and about which a decision must be made as a result of the test. It would seem that these clauses belong under the purview of operations as they are production activities. For the most part, this is true. However, we arguably assigned Clause 4.14 to the purview of management, for the reasons stated in Chapter 5. Clause 4.13, too, involves issues of economic policy that must be established by executive management. The decision about what to do with nonconforming product affects profit and loss. Nevertheless, once the categories of nonconforming product are defined, as applied to a given company, and the policies established, then Clause 4.13 is governed and implemented entirely on the production floor. Therefore, this clause belongs, appropriately, in the purview of operations.

As Exhibit 23-1 shows, a company can do various things with its nonconforming product: rework or scrap, regrade, or

Exhibit 23-1. Disposition of nonconforming product.

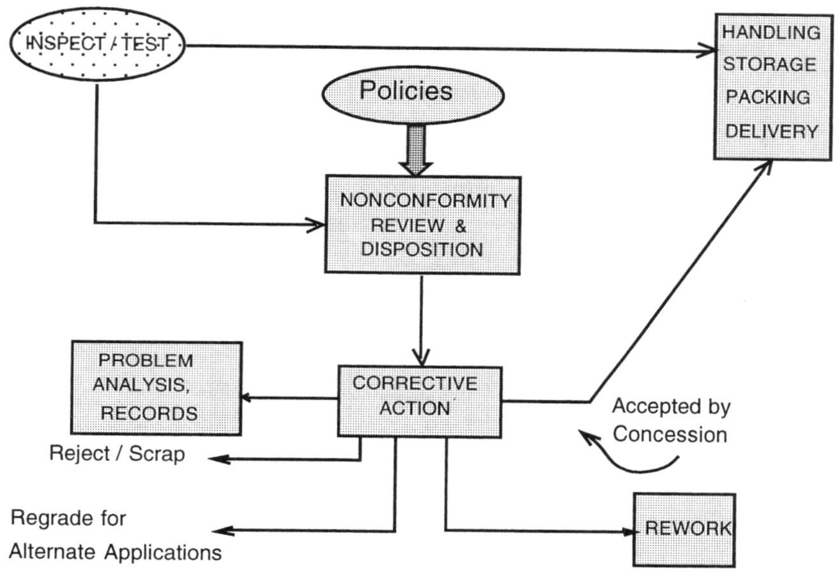

provide to the customer on a concession basis. (The customer agrees to accept the product as is.)

ISO 9000 does not presume to force economic decisions upon management; the marketplace will decide the wisdom of their choices. But the Standard does require that nonconforming product be quickly identified, segregated and prevented from unintended use, classified, documented, and disposed of accordingly. Moreover, this process must be described in a procedure. The procedure will state, as accurately as possible, the criteria for scrap, rework, regrade, or concession. It will describe the identification and segregation process. None of this need be wordy. A procedure for nonconforming product can be written on a single page.

As with the other clauses of the ISO requirements, Clause 4.13 does not specify how it should be implemented. Yet it is better than most because it forces a management review of nonconforming product, the outcome of which should be a set of policies in regard to the matter. It is still possible to make bad policy, but at least the loop is closed. Closed loops enable stability, capability, and improvability.

Nonconformity Review

There are several good practices concerning the occasion of nonconformance. The first is to detect the nonconformance. The second is to decide what to do with the nonconforming product. The third is to investigate the cause of the nonconformance and take some counter action. These steps are nothing more than bottom-up and top-down approaches to the matter. Deciding what to do about the defective product is called disposition. Deciding what action to take to counter nonconformance on the system level is what Clause *4.14: Preventive and Corrective Actions* is all about. Thus, nonconformity review is the activity that relates Clauses 4.13 and 4.14.

It might seem that once a defect is found the inspector has only to label the unit as nonconforming product, then take it out of the production line and dispose of it according to policy. All this is necessary but not sufficient because it limits assessment to the specific unit, time, and place of defect. A policy of resolving every nonconformance at the site of detection may well preclude the recognition of systemic problems.

Nonconformity review should begin simply, with an ad hoc meeting of those on the production floor most closely associated with the defective product. This bottom-up approach provides the technical expertise that is needed to make a first-cut determination of whether the cause is common or assignable, systematic or random. The occurrence and identity of a defect and its tactical assessment of cause should be filed as a defective material report, which will be the first documentation of the review process.

The issues raised by Clause 4.13 can become ambiguous over terminology, so let's clarify certain terms. An *inspector* in the sense of finding a defect might well be an inspector or tester—say, from the quality assurance department. It might also be the craftsman performing the work or the operator overlooking an automatic machine. Modern quality control now assigns quality responsibility to the craftsman, so this person may well be the inspector, functionally. For our purposes, the inspector is whoever has discovered the defect and initiated the failure report. We call this report a *nonconformance report,* or NCR, because the words *bad, failure,* or *defect* have judgmental interpretation. You don't want an inspector wondering if perhaps the defect really isn't all that bad, so . . . Similarly, you want these reports to be filed whether they concern raw material, purchased parts, partial product, or finished product. The title of nonconformance report avoids classifying a unit subjectively. The unit may be good or bad in some relative sense, but it did not conform to an inspection criterion, and therefore an NCR is issued irrespective of the nature of defect or product.

Following this initial assessment, the NCR will go to Quality Assurance because QA provides the best chance of identifying systematic cause. QA keeps the records. The identification of systemic problems is absolutely necessary to a successful and meaningful quality system. Systemic problems will escalate the review process, perhaps to the executive level. Thus, management is brought into the review process appropriately, rather than automatically, through the mechanism of a material review board. This board is usually composed of senior personnel and managers from Quality Assurance, and from Product and Manufacturing Engineering. The purpose of the board is to identify strategic actions that must be taken to eliminate systematic failure, from receipt of materials to finished product. The integration of top-down and bottom-up reviews is provided by Quality Assurance. Preventive and corrective actions in pursuit of the problem is discussed in Clause 4.14.

Disposition

The quality manual will describe the company's policy on the disposition of the nonconforming product. Such products can be disposed of in several ways. Usually it is not difficult to determine the reasonable thing to do. For example, one company produces printed circuit cards that have an end-of-line value of $60 or more. Obviously, rework is a far better alternative than scrap, even for a very low failure rate. Other companies apparently do not put a great deal of thought into the matter, for example, regrading nonconforming product without evaluating the opportunity loss in the lesser market. Although ISO 9000 does not critically review management's economic decisions, it is nevertheless true that cost of quality analyses favorably impress ISO auditors as an indication of competence. In addition to that, they are plain good business. Therefore, we shall assume that such analyses are done and proceed to the disposition of nonconforming product.

Scrap

Scrap is used as a general term to apply to nonconforming product that is rejected. It is not going to the customer. It may be thrown away as trash, it may be returned to the vendor, it may be sold as scrap, but it is not going to be used to make product by your company—any kind of product. Scrap, even when sold as such, is not regrade. It is reject.

The very first thing that must be done is to isolate the nonconforming product from good product. This must take place immediately, at the location of defect discovery, because it is in the vicinity of production that bad product is most likely to be inadvertently reinserted into the mainstream. The designation of nonconformance can be in the form of a colored label or sticker attached to the defective product by the discoverer, usually an inspector or tester.

Once the nonconforming product is identified and labeled, it should be removed from the production area and put into quarantine. If it is not feasible to remove a nonconforming item immediately from the production area, it should in any case be placed in a designated "bad product" cart immediately following its condemned labeling. This step greatly reduces the probability of reinsertion, but as soon as feasible the cart should be taken to quarantine. The quarantine area should be well isolated and well designated as an area of rejection. The inevitable destination of the nonconforming product can be indicated on an attached tag; it is not necessary to have a quarantine area for every disposition.

I once visited a plant that returned incoming bad product to its vendor. The rejection area was located in the supply area along with good product. This is not a good idea and will not be acceptable to many ISO auditors. People associate supply areas as sources of good product, and the chance of randomly selecting a nonconforming product that is nearby is too great to take the risk. Rejection areas should be isolated and well designated.

It is not necessary to keep rejection areas under lock and key. Even a cordoned area can serve as a rejection area if it is well marked and if it is not ambiguously located right next to good material. In fact, cordoned areas are efficient because they can be expanded or contracted as needed.

Rework

Bad product that is to be reworked can be taken immediately from the point of detection to the rework area, or it can remain in a rejection area if this is more efficient. How will it be recognized as rework, in contrast to other defective parts in the rejection area? That is up to the policy of the individual company. Perhaps the label on each defective unit may designate its disposition. Then by some convenient mechanism—say, via a periodic daily schedule—those parts destined for rework can be gathered from the rejection area and carted to the rework station.

Rework is a viable option if a cost-effective repair process can be developed. Usually, this depends on the nature of the product. Complex products are often repairable; fabrics usually are not. In any case, ISO 9000 is noncommittal on the subject, leaving the matter a decision of management. If there are rules of thumb to be used in the decision to rework or not, then they should be included in the policy described in the quality manual. This forces the company to think hard about what it wants to do relative to the business it is in.

A question often arises as to whether a reworked item should be treated differently from an item that had never failed. Again, there is no ISO policy on this matter. Each company should decide for itself, based on technical issues, whether a repaired product is as good as a new one. The governing factor will be the customer because no ISO auditor will second-guess management policy. Most of us purchase things that may well have had rework, such as a television set, and we never know the difference. At least the reworked part has been tested (usually), whereas a newly manufactured piece is often subject to a scheme of acceptance sampling and may not have been tested at all. As a general rule, the reworked unit should be reinserted into production at the point where it failed.

Regrade

As we mentioned, some companies do not admit to nonconformity and regrade or reclassify product as a viable alternative to improving the quality of their premier process. This secondary inventory competes with the top of the line and so adds complexity to the cost of poor quality. For example, a manufacturer of fine fabric realizes high profit for the industry on its top-of-the-line product. Secondary product is sold as remnants at less than a dollar per yard. Tertiary product is sold as rags at a few cents per pound. The manufacturer keeps no records of the ratio of each product to the total weight of manufactured fabric. Two questions arise: What business is the manufacturer in? What is the average profit?

The point is that the regrade option can be a misleading enticement. It may seem clever to sell what would otherwise be scrap, but not if the off-products compete with the top of the line for the company's manufacturing resources. A cost of quality analysis is not free, but must be made if only so the company can know what business it is in! Beyond that, it would be nice to know whether real profits are being achieved. Ellen Goodman (1994), the syndicated columnist, complained that since only 3 or 4 percent of the delivery of the U.S. Postal Service was first-class mail, then despite its name, it was not really in the mail business. If a manufacturer is producing mostly remnants and rags, then it is not in the business of fine fabrics, whatever the claims of the company brochures.

Regraded product will be subject to the ISO purview if that product is part of the process being certified. For example, suppose that an electronics company manufactures narrow- and wide-band amplifiers for use in its own electronic products. Some of the wide-band amplifiers have lower gain than others at the limits of the bandwidth, and so fail inspection. Suppose, however, that these failed units can be used elsewhere in the product in a narrow-band application. Then they are subject to ISO interest. On the other hand, if they are sold to an outside company as an independent secondary product, then they do not come under ISO 9000 if the process making the secondary product is not being certified.

Concession

A nonconforming product is one that fails to meet specifications. If the specifications correctly mirror customer requirements, then why should a customer accept a nonconforming product? In fact, this sort of transaction happens all of the time and is one of the very good reasons why the term *nonconforming* is better than the term *bad*. The U.S. Navy accepts product by concession regularly, from ship repair yards. A typical repair period of a surface combatant might involve thousands of man-days and $20 million or more. There will be hundreds of work items in the package, as well as extensive testing to be achieved. There is also a hard delivery date; the ship will be needed for deployment in order to relieve another ship already deployed. Depending on the nature of incomplete work or of failed tests, the Navy may well determine that it can achieve this effort later, on its own, and waive the nonconformances.

We often do the same thing, and for the same reason. You take your car for a diagnostic because there seems to be a new noise. The mechanic's assessment includes things that must be done and things that ought to be done, but the total price is too high, so you waive the things that ought to be done. When you retake possession of the vehicle, there are known defects in it. Strictly speaking, this is not acceptance by concession if the known defects were not in the final work package, but the idea is the same. A better example might be this: You order a new car with options. All the options are written into the specification, or job order. After waiting five weeks the car arrives, but one of the options is missing. You decide to take the car anyway rather than wait another five weeks.

We saw in Chapter 4 that the quality process consisted of translating customer requirements to specifications, then building a product according to the specifications. Clearly, then, nonconforming product that is delivered to a customer on concession becomes a quality record. The reason is that the delivered product is what the customer received, and not the product that was specified. Although permissible, this is a fundamental discrepancy and policy and procedures must be explicit on all phases of this process.

Summary

Sustainability in Clause 4.13 requires a three-prong system of dealing with nonconforming product as shown in Exhibit 23-1. The elements are: (1) written policies describing the disposition of nonconforming product; (2) a documented and implemented system of product disposition; (3) a nonconforming product review process with executive overview.

References

ANSI/ISO/ASQC. *Q9001-1994. Quality Systems—Model for Quality Assurance in Design, Development, Production, Installation, and Servicing*. Milwaukee: American Society for Quality Control, 1994.

ANSI/ISO/ASQC. *Q9004-1-1994. American National Standard: Quality Management and Quality System Elements and Guidelines.* Milwaukee: American Society for Quality Control, 1994.

Goodman, Ellen, "The Hard Fax on Slow Mail Service." *Boston Globe*, July 3, 1994.

Chapter 24

Clause 4.15: Handling, Storage, Packaging, Preservation, and Delivery

Brief: Clause 4.15 requires a documented system to control postproductive activities, from acceptance testing through delivery of product.

I once saw a cooling system being moved by forklift from a final assembly workstation to the shipping dock. A sizable area of cooling fins was bashed in, not large enough to impede operability or function, but large enough to catch the eye. I knew that if that unit were delivered to me, I would refuse to accept it.

We often think of handling, storage, packaging, preservation, and delivery as secondary efforts, of which only delivery is really all that important. But as the cooling fins story suggests, a good performance in these activities may not make you a superstar, but a bad performance will ruin your reputation.

The Transfer States

If you consider these activities as transfer states, then your reputation transfers with them, *sic transit fama*—for better or for worse. Transfer states touch more directly with the customer than the high flyers of manufacturing: design and production. For this reason, sustainability requires strict attention to details. The transfer states are customer interface.

The manufacturing process is continuously dynamic throughout its cycle. You bring in purchased parts and raw material, add value to those things in a flow of productive activities, and finish with a product that is then delivered to market. Every state is a transient state. How then do the states of handling, storage, packaging, preservation, and delivery differ from any other? Clause 4.15 recognizes these states as applying to finished product. The receiving and productive states are ended and the product is being readied for transfer to market. The ISO 9004 guidelines refer to handling, storage, packaging, preservation, and delivery as postproduction activities. It is a good idea to think of the postproductive dynamics as transfer states in order to stress the close relationship between them and the customer. The product has been in-house for a long time, from design through fabrication and test. Ownership is being transferred to the customer.

Handling

Handling means literally that: the moving about of product on the factory floor. This activity seems simple enough, except that quite often the product is in lots and is heavy. Heavy things require care in lifting, even if a forklift is used. The product container must be balanced on a pallet and the pallet lifted by a skilled forklift operator. Sometimes the product is kept in open cardboard boxes for a few hours (or days), where it is exposed to damage risk.

The company will provide methods of handling product that prevent deterioration or damage. The big sins in handling are almost always on the shop floor, and are caused by careless operation of forklifts. This comes about in two ways. First, damage can be done by a forklift grazing a nearby product with its load or by grazing a nearby object with its product. The second is in picking up and laying down product.

An example of the latter occurs when a forklift operator lays down a length of sheet steel on a bulky object, bending the sheets. This can happen, for example, where a company makes product that is delivered to the customer in an unassembled condition, then is assembled on-site by a trained crew. Suppose that the final product is a mobile steel cabinet. The sheet steel being shipped does not have the structural strength of the assembled product and can bend easily if not stacked properly in the shipping area.

These occasions can be reduced in several ways. The first is to always mark off areas that are not to be used as pathways: isolation, quarantine, shipping, and reject areas should always be well marked, and an effective way to do this is with yellow nylon rope. The second is to ensure the best training for forklift operators. The third is to enact plant floor traffic discipline. Only qualified operators should use forklifts. Traffic rules should be made known to the forklift operators, along with the understanding that they must follow the rules.

Some products are delicate. Others are heavy—too heavy to be used to demonstrate manhood. The best handling of product that I know of takes place on ships in port. Only trained riggers may handle onloading and offloading. This is not featherbedding. Movement of heavy items inside a ship, and from ship to pier, requires special equipment and skill. Everything is steel—decks, bulkheads, and fixtures—and the ladders are steep. The environment for motion in a factory is benign by comparison, but handling rules should still be controlled by procedures.

Even trained riggers can make mistakes if they ignore procedures, or if there are no procedures. A crane operator in Portland was assigned to lift a brand-new automobile aboard ship. The riggers attached a body strap to the underside of the car but failed to put a spacer bar above the vehicle, which would keep the straps parallel. When the crane began to lift the auto, the pull on the strap formed it into an inverted V, caving in the walls of the car. This type of incident, repeated thousands of times daily all over the world, is the reason the ISO 9000 standards are so insistent and strict on procedures. Write them, then use them.

Storage

Resource management is a field under considerable study these days, and storage is one of its components. In modern quality thinking, storage should be an insignificant issue. A company that uses just-in-time inventory and production methods should have little storage problem. However, we have already discussed one industry that has a large storage problem—shipyards. Storage can also be a problem in companies that are part of vertical structure, seen more and more often in the business world. Such companies often cannot establish their in-and-out inventory policies and must store product according to the dictates of some distant corporate headquarters. This structure is recognized by the ISO 9000 requirements, which do not look at how small inventory is so much as at how well it is retained.

There are two principal areas of storage: incoming of purchased parts and outgoing of finished product. Clause 4.15 is concerned that both areas provide freedom from damage and deterioration. For example, things can be stored outside, but must be protected from the elements if they are perishable or diminished in some way. Common sense pertains here. Automobiles are offloaded from a Japanese cargo ship in Port Hueneme, California, and stored in an open field for a time. No problem: The automobile is made for this kind of exposure; many customers will do the same.

On the other hand, things that tend to rust easily must be sheltered. Perishable goods must be refrigerated. One example of perennially bad storage has to do with fresh cheese. It is difficult to buy fresh cheese in many grocery stores, probably because of naivete about how cheese ages and is affected by the environment. It is not unusual to buy cheese that is refrigerated, only to take it home and find that it had been stored unrefrigerated for a period, then re-refrigerated.

According to Clause 4.15, purchased parts must be appropriately stored prior to use; finished product must be appropriately stored pending delivery. This is best accomplished by establishing storage areas, clearly delineated either by chamber or by yellow nylon rope, and by appropriate packaging or cover. When product or parts are stored for a substantial period of time, their condition should be periodically checked. What does *substantial* mean? That decision is up to the company. Storage policies and procedures are required.

Even a reject area should be protected from intrusion. If the products have reject tags there may be little probability of inadvertent use. Nevertheless, the area should be roped off to distinguish its purpose, just as are quarantine and other areas. The reason is that if rejected items are damaged due to intrusion, then certain corrective alternatives are precluded, and how do you explain *that* in a procedure? Roped areas need not be installed permanently. You can designate any area you want for special purpose, whenever you want. But mark the area and provide a procedure for its use.

Storage areas are necessary but not sufficient compliance to this clause. Product labeling is also required within the storage area. Different products can be stored in the same area as long as they have the same status: quarantine, accepted, rejected, ready for delivery, and so on. Color-coded labels can be used to delineate the status, according to written procedures on labeling.

Packaging

Packaging is one of the strong points of American industry. A visit to any city dump will confirm that we use plenty of it. The strength of modern materials is so improved that sometimes it is difficult to open even blister packaging without tools. In sum, most manufacturers do not spare the horses in packaging. They have paid the cost to produce a product and now it is nearing payback time.

The importance that industry places on packaging is indicated by the dynamism of its technology. Many mid-size companies not only employ packaging engineers but also maintain research and development programs in a continual effort toward stronger and cheaper materials and more efficient machines. Basically, packaging materials never change: paper, metal, plastic, and glass. Material preference changes, though, with plastic gaining fast because it is getting stronger and because it provides visibility of product.

The constant development of packaging material is accompanied by a similar dynamic in packaging equipment and operations. These include an increasing use of electronics and of software control. The dynamics of packaging means that, for many companies, a great deal of control is required of this state.

Control procedures are required to ensure appropriate and sufficient packaging of product, with associated security. These controls include policies and procedures. The specifications may well define the requirements, but if not, the responsibility is still there. Procedures would designate the kind of material to be used and the extent of the packing required. If security is a customer requirement, then written policies and procedures are required that define the limits and describe the security process.

Packaging includes marking the package. The marking should be securely affixed to the package, for obvious reasons. Often, the packing material is opaque so that product identity is obscured. The marking label tells what the package contains. It also provides other important information, such as destination, storage date, delivery date, and special characteristics.

These ideas are the minimum concerns of Clause 4.15, but sustainability requires more, particularly in the area of training. In an article titled "Slaying the Technology Beast," *Packaging World* (1996) gives an indication of the training dimension in an article on the fundamental role of the packaging engineer. This person maintains, improves, specifies, and integrates packaging machinery and packaging operations. The required skills stress an understanding of materials and machines. The objective is a common engineering one of continual optimization. Even smaller companies that have no R&D effort must train their technical people in the packaging art. *Packaging World* reports that roughly two-thirds of manufacturers believe training is necessary in machinery operation and even in machinery selection. This training is usually provided by the OEM, but whatever the source, a formal training program is needed in machine operation and maintenance.

Preservation

Preservation is a new requirement, added into the 1994 revision of the Standard. It assigns responsibility to the company for appropriate methods of preservation and segregation of product during the time the product is under the company's control. This also may seem to be a motherhood requirement, in that most companies are eager to ensure that their product is appropriately preserved. A refusal of the product by the customer is an ignominious end to the productive effort. However, even meticulous companies may not have written procedures governing preservation of product. This clause rectifies that shortcoming.

Packaging and preservation may seem closely related. Both activities have the same objective—to safeguard the effectiveness of the product. If a pack of razor blades is encased in plastic film, is that packaging or preservation? We normally think of preservation as the act of preventing chemical decomposition. Aspirin subject to the weather will decompose, but so will some razor blades, although we call it rust. Exposure to weather renders both products ineffective.

It is not necessary to delineate packaging and preservation as activities. They are delineated in their effect on the motivation of the supplier. The purpose in adding preservation to the ISO 9000 standards is to remind the supplier that packaging, per se, is necessary but not sufficient. The product must be preserved, too. Ineffective packaging is unacceptable.

Delivery

Delivery is a transfer state in two ways. It physically transfers the product from the performer to the customer, and it transfers the contract from the cost column to accounts receivable. A company is well motivated to complete this function effectively. There are several issues to consider in creating a sustainable delivery system. They are traffic and protection.

Traffic

Traffic defines the method and conditions of transport of product. A manufacturer can effect traffic in one or several of three options: do it yourself, by contract carrier, or by common carrier. Of the three, the first provides the greatest control because all the factors are under the authority of the company: conveyances, drivers, loaders, routes, and schedules. On the other hand, doing it yourself requires that a fleet of vehicles of some sort be retained, with associated purchasing, maintenance, and full-time labor costs.

Contract carriers—moving companies, for example—offer door-to-door delivery service that you pay for only when you need it. The manufacturer has little control over the traffic factors, but can negotiate schedules and freight rates. Similarly, the manufacturer can use common carriers, claiming the same alternatives. Common carriers do not guarantee door-to-door delivery, but may off- and onload freight at various terminals.

All of these issues are a matter of negotiated cost and may also be an ISO 9000 matter if the quality of the product is somehow put at risk, depending on the traffic method chosen. For example, it is probably better, from the quality point of view, that the product be delivered directly from manufacturer to customer, nonstop, in order to reduce the risk of damage. Traffic policies must be defined in the quality manual, and delivery procedures should spell out how a delivery is effected. There will be a paper trail of product traceability and signatories from shipping to customer that verify quality of product upon arrival.

Protection

The company is obligated to arrange protection of product after final inspection and pending delivery. In some cases the contract will specify that this protection be extended through delivery. This is no small accomplishment, particularly when many manufacturers use common carriers for the delivery. The spirit of the requirement is met when the contract with the common carrier includes the requirement of protection. In this case, the carrier is simply a subcontractor and is subject to the evaluation and control required by the company of all its subcontractors.

Many manufacturers use dealerships to reach the marketplace. The arrangement between manufacturer and dealer is an ISO 9000 concern. The relationship will be either supplier-customer or supplier-subcontractor. In the first case, where the dealer is a customer, then the ISO 9000 view is one of simple delivery of goods for customer satisfaction. The end user may well be dissatisfied if the dealer is negligent, but this is a manufacturer's problem and is not strictly within the purview of ISO 9000. It is in the purview of sustainability, however, and the sagacious company will maintain an evaluation program of its dealerships. In the second case, the dealer acts as agent to the manufacturer and a dealership performance evaluation is required by ISO 9000 standards. The evaluation program should be defined in policies and procedures.

Summary

Sustainability in Clause 4.15 requires a realization that the transfer states touch the final customer more intimately than any other. Therefore, focus and attention should be concentrated on them even though they are usually active only at the end of the productive cycle. The key issues of the transfer states are quality of product *as delivered*, timely delivery, and acknowledgment of satisfaction by the customer.

References

ANSI/ISO/ASQC. *Q9001-1994. Quality Systems—Model for Quality Assurance in Design, Development, Production, Installation, and Servicing*. Milwaukee: American Society for Quality Control, 1994.

ANSI/ISO/ASQC. *Q9004-1-1994. American National Standard: Quality Management and Quality System Elements and Guidelines*. Milwaukee: American Society for Quality Control, 1994.

"Slaying the Technology Beast," *Packaging World*, November 1996, pp. 77–87.

Part Six

Quality System Requirements: Sales and Service Purview

Chapter 25

Clause 4.3: Contract Review

Brief: Clause 4.3 requires a documented system for review and amendment of the contract, to ensure customer-performer agreement of expectations.

A contract is a formal agreement, usually written, between two parties. Moreover, if you agree to provide a product or service to a client, the contract between you defines its quality. How can this be? Recall the ISO definition of quality: "the totality of features and characteristics of a product or service that bear on its ability to satisfy stated or implied needs." The stated needs are expressed in the contract. The implied needs are not in the contract but are part of the customer's expectations. As it becomes apparent that an implied need is not being met, the contract as written becomes inadequate.

When we think of contracts we often think of the simple case. One party agrees to this, the other to that, then the whole deal is engraved in stone. This kind of simplistic obligation is not the usual case in modern affairs because so many contracts nowadays require interactive activities, state-of-the-art materials, and extended performance. In other words, even the world of contracts must keep pace with the changing environments of the global economy. Except in the briefest of performance periods, there is a good chance that one or more conditions in a contract may have to be renegotiated by one or the other party to it.

As Hybert (1996) puts it, "contracting is the process by which customized systems are designed and delivered." This view goes much further than convention. Most people will agree that the contract is not over until delivery, but Hybert is saying that *contracting* is not over until delivery.

An Agreement of Expectations

Roshomon was a 1950 Japanese film by Kurosawa that told the story of a couple in the Middle Ages who left their village to visit the wife's parents. On the way they were set upon by a bandit. The story opened at the trial of the bandit, where the tribunal required that each party—husband, wife, bandit—tell the story in his own words. The denouement was that there were three entirely different narrations—thus the *Roshomon effect*: Given a single event, each observer sees a different reality.

A contract performance often reflects this dichotomy. The single event is the contract. The customer expects a certain result from a contract. The performer expects a different result from the same contract. They are reading the same words differently. In some cases, the customer wants to make "insignificant" changes that are not at all insignificant to the performer. Conversely, the performer might elect to change a material called for in the contract, but that may be unavailable or too expensive at the time of need. "No problem," thinks the performer, except that the customer may consider the change unacceptable.

Sometimes the customer and performer focus on the front end of the product—what it can do and how much it will cost—and fail to include product life-cycle issues, even though both parties may have them in the back of their mind. At first cut the contract is incomplete.

Hybert points out that sometimes even the specifications are incomplete. They usually satisfy the technical evaluators in some limited sense, but don't cover all the customer expectations. This can happen, for example, when they are written by sales and service personnel working from a boilerplate. If the customer wants changes to an off-the-shelf product, then the risk of adequate specifications are in proportion to the quantity and quality of the changes.

Initial Review

The best way to ensure an agreement of expectations between customer and performer is to have an initial review of the contract, to include the job order. In some cases, the contract contains only the customer requirements and not the specifications. In other cases, the contract will contain both. In all cases, the production force works from the job order. Thus, even if the customer is able to verify from the contract that the specifications meet the requirements, this does not verify the job order, which may contain more, fewer, or different specifications.

Chapter 15 mentioned a case concerning the specifications on a roofing job. Suppose that you are a builder of a housing development and you have contracted with a roofing company. You may state your requirements as thirty-year asphalt tiles, waterproof underlay, chimney flashings, and ridge vents. There is a great deal of variance possible on all items. For example, there are metal and plastic ridge vents, and even among the latter the designs can be a difference in kind. As the customer, it is absolutely necessary that you review the specifications in order to approve the translations. Again, your review of the job order is necessary because if it does not exactly repeat the contract specs, then the roofers may well diverge from your expectations and may even install whatever happens to be in the shop that day.

ISO standards recognize the possibility of divergence and therefore require an initial review of the contract to ensure that:

1. The requirements are adequately defined and documented.
2. Requirements differing from those in the tender are resolved.
3. The supplier has the capability to meet contractual requirements.

Review Team

Companies differ in their primary interface agent with the customer. In some cases, the primary agent is the marketing department. In others, a customer service department is the main point of contact. In still others, a comprehensive team representing all affected departments meets with the customer. Except in the latter case, any company agent is limited in his ability to exactly understand how a customer's requirements meet the capability of the company.

It is equally true that a single customer agent is limited in her ability to exactly express the requirements for all but the simplest of products. If the product is to be a system of some sort, then the contract review team should consist of members representing both customer and performer. The performer's team might have members from marketing, sales and service, design, manufacturing engineering, and purchasing. The customer's team will consist of those functions who will be owners of one or more of the modes that the system will provide. There are almost always multiple end users for systems. Examples are many: materials planning requirements (MRP) systems, management information systems, communications systems, a fleet of aircraft. A customer contracting for a passenger airplane will want people in the contract review process who represent its own marketing, customer service, technical support, and maintenance functions.

A Structure of Agreement

A sustainable contract process will be structured to maintain an agreement of expectations between performer and customer throughout the performance period. The process can be informal and yet be suited to a particular business; an example structure is shown in Exhibit 25-1. Through one agent or another, the performer (supplier, in the exhibit) will take requirements from a customer and pass them to an assessment team of, perhaps, purchasing and manufacturing and product engineering. Then an evaluation of the performer's capability and of the customer's requirements is made, and perhaps a new design is needed. The job is sized and estimates of cost in time and materials are made.

When there seems to be tentative agreement that the customer's requirements are understood and the company has the capability to meet them, an initial contract is formulated and agreed to by all parties. At some point, the requirements are translated to specifications, and a job order is defined and begins its process through production and operations.

In keeping with the ISO philosophy, there is, of course, a paper trail for all this. Much of the transaction may take place by

Exhibit 25-1. Contract review process that enhances agreement of expectations.

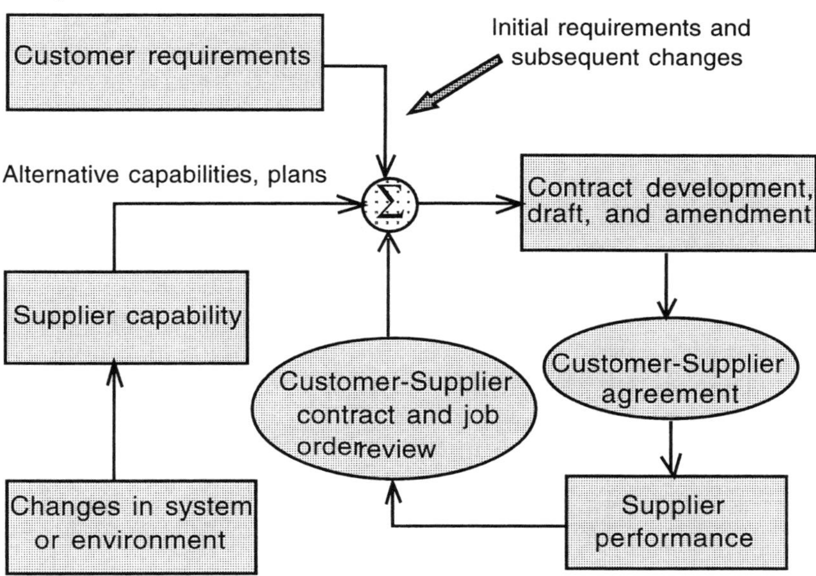

telephone, but there must be supporting documentation as testamentary to taking and filling an order. Some orders are relatively simple and can be finalized by facsimile, but the initial agreement should always be written down and approved by both parties as written. The requirement to perform to a written contract is almost trivial because the practice is widespread. But curiously, the written obligation can sometimes appear conveniently ambiguous. Many suppliers act on the notion that unilateral changes to the terms of the contract are permissible if the substitutions—time or material—are "equivalent." A sustainable structure differs from this notion because unilateral changes by either side are inadmissible. Changes must be preceded by a review process.

Continual Review

The process thus described will get the job started, but it will not maintain an agreement of expectations. If there is an appreciable period of performance, then the agreement of expectations will be dynamic and a mechanism will be needed for a validation and verification accord. The customer may change his mind, or labor or weather problems or delayed delivery of material may alter schedules. Substitute materials may be advised. Periodic contract reviews provide this mechanism. It keeps the customer aware of the dynamics of the performance and allows both sides a voice in proposed changes of material or schedule.

The idea of continual contract review is shown in the closed loop of Exhibit 25-1 as a fixed feedback element of the system. At the beginning it provides the customer the ability to verify that requirements were recorded as they were transmitted and that the specifications are a valid translation of the requirements. During the period of performance it provides the customer and performer the occasion to review progress and resolve problems together. This common view of reality is a maturing process, too, helping the customer to understand what must be done, the options available, and their cost. The customer's expectations may rise or fall as a result of the review, which enhances an agreement and satisfaction at the end of the contract.

A ship repair contract is a good example of the need for continual review between customer and performer. The period of performance for a Navy surface combatant is typically six to twelve months and may cost between $10 and $30 million. There will be hundreds of change orders resulting in a growth of a work package of perhaps 30 percent or more. Clearly, if the customer's expectations were frozen at the signing of the contract, disappointment would be assured. The process of continual review permits the customer information of emergent and new work, and provides the opportunity for choices such as rescreening.

Other examples show the different ways in which the customer's expectations are dynamic. Suppose a power company is negotiating with a large consumer for its product. The customer is concerned with both rate and reliability. Both parties finally agree on a price per megawatt and on a reliability factor of, say, 98.5 percent, with a decreasing rate structure if reliability drops below the index. This reliability is known as *mean time between failure*, or MTBF. No word appears in the contract about an associated index of availability called *mean time to repair*, or MTTR. As time goes by, the power company lives up to its MTBF, but in the very infrequent occasions when power is lost, the down time is unacceptable to the customer. Questions arise about it in review meetings and the performer and customer agree that MTTR should be a factor in renegotiations. If there can be no renegotiation, or if there were never a review process, then the customer's initial high expectations will certainly lead to disappointment by the end of the contract.

Some contracts require continual review by their very nature. An oil company contracts to a customer to provide a volume of crude oil from time to time over a performance period. On occasion the customer will call for changes in the order, either up or down. If down, there may well be a quid pro quo clause in the contract that protects the performer from loss. If up, the performer must locate the extra crude, either through a spot market or through affiliates.

You can see from these examples that there are two considerations in contract review. The first is that a continual review process of contract is needed for complex products, or for an extended period of performance, if the performer is to maintain a sustainable quality system. The second is that a dynamic contract requires a great deal of thought in terms of the possible permutations of product or performance. It may be necessary to change one or more product characteristics. It may be necessary to change the time, schedule, or cost of the performance.

This is why it is so important to use the team concept in contract review—a broad range and diversity of experience is better suited to foresee those possibilities. Marketing and service personnel know the customer and have the best feel for her expectations. Purchasing has insight into the variance of cost. Product engineers are most familiar with the possible variations of product, and manufacturing engineers are most familiar with the scope of process.

Amendment

After an agreement on the contract is reached, the company may initiate the various phases of execution: design, development, and production. Periodic contract reviews are conducted, during which both the customer and the performer may request changes.

Perhaps a material is no longer available, or its price has greatly increased, changing the scope or the cost of the product. Or perhaps the customer's own requirements have changed. We discussed some examples in which changes to the contract might be attractive to one signatory or the other.

A well-written contract will contain clauses that define this flexibility. The contract will admit the review process and describe the implementation procedures for change. A reasonable amendment process will recognize the cost incurred by the performer for production already begun and spell out the trade-offs for alteration. Most companies already do this sort of thing routinely, but the ISO standards require that the amendment process be described in a procedure.

For example, the customer has ordered wood cabinets, then finds that load projections will require metal ones, preferably lightweight. Lightweight but strong metal cabinet options may be magnesium alloy, aluminum, or titanium, and each has trade-offs. The cost of changing the contract will be an increasing one, depending on whether the job order is in design, in queue awaiting materials, or in production. The performer must be paid for his costs thus far, and the customer is due an explanation of those costs, and of the trade-offs in cost and performance characteristics of the alternate materials. The elements of the amendment process then would be:

1. Declaration by customer or justification by performer
2. Development costs thus far
3. Projected costs for new or emergent work, including new design and drawings
4. Rewrite of contract or of attachment thereto.

Records

We noted at the outset of this chapter that a contract literally defines the quality of the product. The contract is therefore a quality record within the meaning of the ISO standards. The job order represents the implementation of the contract, and so is also a quality record. By the same reasoning, amendments to the contract are quality records. Finally, the ISO standards extend this reasoning even further, declaring that the records of contract reviews are quality records. Therefore, the records of contract reviews must be retained.

Summary

Sustainability in Clause 4.3 requires a contract-and-performance dynamic similar to that shown in Exhibit 25-1. The key to achieving customer satisfaction lies in correct translation of customer requirements through the productive process; and maintaining conformance to customer expectations through the productive process. This flexibility is obtained by a continual review system with amendment capability. By *productive process* is meant the entire process from contract negotiation through design, production, and delivery.

References

ANSI/ISO/ASQC. *Q9001-1994. Quality Systems—Model for Quality Assurance in Design, Development, Production, Installation, and Servicing*. Milwaukee: American Society for Quality Control, 1994.

Hybert, Pete. "Five Ways to Improve the Contracting Process." *Quality Progress*, February 1996, pp. 65–70.

Chapter 26

Clause 4.19: Servicing

Brief: Clause 4.19 governs the performance of service activities when they are specified in the contract. Procedures will verify that the service meets specifications.

Within the context of an ISO standard, servicing does not mean customer service as it is usually understood. Blanding (1991) describes customer service as a process by which an agent of the performing company attempts to match customer requirements to performer capability. Clause 4.19 refers to service that may be provided to the customer in the postproductive period. This service includes installation, in service engineering, and product support, and does not apply to companies that exclude service from their contracts.

Examples of installation service are PBX communications systems and mobile storage systems. Copying machines represent an example of in-service engineering, and product support services might include replacement of nondurable goods such as office supplies, printing inks and paper, and fuel supplies.

Generally, warranty work is not a service within the meaning of this clause. Presumably a product that failed to perform as specified would fall under the purview of Clause *4.13: Control of Nonconforming Product*. Nevertheless, the processes that control nonconforming product are internal in most companies. Their service departments are set up to support technical matters in the field, and warranty work is most efficiently handled through these agents. The important issue is service, not bureaucracy. If you want to handle warranty work through the service department, then simply put the relevant responsibility, policies, and procedures in that department.

To Serve or Not to Serve

Clause 4.19 is one of the requirements of ISO 9001 that is deleted as a requirement from ISO 9002. Not too much should be made of this because even in the ISO 9001 requirements the clause reads "where servicing is a specified requirement. . . ." In other words, if the contract does not specify a service, then even an ISO 9001 company need not bother with it. On the other hand, a company lacking a design function may well apply for ISO 9002 certification even though it provides some postproductive support in its contracts. The bottom line is that ISO standards are meant to be flexible. If you have a specific function, then policies and procedures must be defined for it.

Sometimes companies do not offer a service in their contracts but provide it anyway, as a matter of policy. For example, many mail order computer manufacturers and software houses provide warranties, but in addition provide a telephone information service for an undefined period of time, in order to help the customer get up to speed. The performing company is under no contractual obligation to provide this service, but wants to maintain good relationships with the customer in the expectation of repeat or extended business. If a company provides a service, under contract or not, then Clause 4.19 pertains and the system must be documented.

The Anatomy of Service

Exhibit 26-1 shows a closed-loop structure that provides a sustainable system of service in a dynamic environment. It refers to both installation activities and postinstallation service. The installation activity is easily understood and is usually made clear in the contract. Service, on the other hand, has a dual nature. Sometimes it is scheduled by the performer and some-

Exhibit 26-1. Dynamic closed loop for postproduction servicing.

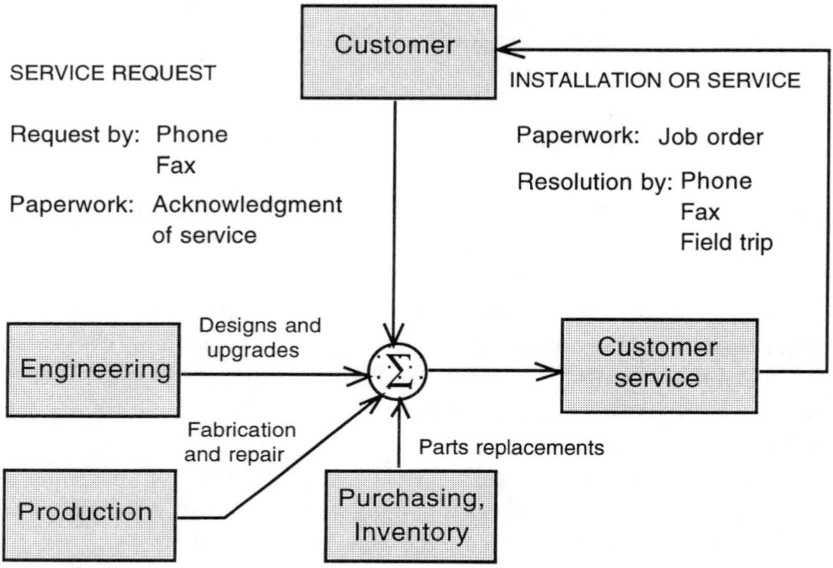

Customer

SERVICE REQUEST

Request by: Phone
Fax

Paperwork: Acknowledgment of service

INSTALLATION OR SERVICE

Paperwork: Job order

Resolution by: Phone
Fax
Field trip

Engineering

Designs and upgrades

Σ

Customer service

Fabrication and repair

Parts replacements

Production

Purchasing, Inventory

times it is a random event initiated by the customer, perhaps because of a problem.

Scheduled service is provided for certain products that have extended term maintenance requirements, where the maintenance capability is either proprietary to the performer or too complex and costly for the customer to assume its responsibility. It may thus be cost feasible for the performer to pay for maintenance service. This service will be in the contract, of course, along with the maintenance schedule and other foreseeable issues, such as expendable supplies that might be a by-product of maintenance. A job order will be written up and the service will be resolved, usually by an agent in the field. After the job is completed, there will be some written acknowledgment of satisfactory product performance because such performance is de facto evidence of product quality, and is therefore a quality record.

On the other hand, random failures of the product, during or after the warranty period, will result in the customer's initiating the contact. This process should not be so complicated as to discourage the customer. A telephone call, E-mail, or facsimile transmission should be all that is needed to initiate support service.

The problem may be resolvable by a telephone call to a company expert familiar with the symptoms. Even so, the call will be logged in, a job order will be filled out, and a customer satisfaction acknowledgment received, perhaps by fax.

Why? First and foremost, the transaction is a quality record. It attests to restoration of a product from a degraded or nonfunctional mode. Second, the event will provide product reliability information and service quality data. Even when problems are resolved relatively easily and inexpensively, they provide insight into the integrity of the quality system.

The format of the report is important, too. After the service is performed, the company's field representative may submit a travel report, but this is not an adequate quality record. There should be some document, if only a Tier 4 form, that specifies the work that was done and relates the customer's agreement in the form of a signature. This document is necessary because it may be a quality record. The customer service process must be defined in a written procedure. As with most procedures, it can be brief, but should describe the alternate ways of handling customer calls and how problems may be addressed.

Summary

Within the context of Clause 4.19, customer service refers to that service offered in the postproductive period. Sustainability requires a closed-loop structure of customer service as indicated in Exhibit 26-1. Surprisingly, many companies that offer service after sales do not always require an expression of customer satisfaction, for example, by signing off on a work order. Until the company obtains such an expression, customer satisfaction cannot be assumed.

References

ANSI/ISO/ASQC. *Q9001-1994. Quality Systems—Model for Quality Assurance in Design, Development, Production, Installation, and Servicing*. Milwaukee: American Society for Quality Control, 1994.

ANSI/ISO/ASQC. *Q9004-1-1994. American National Standard: Quality Management and Quality System Elements and Guidelines.* Milwaukee: American Society for Quality Control, 1994.

Blanding, Warren. *Customer Service Operations*. New York: AMACOM, 1991.

Chapter 27
Down the Road

Those who have gone through an ISO 9000 certification, or who plan to do so, are fully justified in wondering about the long-term prospects of their investment. That investment really has two parts to it—one in quality itself, the other in the ISO program. Put another way, the investment has form and substance. An ISO standard provides form; quality methods provide substance.

Systems, processes, institutions—all structures of endeavor—have both form and substance. Yet the relationship between these two properties is often not fully appreciated. We sometimes hear complaints, for example, that the civil service is strong on form and weak on substance. They say that, in government, things should look good even if the product is not evident. Conversely, some dynamic individuals boast that their company is all substance, form being unimportant. We might hear this boast from new industries such as the world of cyberspace, perhaps from a hard-driving start-up entrepreneur with a hot product and no history.

Form and Substance

The fact is that processes and institutions need both form *and* substance. It is clear what substance does for you: It provides the brains and muscle that create, build, and get things done. But form, too, has its purpose. It provides the skin and bones. Form provides the framework upon which hangs substance. Form is the collection of traditions, customs, and values that assure reliability. Form holds things together. Institutions with all substance and no form tend to patricide and reinvention of the wheel every generation. Each new leader abrogates the position of the predecessor with an arrogance that denies the need of reference points.

I noted early on in this book that ISO 9000 standards provide neither stability, capability, nor improvability. Therefore, what good are they? Well, they do not provide stability in the sense of Liapunov or of Shewhart, true. These are substantive measures of stability. But ISO 9000 standards do provide stability of form. By requiring widespread use of procedures and written policies, the standards force a consistency and repeatability of action. This is what I mean by stability of form. When combined with substance, ISO 9000 standards ensure that if what you are doing is good, you will keep doing it.

The Future of Form

Can standards of process have durability? Do they withstand change? There are several examples to show that the answer to both questions is yes. The best example is that of the Constitution of the United States, which is a standard of governance that has endured for 210 years. The original document remains unchanged. The living document adapts to the requirements of each generation according to court decisions. Nevertheless, the original document remains the point of reference from which all departure is made. This adaptability provides the endurance of the standard. As with any standard, the life of the Constitution depends on a general agreement to abide by it, as interpreted contemporarily.

Another example, perhaps more easily related to our concerns, is Mil-Q-9858A, which dates to 1963. Canceled in 1994, the document provided the standard of quality organization of defense contractors for over thirty years. If its closely related antecedents are included, the standard can be traced to World War II, yielding an operating life span of over half a century. Admittedly, the standard had special protection, being championed by the government of the United States and operating only on government contracts.

Standards are by definition a convention, an agreement among participants to recognize a reference. Thus, there are always political and social compromises to be made. The final form of the standard will reflect the traditions, customs, and values of the signatories. Although these things may not change much from generation to generation, relative power and influence among the membership will change. Therefore, we must expect to see changes in process standards. We can certainly expect changes in high-level standards such as ISO 9000, ISO 14000, and QS 9000 because these norms get into organizational structure and management purview. In contrast to substantive quality methods, which operate at a level of effectiveness, process standards operate at a level where subjective values weigh in. In particular, they act across functional barriers, which scope invariably meets resistance.

Form, then, can be expected to change with the ebb and flow of the influence of its subscribing members. Yes, we shall see changes in ISO 9000 and shall discuss them momentarily. I also argue that those companies who have organized for sustainability will be the least affected by these changes.

The Future of Substance

The technical methods of quality provide its substance. Examples abound: Taguchi techniques, design of experiments, total quality management (TQM) methods, control charting, quality function deployment, *kaizen*. If upon its introduction, a substantive method survives the critique of the technical community, then it will probably have long life. Most of the methods have been around a long time because they are effective and because they function at a level at which effectiveness is highly regarded. Even the technique of quality circles still enjoys widespread use, although it had to change its name. As Vaughn (1990) recounts it, when first introduced from Japan, quality circles were misunderstood. They were regarded as low-level activities in which production workers could get together to discuss problems on the floor. They failed because decision makers were absent. Today we see similar activities under other names, and this time with management involved.

Some of the substantive methods will develop variants. *Kanban* is a good example. Deming (1986) reports that *kanban* is a just-in-time inventory control method in Japan. In the United States a wide variety of work-in-process inventory control methods are called *kanban*. It makes sense to adapt technical methods to local conditions, so long as the underlying principles are understood and their integrity is retained.

There will be trends and development in substantive methods. We already see a vast expansion of techniques in application because of the versatility of the personal computer. Techniques that were simply too exotic a few years ago now have the potential for application as quickly as user-friendly software can be written. We shall explore the direction that all this will take in the following paragraphs.

The Future of ISO 9000

Before we can estimate the future of a quality standard, we must agree on what the future is—the period of interest, so to speak. Hayes and Wheelwright (1984) provide ample evidence that American managers have a rather brief definition of "the future," for which they are roundly and universally criticized. The authors claim that since the 1950s, management lore has focused on short-term results rather than on long-term goals and capabilities. The validity of this criticism is being increasingly recognized by American graduate schools of business. On the other hand, the pressure of quarterly earnings tends to keep management focus on the very near term.

Rather than speculate on what American industry might consider the long term to be, we shall focus on the intermediate term—say, five to ten years. The task at hand, then, is to estimate the direction that the ISO program will take in the next ten years. At this time there are four major forces acting upon the Standards, in no particular order: the U.S. government, QS 9000, ISO 14000, and the loyal opposition.

The Government

In Chapter 1 we saw that, unlike the European nations, the U.S. federal government has stepped aside as overseer of the ISO 9000 program, leaving this duty to private organizations. This abrogation is in such profound accord with the American notion of the proper role of government that we can safely predict there will be no change in this policy. Does this mean that the government will have no role or influence at all? I hope not, because a national quality standard is sorely needed, in my judgment, and government interest can be a catalyst to make it happen. The arena of involvement may well be in defense contracting.

The Department of Defense canceled Mil-Q-9858A in November 1994. Many of us expected an official recognition of ISO 9000 to fill the vacuum, but no such recognition has been forthcoming. Nothing is advanced to replace the former standard and, as a result, much of the defense industry finds itself in a dilemma. A government agency can proffer a standard in a given solicitation. Companies that bid on a dozen or more solicitations per year are then faced with a variety of standards to which they must respond. On the other hand, the government can offer to accept a proffered standard from each bidder, in which case the government is faced with a variety of standards to which it must respond. No one can be satisfied with this situation.

The solution is to adopt a replacement for Mil-Q-9858A, and there can be little doubt which standard is most advantageous. Some defense manufacturers are increasing their foreign sales and are required to certify to some ISO standard. And increasing sophistication in the marketplace demands quality, so it is to everyone's benefit to march to a single standard. The most readily available and most widely recognized is ISO 9000.

Many experts believe that the government will eventually select ISO 9000 as its quality process standard. Lamprecht (1992) writes that "although the DOD will eventually replace Mil-Q-9858A and Mil-I-45028A with the ISO 9001 standard, it does not (yet) require its supplier to be registered to ISO 9001." I share Lamprecht's (1992) prediction, but do not believe that the government will initiate this selection. My experience indicates the force for policy change will come from the private sector. Pursuing international business, more and more very large defense companies will become ISO 9001–certified and bring pressure to bear upon the government to give their quality systems official recognition.

QS 9000

The Big Three automobile makers—Chrysler, Ford, and General Motors—created and ratified in 1994 the quality standard known as QS 9000. Lovitt (1996) writes that they did this because they recognized the economic advantage in adopting common standards for their supplier base. Desiring to be in harmony with international standards, the Big Three adopted ISO 9001 as the basic reference for QS 9000. The fundamental difference between the automotive standard and the ISO 9001 standard is that there are substantive measures associated with the former. These include improvement mechanisms and statistical techniques.

In short, QS 9000 has both form and substance and is clearly the superior standard. Will it therefore replace or displace ISO 9000? We should review the nature of a standard in order to best answer this question. A standard is a convention agreed to by signatories. The ISO standards have hundreds of volunteer signatories—perhaps thousands, depending on your point of view. The terms of the standard must be acceptable to all. Necessarily, then, the terms will be less strict than might be a requirement mandated by a few.

At present the QS 9000 standard has only three signatories. The terms of the standard can be as strict as the three wish them to be. The signatories are powerful within their own realm and can virtually dictate to their subcontractors, who number in the thousands. The vast majority of these subcontractors are located in the Midwest, but as new auto plants are built elsewhere, particularly in the South, the geographic scope of the QS 9000 influence will greatly increase.

The number of QS 9000 signatories with authority will increase, too, however. Struebing (1995) reports that the demand for copies of the standard is worldwide, and that QS 9000 programs are being launched in Australia, Europe, and Latin and South America. As authority spreads, a susceptibility to deviation will follow, so that an estimate of what the QS 9000 standard will look like in ten years is rather difficult to make.

Countering the QS 9000 force, manufacturers who do not supply the automobile industry will resist a standard that imposes upon them terms more strict than necessary. Both QS 9000 and ISO 9001 have value. QS 9000 provides automakers with a substantive instrument that gives them improved control over a truly massive supplier problem. ISO 9000 gives the general service provider or manufacturer a framework on which to build a quality system as effective as it needs to be. Since an effective quality system needs at least some substantive techniques, it is possible that ISO 9001 and QS 9000 will eventually come to resemble one another, at least in substance.

Ironically, Scicchitano (1997) reports that the Big Three have announced their intention to depart from the text of ISO 9000. Thus, the possibility that the two standards will converge in substance is offset by the probability that they will diverge in form. Although there has been talk of one standard replacing the other, they have different purposes and each has powerful champions. My belief is that ISO 9001 and QS 9000 will continue to live side by side.

ISO 14000

Worldwide concerns about the environment led to an international congress in Rio de Janeiro in 1992, in which policies and procedures were developed and agreed upon. These proceedings led eventually to an international series of environmental management system standards (EMS), known as ISO 14000. One of the standards, ISO 14001, is applicable to the way manufacturers do business and provides an opportunity for third-party registration. Meeting the terms of an ISO 14001 standard offers a company regulatory relief, decreased liability, and improved relations with environmentally conscious stockholders and the general public.

Attraction to ISO 14000 is lukewarm at present; Rubach (1995) cites ISO registrars as reporting that less than half of their clients are interested in it. On the other hand, House (1995) expects to see a sudden increase in interest, as happened with ISO 9000. This notion seems entirely reasonable, as EMS programs help manage what must be done anyway—satisfy regulatory requirements.

The government's view of its role in support of ISO 14000 is an important factor in the growth of the standard. The trend is to allow a market-driven approach, according to Miller (1995). Barlas (1996) reports that the Environmental Protection Agency

(EPA) has no plans to encode the standard into any regulatory requirement, and is presently only considering what leeway, if any, it might grant a company certified to the standard. Some government officials are opposed to ISO 14000 on the grounds that it can be used to erect trade barriers.

The same argument used to champion ISO 9000 can be used to champion ISO 14000. If concern for the environment is a good idea, then systems that enhance environmental care are also a good idea. If there is a positive correlation between management and objectives, then one can reasonably conclude that there is a positive correlation between management system standards and objectives. ISO 14000 has many firm advocates and their number will grow, although it is difficult to project its rate of growth. The resistance of business and labor to environmental issues, including standards, is deeply founded in a short view of economics and is widespread. Many nations have no environmental regulations at all, and we have trade agreements with them. It is not likely that American business will submit to costs that are not imposed upon its foreign competition.

ISO 14001 does not directly relate to ISO 9001. The former has to do with the quality of the environment, the latter with the quality of product or service. House believes that the two standards will reinforce one another. The form of this duality might be that the two standards exist side by side, since their objectives are disjointed. Or there might be a unification of ISO 9000 and ISO 14000 into a single standard, because there is a similarity of internal structure and because it is an economic alternative for those companies desiring both capabilities.

The Loyal Opposition

In a widely read paper, Zuckerman (1994) rattled a few cages of ISO 9000 complacency when she recounted significant resistance to the standards. The general reason given was simply that the standards do not go far enough—they do not ensure quality. Zuckerman may have been the first to point out that the government was not rushing to embrace ISO 9000, and that many industry leaders already use more-stringent standards. These objections are true enough and are the basis for why this book is written. We concede the point. Those loyal to the idea of quality have many reasons to look elsewhere—in fact, they must look elsewhere for substance.

On the other hand, there is a considerable voice raised against the standards because they are viewed as being European. Part of this complaint is justified on grounds similar to those of James Thomas, president of the American Society of Testing and Materials. Barlas quotes Thomas: "We often hear from our technical advisory groups that the members of the European Union vote as a bloc on particular issues and that standards coming from ISO are reflections of European, not American, technology." This argument may have some merit in regard to product standards, but is not effective when applied to process standards. ISO 9000 addresses policy, procedures, and organization, not technology. Europeans use the same systems theory and principles that are used in the United States and have developed their share of them.

Another manifestation of the anti-European complaint is that ISO 9000 "raises trade barriers." Perhaps. It may be true that ISO 9000 standards raise trade barriers against inferior product. They ought to. Let's explore the mystique of trade barriers. Sometimes the term is legitimate and sometimes it is used as code. For example, Germany's purity-in-beer laws proscribe a number of imports that do not meet the standard. Those beer makers that cannot export their product to Germany cry "trade barriers." But if you read the table of contents of modern beer, it can scare the daylights out of you. The rise in popularity of microbreweries may be due in large part to an unwillingness on the part of many beer drinkers to put all those chemicals in their body.

ISO 9000 provides stability of form. Nothing in the standard precludes use of substantive quality techniques. On the contrary, the standards will lock in whatever quality methods are put into the quality manual. We return to the theme of form and substance. Both are needed in any process. The loyal opposition has not come up with an alternative standard of form. The demand for quality standards of product and process is universal. Quality experts everywhere, and business managers in tune with their customers, want them. Market forces and the principle of efficiency will move toward a common process standard, and ISO 9000 appears, at this time, to be the best alternative.

Compromise

ISO 9000 and ISO 14000 are not the only process standards coming down the pike. Zuckerman (1996) reports that the International Organization for Standardization is considering yet another standard, covering occupational health and safety. The ISO is well aware that a requirement of three different certifications will meet with mighty resistance and is trying to develop ways to simplify the process. They estimate that within five years there should be one or possibly two approaches. The first will be a single certification for process management, environmental protection, and issues of occupational health and safety. The alternative might be a selective process in which a company might certify a single operation, but demonstrate competence in others. The idea is to increase quality, not bureaucracy.

Finding a happy medium in the tangle of ISO standards will be difficult because, as Zuckerman reminds us, the registrars have a vested financial interest in the certification process. My own feeling is that bureaucracy seems to have an entropic property. It simply increases. In fact, there are two bureaucracies at work. One is government, which can generate untold volumes of rules and regulations with respect to the environment, safety, and health. The other is the ISO, which is attempting to ensure that companies can correctly manage all this paperwork, and oh, by the way, maintain quality in their productive processes while doing it.

In sum, we shall probably see some sort of unification of the different standards into a single certification, with ISO 9000 the dominant one. A commercial enterprise is in business to make a profit, and quality improves that profit. Environmental, health, and safety issues can have a negative effect on profit in the sense of punitive costs, but they cannot provide positive effects. This view is by no means an aspersion. The days of dumping toxic waste into drinking water, of working children in factories, of holding unsafe working conditions as part of the job, are numbered. Nevertheless, a company that ranks very high on a scale of social awareness, but that cannot produce a quality product at a competitive price, will fail in business.

The Direction of Substance

Most of the technical tools used in quality today have been around a long time. Some of them, such as response surface methods, require a significant mathematical and statistical background. Others, such as factorial arrays, were too cumbersome except in the most simple applications. Genichi Taguchi and others have developed fractional factorial methods that reduce the number of experiments in a design effort, but this reduction has a price in terms of confounded results. Confounding occurs where, in order to keep the arrays within manageable dimensions, factors of interest are arrayed in positions that reflect the influence of factors not of interest but thought to be insignificant. This tactic is called aliasing. If the experimenter is wrong about this insignificance, then aliasing results are ambiguous.

The high-speed personal computer with pentium processor and enormous memory capacity is changing all that. For example, design of experiments software is being developed, or is already available, that can solve very large arrays but remain user friendly. Perhaps too user friendly, because the programs require less expertise to run than does the understanding of results. But given that the programs are used by people with the appropriate technical skills, the new software permits an increasing application of statistical methods.

There are now software packages for organization, such as flowchart analysis, simulation, and calibration management: for statistical process control, including detection and failure analysis; for experimental design, including analysis of variance and multiple regression techniques; and for life cycle analysis, such as reliability and failure modes and effects analysis. The gap is closing between the world of theory and the world of application.

The new horizon created by developing software is causing a major change in substantive measures—a trend from statistical process control to design of experiments. This does not mean that SPC is dropping by the wayside; on the contrary, I believe that SPC and DOE have different objectives, and one cannot replace the other. But companies have a fixed quality budget, and as more of that budget is spent on DOE, less is available for SPC—thus the trend. In general it is a good thing because experimental design optimizes quality up front and increases product reliability. Effectively, DOE shifts the burden of quality activity from correction to prevention and thus is in tune with the general trend in every field. For example, in health there is a new focus away from corrective measures and on preventive medicine. Quality is on the same trend.

The Big Picture

The trends of the future follow a systems approach, a widening of scope in order to achieve a broader influence of quality. One example is total quality management (TQM), which is a collection of quality techniques applied throughout the company. Although ISO 14000 has not yet quite arrived, industry is developing the notion of TQEM—total quality environmental management. Hemingway and Hale (1996) trace the outline of the TQEM method, which is a classic systems approach: Model the business and its processes; identify critical measures; develop standards; adopt strategies and tactics that are customer oriented. If you substitute state variables for critical measures, this method is closely related to the methodology of this book.

A perusal of research areas indicates the direction that substantive quality methods are taking. Staff writers at *Quality Progress* (October 1966) list some of the research projects for the next generation of quality: leadership of technical teams, multifaceted investigations, roles of strategic planning in TQM, quality system assessment for organizational improvement, integration of suppliers, computational enterprise modeling, participatory human resource management, and design of sustainable quality improvement mechanisms, to name a few.

These research activities reinforce the idea that quality is moving to a big picture view, both company-wide and industry-wide. This does not mean that research and development of quality tools will diminish; a perusal of the professional journals verifies that statistical and technical methods remain bountiful fields for doctoral research. But we are moving into an era of increasing research in quality methodologies at the managerial level. The ten-year prediction is that in visionary companies, executive management on down the hierarchy will have substantive quality roles. They will not be cheerleaders or monitors; they will be doers.

The Future of Sustainable Quality

Although this overview of the future of quality is brief and its predictions guarded, there is one fairly safe conclusion: The field of quality is dynamic and becoming more so. Whether form or substance, change will happen. Whatever you are doing now will be upgraded over the next ten years if you want to remain competitive. But how can you know which way to go, particularly in the arena of process standards? There seems to be renewed activity at ISO headquarters in the reform of ISO 9000 standards. Struebing (1997) reports efforts to make the standards more comprehensive in order to bridge the gap between ISO 9001 and the national quality awards.

The sustainable company will not have to worry about it. The manufacturer or service provider who has installed sustainable processes will have in place the form and substance that are in accord with any standard likely to come down the pike. The battle for standards revolves around two issues: authority and substance. Sustainable processes will have substance because they measure and control the three essential properties of stability, capability, and improvability. As such, they will meet the criteria of any foreseeable standard, including QS 9000.

The sustainable company will have in place documented policies, procedures, and audit systems that will satisfy any foreseeable standard of form. Even ISO 9000 does not mandate a particular documentation format, simply a comprehensive one. A review of ISO 9001, QS 9000, ISO 14001, and Mil-Q-9858A shows an extraordinary agreement on form, indicating that there is apparently an optimal one. Changes in form over the next ten years may demand an inclusion of, or accommodation to, some new notion, but they will not require a difference in kind.

The sustainable company will be immune to changes in authority. Whether a universal standard is governed from Geneva or Milwaukee will not affect its operations, which will have achieved optimal performance in form and substance.

Summary

By its very nature, the global market requires agreements on tariffs, trades, and standards, including quality standards. The United States is a signatory to some of these agreements. Sooner or later, we shall need to adopt one of the universal quality standards.

A dynamic marketplace will have many participants—the more the better. This means that agreements will be more difficult to come by and will require more compromise. It also means that there will be an ebb and flow to the details of a standard, in terms of its form and substance, and its depth and breadth. Therefore, predictions about standards are not worthwhile.

Forecasting the standard of the future should not be the strategy of a company seeking to build a quality system. In building for the future, the low-risk strategy is to adopt an ISO 9000 standard because of its universal, best practices form, then build in processes of stability, capability, and improvability. This provides sustainability. First and foremost, it offers the best opportunities for customer satisfaction. Second, it enhances the probability that new ideas in standards requirements can be accommodated with minimal effort and incremental adaptation.

References

Barlas, Stephen."Standards." *Quality Progress*, November 1996, p. 23.

Deming, W. E. *Out of the Crisis*. Cambridge: Center for Advanced Engineering Study, Massachusetts Institute of Technology, 1986.

Hayes, Robert H., and Steven C. Wheelwright. *Restoring Our Competitive Edge: Competing Through Manufacturing*. New York: Wiley, 1984.

Hemingway, C. G., and G. J. Hale. "The TQEM-ISO 14001 Connection." *Quality Progress*, June 1996, pp. 29–32.

House, Gaff. "Raising a Green Standard." *Industry Week*, July 21, 1995, pp. 73–74.

Lamprecht, J. L. *ISO 9000: Preparing for Registration*. New York: Decker, 1992.

Lovitt, Mike. "Continuous Improvement Through the QS 9000 Road Map." *Quality Progress,* February 1996, pp. 39–43.

Miller, W. H. "A New Look in Regulation," *Industry Week,* July 3, 1995, p. 10.

Rubach, Aura. "Standards." *Quality Progress,* October 1995, p. 27.

Scicchitano, P. "Warning: Danger Curve." *Quality Digest,* May 1997, p. 21.

Struebing, L. "Standards." *Quality Progress,* November 1995, p. 23.

———."Standards." *Quality Progress,* February 1997, p. 19.

Vaughn, R. C. *Quality Assurance.* Aces: Iowa State University Press, 1990.

Zuckerman, Amy. "ISO 9000 Skepticism." *Industry Week,* July 4, 1994, pp. 43–44.

———. "European Standards Officials Push Reform of ISO 9000 and QS 9000 Registration." *Quality Progress,* September 1996, pp. 131–134.

Author Index

Subject Index